TWENTIETH CENTURY
FASHIONABLE

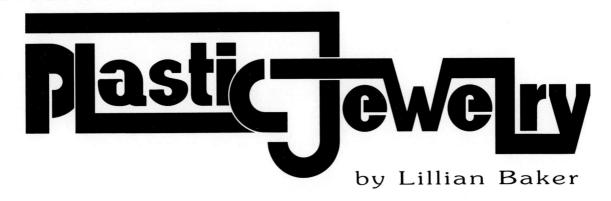

Plastic Jewelry

by Lillian Baker

COLLECTOR BOOKS
A Division of Schroeder Publishing Co., Inc.

Searching For A Publisher?

We are always looking for knowledgeable people considered to be experts in their field. If you feel that there is a real need for a book on your collectible subject and have a large comprehensive collection, please contact us.

COLLECTOR BOOKS
P.O. Box 3009
Paducah, Kentucky 42002-3009

Additional copies of this book may be ordered from:

COLLECTOR BOOKS
P.O. Box 3009
Paducah, Kentucky 42002-3009

or

Lillian Baker
15237 Chanera Avenue
Gardena, California 90249

@$19.95. Add $2.00 for postage and handling.

Copyright: Lillian Baker, 1992

Dedication

For Loving Family
and
Loyal Friends
Here and Beyond

Cover Credits

Design and layout by Lillian Baker
Photography by Dave Hammell

Collections on Cover and Credits

Bracelets: Lillian Baker, Ginger Moro, Christie Romero

Pins & Brooches: Lillian Baker and Christie Romero

Beads, Necklaces & Pendant: Ginger Moro

Hatpins: Lillian Baker

Tall Bakelite Vase: Ginger Moro

Vinyl-Plastic Coated Yellow Basket: Lillian Baker

Yellow Thermoplastic 3-drawer Utility Box: Lillian Baker

(The majority of pieces shown on the cover of
this book are displayed on inside pages
and evaluated in the price guide.)

Back Cover: Photo by Lucile Nisen

Lillian Baker wears *Emmons Jewelers*
"All Season's Favorite,"
necklace and earrings made of plastic
combined with patented goldtone metal

Jewelry Collections Featured
(Numerals in Italics Indicate Black & White Plates)

Acknowledgments

Heartfelt thanks for the valuable assistance, cooperation, and special skills of the following persons who are listed alphabetically:

Jewelry Collections

Dorothy Buhrman, Milly Combs, Rex Franz, Joan Castle Joseff, Kenneth Jay Lane, Ginger Moro, Christie Romero, Stella Tarr, and the collection jointly owned by Catherine Yronwode and Dean Mullaney.

Photography
(Unless Otherwise Noted)

Dave Hammell, national award-winning photo-artist, assisted by his wife, Barbara Lee Hammell.

Library Resources & Archival Materials

In addition to my own collection of resource materials, I'm indebted to the following individuals for the loan and/or sharing of further research materials and photographs from their personal archives: Sharon Hepburn, Joan Castle Joseff, Kenneth Jay Lane, Ginger Moro, Christie Romero, Catherine Yronwode and Dean Mullaney.

Thanks are due Kyle Husfloen, Editor, *The Antique Trader*, and Davida Baron, co-founder/publisher of *Vintage Fashion & Costume Jewelry Newsletter and Club* for permission to reprint articles pertinent to this publication.

Typing and Clerical Assistance

Lucile Nisen, longtime friend, helped considerably in the important technical and time-consuming duties required of an able assistant and secretary. I appreciate the long wearisome hours she spent taking dictation and the other demands of desk-work. How fortunate I am to have her almost "at beck and call," and to enjoy her faithful companionship for many years.

Special Kudos

Unforseen circumstances caused the longtime postponement of the final manuscript for this book. I sincerely appreciate the understanding and consideration shown to me by the publisher and staff of Collector Books: Bill Schroeder, President; Steve Quertermous, (who has since left to begin a new career in an unrelated field), and Lisa Stroup, the new editor who is responsible for the completion of this work from manuscript to book-form. Lisa immediately put my mind at rest when "changing the horse in mid-stream" occurred. My relationship with **Collector Books** which began in the early 1970's, has been a rewarding one based on mutual respect, admiration, and reciprocity.

Special Acknowledgment

A special acknowledgment is extended to my husband for his decades of devotion. Our marriage vow, "to love in sickness..." was sorely tested in June 1990. He passed the test with flying colors through early 1992, and the completion of this manuscript. This book would not have reached fruition without his untiring efforts during recovery from a serious accident.

I'm glad to be able to acknowledge the loving assistance of family and friends whose encouragement gave me the extra spiritual strength which transferred itself to the physical effort needed to complete this longtime project.

Table of Contents

Section I
Introduction

Unit I - New Conceptions of Plastic Jewelry: a challenge to "conventional wisdom"

Unit II - Evaluating Plastic Jewelry: a commentary on pricing

Unit III - Fifty Thumbnail Sketches

"Primitive man was probably not aware
of the fact that his rude hut of stone
or wood was limited in its size and
shape by the character of the very
substances of which it was built...
Almost daily, man is discovering new
substances and developing products
that will eventually find their proper
niche in the galaxy of available materials.
Unfortunately these products developed
by scientists and engineers are at
the mercy of persons of lesser
knowledge, insofar as their use
is concerned, who apply a
time-worn measuring stick to
their judgment."

The Architect, The Theatre and Plastics
by Wm. L. Pereira
(*Modern Plastics*, February 1935)

Section I
Introduction

Unit I - New Conceptions of Plastic Jewelry: a challenge to "conventional wisdom"

"...the world of fashion
are the 'movie stars' of
Hollywood. What they wear,
from shorts to zippers, the
rest of the world obediently
dons the day after. Thus dress
follows the celluloid trail..."

Dr. Fairfax Proudfit Walkup,
Dressing the Part
(Crofts & Co., Inc. 1938)

On May 17, 1968, I worked enthusiastically with Dr. Walkup on updating and revising her book which provided a source for costume to be used by the theatre. She inscribed a copy of her book to me with these flattering words: "To Lillian, my co-worker in costume bits and pieces...," adding a very personal note which she signed,"Devotedly, Fairfax."

Frankly, it was a joyful relationship based on mutual admiration and a longtime friendship during which time I must confess that I was a mere novice seated at the knee of a top professional.

That seat of learning and the lessons taught have remained an important mainstay throughout my writing career. I happily share with my readers some of the results of that experience.

The "Celluloid" Trail
When Dr. Walkup wrote about the influence on dress and accessories that were coming from Hollywood, and the masses who followed "the Celluloid trail,"she was of course referring to Celluloid film, a kind of slate upon which was projected moviedom's fashion plates. These fashions, worn by the stars, inevitably dictated dress fashions for mass production.

Although Celluloid was a 19th century invention, (originally called xylonite), its popularity peaked at the turn-of-the-century when mass production supplied imitation coral, tortoiseshell, amber, and a variety of gemstones to a newly created market spurred on by the ever-expanding industrial revolution.

Celluloid, a patented trademark of Hyatt Bros., Newark, New Jersey (1868), is the word most often used to describe *any* synthetic ivory, bone, or tortoise.

However, there were many other innovations of natural elements commercially sold as "ivorine," "tortine," and the familiar designation, "French Ivory."

Phenolic resins versus Celluloid
Because early Celluloid was highly flammable, it was substituted or replaced for all general purposes by the phenolic resins of the 1930's, such as Bakelite, Catalin, and Marblette which were inflammable, were harder and more resilient, and because these newer materials were made of thermoset plastic substances.

Many books listed in the Bibliography, are provided for further reading and reference work. They give, in some instances, technical information about the chemistry of plastics.

As an *essayist*, I hardly pretend or presume to be an *assayist*, nor am I a *chemist*. Therefore, for those who are interested in the making of plastic products, a chapter is devoted to an excellent article written by John A. Mallinak. The article first appeared in *The Antique Trader*, (Dec. 3, 1986). Kyle Husfloen, editor of this widely read newspaper, has given permission to reprint the complete article entitled *The A B C's of Plastics*. Readers can refer to this highly informative and well-researched dissertation by Mr. Mallinak, by turning to Appendix A.

Lucite, "an amazing new plastic"
As an aside, I found it interesting and rewarding that through proper research I was able to pinpoint some exact dates when certain plastic products were introduced. For instance, in Mr. Mallinak's article (mentioned above), he correctly refers to Lucite as a plastic product produced by duPont

Plastics, plastics division of E.I. duPont de Nemours & Co., Inc., Arlington, New Jersey. It was produced, Mr. Mallinak states, "sometime in the 1930's."

Feeling much like the forty-niner panning for gold who strikes it rich, I had the same tendency to shout, "Eureka! I found it!" So it was when scanning the pages of the June 1937 issue of *Modern Plastics* magazine, I came upon the advertisement headlined:

DuPont Announces an Amazing New Plastic
Here is the finest plastic modern chemistry
has yet developed! It is "Lucite"...
"Lucite" is duPont's registered trademark
for its methyl methacrylate plastic,
formerly known as "Pontalite."

We *now* know the exact moment in time–June 1937–when the word "Lucite" became a part of our everyday language. We can now more easily date the fashionable Lucite jewelry and accessories, such as buttons, buckles, and slides, because of this dated advertisement.

"Bakelite" as a Generic Term

Mr. Mallinak's article confirms what some other authors have recently stated about the use of the term "Bakelite" as a cover name for plastics. The fact is that Bakelite is and should be used as a "generic" term for thermoset phenolic resins or plastics.

It's generic in the same sense that other words are similarly used. In bygone days one remembers, "bring along your Kodak," meaning, of course, not to forget one's camera.

"Don't forget the *Thermos*," "How's about a *Coke*," "I need a *Kleenex*," "Make me a *Xerox* copy"—all terms in common usage which are actually fully patented and trademarked.

Imitation being the proverbial best form of flattery may be true, but one can feel somewhat resentful by the intrusion of a galaxy of imitators and copyists who have profited by a word I shall coin: *generiactric*. It would be fairer, it seems, that if a shopper asks for *"Jello,"* or a "box of *Kellogg's,"* one should not have to settle for a competitive product. Unfortunately, the common marketplace today has in effect become common to the trade.

Baekeland, Bakelite, and Baker

I was born in Yonkers, New York, almost within walking distance of Dr. Leo Hendrik Baekeland's laboratory where he conducted his experiments in the early 1900's. It's an ironic twist of fate that I should now be writing about the man who was a neighbor and contemporary of my parents who also immigrated and settled in the small but thriving community of Yonkers, New York.

Although the Doctor's laboratory was within walking distance of my parents' home, long before I wore "walking shoes," my family resettled in uptown New York City. Nonetheless, several of my relatives remained to spend their lifetimes in Yonkers and we visited them quite often.

I remember the children's library in Yonkers, where the sweet librarian devoted Saturday afternoons to the reading of classic tales to an eager and excited young audience of which I was a part. Our weekend visits to Yonkers always included my participation in this event. I must confess that I do not recall the decorative attributes of this library, but I have since come upon information about a trio of murals for the children's room of the Yonkers, New York Public Library.

These murals were painted during the 1930's by David Hutchinson. The theme of the last of three murals was called, "The Age of Invention," and depicted a panoramic view of Yonkers, looking out over the city toward the Hudson River and the Palisades hills of New Jersey.

The Age of Invention

The figures represented in the mural were of famous men who had contributed to invention and science, including the inventor of Bakelite resinoid, Dr. Baekeland. Four other Yonkers residents were also shown: Rudolf Eickemeyer, (trolley motor); Charles Proteus Steinmetz, (electrical wizard); Halcyon Skinner, (Axminster loom, for the *must-have* Axminster carpets); and Dr. Michael Pupin, (research scientist).

Other outstanding pioneers depicted on this mural, *The Age of Invention*, could be readily recognized. They were: Thomas A. Edison, the Wright Brothers, Robert Fulton, Alexander Graham Bell, Henry Ford, Charles A. Lindbergh, and George Eastman. So well known are they to this date, that it isn't necessary to identify them by their inventions or deeds, even so many decades later.

The author knows not if these three murals remain, or if the Yonkers Public Library still stands. Has it, like so many older edifices and landmarks, been razed in the name of "community redevelopment?" It would be nice to know that those three murals still exist as tributes to these men who were more than people "just passin' through."

More About Dr. Leo Hendrik Baekland

Because of this book's subject matter, the author has singled out one man from that mural whose discovery of phenolic resinous materials in 1907, greatly stimulated further research in the "new field" of industrial chemistry.

Collectors of plastic jewelry automatically associate this good doctor with "Bakelite" jewelry, the copyright name honoring the inventor. Few realize that among Dr. Baekeland's inventions besides "Bakelite Resinoid," was Velox photographic paper, and two years prior to his 1907 discovery which truly marks the beginning of our modern world of plastics, came his important association with Hooker Electro-Chemical Company where he was instrumental in the development of the Townsend electrolytic cell.

The year 1907 was just the beginning of "Bakelite,"

and his further extensive study and research in the field of plastics brought forth multiple uses for this resinoid.

Dr. Baekeland became the president of the Bakelite Corporation, and he employed skilled chemists and engineers to promote and project his work and product into industries too numerous to mention herein. Bakelite cast resinoids were used for items requiring a hard, transparent, water-resistant material. Some of the important plastic products produced by his company were formally presented during the 1935–1937 period, by an exciting and vivid exhibition which began at the Museum of Science & Industry (Rockefeller Center, New York), and was shown via a "Travelcade" on a city-to-city two month tour which ended at the Franklin Institute in Philadelphia.

In December 1934, the inventor of "Bakelite" was bestowed with the honorary degree of Doctor of Applied Sciences, at the University of Brussels (Belgium). "Hometown boy makes good," as he returned for a visit to his 1893 birthplace, Ghent, where he spent his youth; then his early years studying and teaching science and chemistry in Belgian universities. When, in 1889, he immigrated to the United States, he became a great contributor to its society and one who fully realized "the American dream."

Three years later, on September 30, 1937, in the presence of the President of France, Dr. Leo Hendrik Baekeland, by now internationally known and respected, was named Honorary Member of the Societe De Chimie Industrielle, France, for the eminent services he had rendered to science and industry.

At Christmastime, 1937, "Scotty Toys" molded of Bakelite came out of the same product which served major industrial plants.

The Bakelite company also made thermoplastics for electrical products and "polystyrene" molding materials, although the firm is usually associated with thermoset phenolic resins.

Although in April and May 1938, 45,000 visitors came to the New York exhibit of modern plastics, the New York World's Fair (1939), "World of Tomorrow" had only three exhibitors of plastics! The Bakelite exhibit showed how jewelry, notions, crib toys, and "the evolution of buttons," were influencing a coming age of plastics as a new force in a "new world."

Because of Dr. Baekeland's discovery and development of his plastic material, modern living has been dramatically enhanced by the part plastics play in its uses in commercial and military aviation, space exploration, everyday household appliances and furnishings, photography and optics, communications, automobiles, and last but not least, its contributions to the fashion world via buttons, bows, accessories, and jewelry.

The "Bakelite" Market

Today, in the selling and trading of fashionable plastic jewelry, the key word seems to be **Bakelite**. Frankly, Bakelite has become the cover-name for just about every thermoset or phenolic plastic. In using the term Bakelite to describe some of the jewelry pictured within the pages of this book, the reader is asked to accept the premise that no chemical tests have been actually made to determine the plastic composition of each piece of jewelry represented herein. Each piece has been described as faithfully as possible by a group of collectors and/or collector-dealers who have most graciously allowed the author to photograph the myriad of fashionable plastic jewelry in its widest variety of design, color, form, and fashion.

The market for so-called "Bakelite" jewelry has caused a tidal wave of buyers who have drowned themselves in oceans of enthusiasm for a recently rediscovered collectible. The competition between foreign and domestic buyers and sellers, tagging the majority of pieces as Bakelite, caused Catherine Yronwode, editor of the newsletter, *Collectible Plastics*, to label a horde of newcomers in the field as "the Bakelite mafia"! (*Collectible Plastics* is published by "The Society of Decorative Plastics.") The collection of plastic jewelry owned by Catherine Yronwode and Dean Mullaney, editors of the newsletter, are well represented by several color plates in this book. For the collector of fashionable plastic jewelry, these newsletters contain a wealth of information and photographs from period publications which were printed at the height of the Celluloid and Bakelite jewelry production.

Of course an author cannot help but be pleased when recognition is given, as had been printed in *Collectible Plastics*, (Vol. 1, No. 7, Oct-Nov 1985):

Scotty Jewelry and Buttons
Probably the first person to "officially" recognize the collectibility of costume jewelry was Lillian Baker, and in her seminal work, *"100 Years of Collectible Jewelry"* (Collector Books, Paducah, Ky., 1978), she shows a nice carved scotty pin, then valued at $10.00. Says Lillian, "We've come a long way since then. Interest and demand for good old hand-carved plastic jewelry has grown and the prices have risen accordingly."

The Merits of Collecting Plastic Jewelry

Serious collectors of fashionable twentieth century plastic jewelry often meet to discuss the merits of these collectibles. What makes them popular and so desirable? Is it the medium, the artistry, the conceptual rendering on paper drawn from unlimited imagination? Is it simply the joy of color or the humor in a brooch's design which sometimes rests on its absurdity? Is it the *timeliness* or the *timelessness* of the patterns? Why *plastic* jewelry?

Is it the Hyatt brothers or Dr. Leo H. Baekeland, inventors of Celluloid and Bakelite, respectively, who deserve the credit, or is it the simple sculptors in cottage industries or who worked behind factory benches who should receive our accolades? After all, where would Frank Lloyd Wright be without the stone-mason or the landscape artist? What came first, "the chicken or the egg?"

What affect did merchandising and advertising have on the gradual acceptance of, and the unquenchable "thirst" for, the bulky bangles which braved the clang against an inherited sentimental brooch—both sharing the same compartment in a jewelry box or drawer, no less the same wrist or arm?

Fashionable Plastic Jewelry is a Partnership

An inventive mind is complemented by many hands in an industrial world, but even more so in a dream-world of imagination. To have a masterful painting, it is not enough to have a proficient artist. He first needs brush and canvas and earth colors on his palette. Inspiration is not enough. Materials must be supplied by others or the artist could not paint. So it is with plastic jewelry.

A sculptor cannot work without a chisel. That chisel must be forged. The marble, stone, and wood, must first be cut. An architect would hardly render a drawing if he had not assurance that a mason could build the foundation upon which his structure would rise. So it is with scupltured renderings in plastic jewelry.

We begin to realize the interdependence of people and can then quite logically accept the fact that all men are not gifted or inspired in the same way. Without demeaning anyone, we understand diversification of individuals and the balance of "equality" and endowment.

For some, inspiration is a physical encounter. Others pursue the mental task more vigorously. There are those who can do both, and do both well; they are classed as the gifted who are doubly blessed.

The real secret of success, in my opinion, is the desire to do the physical or mental job to the best of one's natural inborn ability. There must be a sense of personal pride in both physical and mental achievement. Thus we can applaud inventor and maker alike, as we make a decision to purchase and physically possess wearable, fashionable, plastic jewelry. We take physical possession as the result of a mental decision.

Enjoying the Hunt and Not the Target

A reader may reasonably ask what all these words have to do with a book about twentieth century fashionable plastic jewelry. And as the author, I must respond accordingly. May I therefore suggest that the successful longtime collector will find that success has little to do with competing with other collectors. Success has much more to do with a sense of personal accomplishment. The joy of collecting is in the hunt and not in the target.

There should be personal pride in laying out plans for collecting. Without pride in that planning, there's little pleasure or profit. Just as the medium used in painting must be skillfully blended for the colors to be true, so must the collector become

educated as to what makes a good palette for his own skills in collecting plastic jewelry. Marble and wood must be carefully struck for perfection of grain, or the statue will look bruised. So, too, will plastic jewelry appear flawed if it has been worked against its structure. Plastics require serious study.

One of the more quiet controversies in a time of many conflicts, is the contention that a desire for material possessions is the disease of the establishment. How much plastic jewelry is "enough"?

Some quarters condemn "collecting" in words used by Gibran who cites the dog burying bones while following Pilgrims to the Holy Land, since we, too, shall not pass this way again. Thus, one may perhaps correctly question the seemingly futile quest for an accumulation or a collection of mere "objects" in the form of high fashion twentieth century plastic jewelry.

However, it is my opinion that collecting antiques, "collectibles," and other jeweled artifacts is in truth an appreciation for materials which have gained real substance in the hands of gifted mortals. And this includes plastics.

The most simple of Earth's materials—wood, clay, sand, rock, ore—have been transformed by both primitive and skilled artisans into objects that are artistic, imaginative, inventive, unique, functional and wearable. Indeed, in some mysterious way, human creativity such as is represented in the fields of plastics oftentimes gives new "life" to inanimate objects.

The intangible magic of mortal inspiration thereupon becomes tangible and possibly eternal.

Of "Fools," the "Foolish" and the "Foolhardy"

Surely nothing else on earth makes more of nature's elements than do we mortals who the famous Bard once called "fools." Foolish, perhaps, but not fools.

To play the fool is to trifle with time; whereas to be foolish may merely denote amusement. To be foolhardy signifies, at times, an adventuresome experience. What better description than this for those inventors of plastics whose "foolhardy" experiments and preseverance resulted in such charming pieces of plastic adornments!

What seems intangible can, through mortal experiment, become eternally inspiring.

For instance, a shepherd notches a hollow reed, gives it his breath, and there's a tuneful whistle in the wind.

A sculptor molds the earth into a clay of dancing figures postured to whirl off a pedestal.

A composer scales mountains of arpeggios and unfamiliar sounds echo from a mysterious valley somewhere beyond our universe.

An artist gives dimension to a flat canvas and his soul seems to emerge from its depth.

An author creates a fictional character by words and phrases, thereby creating a breathing being recognized by others.

Thus, when a collector of music boxes, figurines, paintings, books, primitives, and the wearable arts known as plastic "jewelry" expresses sheer delight in such collections, the chances are that the joy is not truly related to monetary value. Rather the elation such objects provide, are cultural and spiritual gain, realized by temporary stewardship.

The author's appreciation for the advantages of living with antiques and collectibles, and her lifelong fascination for wearable accessories, began early in her youth and has not diminished over the years. In fact it accelerated in the fifties, to wit:

In 1956, Picasso's 75th Anniversary Exhibit at New York City's Modern Museum of Art, took in the entire exhibit floors of this beautiful edifice. At the same time, within the museum there was a showing of an experimental film which I shall never forget. It was a movie that proved to me the beauty of machinery as a rhythmical life-force, and not merely as a functional item.

To a quiet musical Etude, the steel pistons of the great piece of machinery were transformed into the graceful legs of a ballerina. There was perfect harmony between the music and the regular pulsations of the rotating motor components. All became as one, in a symphony of mechanical coordination.

The machine was made of modern plastic components which enabled the pistons to run smoother and quieter. But even that noise was hushed as the film progressed, and all one could see was the constancy of movement; the machine seemed to be imitating nature's own dependable cycle.

All this was an unforgettable lesson in the ability of an inanimate object to transfer a spiritual or aesthetic message. Picasso's profusion of color in some of his more graphic works, provide no more pleasure to me than in my happy chance of finding an assortment of bright plastic jewelry in the museum's gift shop.

Some years later, the above-related experience taught me more tolerance for several young people whose mutual hobby was collecting tools of all shapes, sizes, and functions. Close inspection of these "collectibles" reminded me of the value of ingenuity of design and the limitless scope of "foolhardy" imagination and inventiveness. It taught me the simple pleasure of enjoying things of small intrinsic value, like the colorful armful of bangles I purchased that memorable day.

Ironically, the collectors of yesteryear tools search for wood and metal implements because today's tools are made of "high tech" plastics. Many of the modern tools manufactured in colorful plastics, are beautifully designed while at the same time are functional. Plastic decorative adornments can give one the pleasure of beauty and function, a necessary attribute of jewelry.

Collecting and Preservation

The preservation of products that are artistic and inventive was in the not so distant past, the sole responsibility of curators who relied heavily upon their patrons. But today we find heightened interest in every age group and in every walk of life. Curators are now influenced by collectors, and not simply patrons of the arts.

Thanks to the resurgence of interest in the plastic jewelry field, we learn that many more young people will devote time to preserving the material things of yesteryear, be they genuine antiques or items classified in the single category of "collectibles." Strangely enough—and I write this with a smile—it's often the same young folk who, a decade ago held in disdain the so-called material things of the "establishment," and have become the most avid collectors. But perhaps they have decided that the distinction in "material" lies in definition. That is, objects of finely fashioned or homely handicraft, versus machine-made assembly-line products and reproductions. Perhaps it's the hand work required on a carved Bakelite bracelet or the handpainting on an early Celluloid pin or bangle, that the young collectors find so appealing. If so, the new generation of collectors are in good company and have closed the "generation gap."

Perhaps a certain crudeness gives character to plastics or glass or pottery, and this intrigues most of us. Perhaps machine tooling and rubber-stamped replicas have resulted in the loss of homely handmade charm.

Whatever the reason, certainly in the last two decades, there has been a rebirth of interest in creativity and craftsmanship, the same kind as represented in older plastic pieces which have now become part of the new phenolic "space-age" high tech plastic jewelry c.1980-1990. Surely this should provide an optimistic trend with respect to individual expression *versus* the computerized society in which we find ourselves cast...or as outcasts.

However, for every offensive "experiment" accepted in some circles as "freedom of expression," there are many persons with enough honesty not to flatter mediocrity. The result is a decade of delightful pieces of "high tech" plastic jewelry which deserves more than a mere mention. (Perhaps another book about "space age" jewelry in the making?)

Surely none can deny admiration and much awe for the computerized electrical robot that stamps out some of today's jewelry. However, it is still mastered by the inventor who programs it. The hold on the reins when driving the 1890's horse'n buggy, surely gave no less sense of power than that which is felt by the one who programs a computer or controls the electrical switch or wall-plug.

What we need today are inventors with imagination and vision. In 1930, Henry Ford said that he "expects to see the day when automobile bodies will be molded of some plastic material, much lighter than metal..." Now that's the kind of vision we need today!

Collecting and the Environment

All around us are new collectors dedicated to

searching out the forgotten or discarded "oldies but goodies," thus creating a demand for the outmoded or obsolete. Of course jewelry is never really "obsolete" to anyone obsessed with it.

Who can tell if today's high tech plastics will become tomorrow's compost? And how will future generations utilize these discarded components via ever-promising recycling? This question is answered by the following observation.

Modern day environmentalists have convinced many that preservation and the conservation of Mother Earth is a movement founded by them. The concern for the environment is decades old, as proven by an excerpt from *Modern Plastics*, (August 1938). This report, printed below, should make them sit up and rethink their premise.

News

About three months ago, (May 1938), newspapers announced that William S. Murray, chairman of the Republican State Committee, had disclosed "his invention of a new plastic which may utilize a large portion of the nation's surplus milk." Since that time, many inquiries have come to us asking how this new plastic differs from the well-known product, casein. Rather than try to draw a comparison between the two materials, let us tell you in Mr. Murray's own words just what his product is and how its discovery came about.

For a good many years, Mr. Murray has been engaged in chemical research in the vicinity of Utica, N.Y., and maintains a laboratory under the name, William S. Murray, Inc., 805 Watson Place. Among his clients is a century-old tanning company which in the spring of 1932 was ordered closed by the Conservation Commission because the tannery was polluting a nearby stream. The pollution was caused by the geletinous waste involved in tanning. Mr. Murray obtained a thirty-day stay and promptly worked out an acid treatment which solidified the waste so that it could not harm the stream.

"This set me to thinking," says Mr. Murray, "about all the waste milk in that vicinity which is the by-product of the milk powder industry which uses the cream, and discards the skimmed milk. I wondered if that, too, couldn't be solidified and put to some useful purpose in the plastic field. It is a known fact that casein is separated by treating skimmed milk with a weak acid which throws the casein out of solution. Then it is washed, dried and formed into rods or sheets and hardened with formaldehyde, an expensive process which keeps the cost high.

"Now my thought was to try to change the natural sugar to aldehyde by chemical reaction in the presence of casein which would avoid the curing or hardening process and reduce the cost. I explored that very carefully and finally found that I was able to do it. And I also found that under those conditions of treatment, I was getting a molding powder that was stable after pressing."

The process is simple, requiring but two pieces of apparatus, a digester and dryer. All the elements including woodflour or other filler are put in the digester where they are treated and stirred for 15 to 25 minutes. When dried in an ordinary rotary dryer, the product is removed in the form of powder capable of molding in any hydraulic press....

The product when molded appears much like phenolics; dark colors alone have been produced. It is fully described in *U.S. Patent No. 2, 115, 316*, granted April 26, 1938, assigned to Dairymen's League Co-Operative Association, Inc.

Mr. Murray says he believes the plastic will be used in making heavy pieces such as cases, cabinets, housings, even caskets, where other plastics would be too costly....

We called the Dairymen's League on the telephone to ask what, if anything, was being done about putting the material into production. The answer was: "nothing, yet, but we expect to license the process on a royalty basis eventually and are willing to listen to any proposition."

Because of deadlines, further research about the end result of the above experiment and patent rights could not be reported herein. But the story as told, shows how yesteryear's plastic industry forged ahead with environmental concerns even as today's "space age" plastics industries must face the challenge of what to do with "waste," and how to overcome pollution of the earth's watershed. "We live in a plastic world," is the refrain we hear over and over again. Yet somehow there must come encouragement from the past efforts which can be applied to our present situation.

Curiosity, Reality, and the World of Collecting

But let me return the reader to the reality of the world of collecting. Some people say that "collecting" is self-serving and self-centered. It definitely is *not*.

Collecting has become a new and vital source of monetary exchange. It also produces a healthy interest in what could otherwise prove to be *un*healthy in a too-much-leisure world of tomorrow. Both young and old welcome an incentive for collecting, for it relieves boredom and creates an eagerness to experience nostalgia.

To awaken such interest is to excite emotions and heighten a passion for collecting. It also rouses sleeping curiosity.

True, curiosity may "kill the cat," but for us foolish mortals, curiosity gives birth to further exploration; to a new learning experience; to reaching for a book on a subject, reading it and learning from it.

Collecting is a form of recycling yesteryear's nostalgia. It preserves the products of past generations which would otherwise join the league of the "endangered species" of "old world" creativity.

"Collectibles" provide the concrete evidence and the authentic historical background needed to show how our forefathers lived. Such telltale tangible articles can provide many hints of the mores and manners of generations past. By virtue of this book, we can preserve a history of plastic products facing "extinction," such as the earliest man-made plastics which are endangered by the elements of light, heat, and atmospheric changes. The early Celluloid products are now well over 100 years old and are in their own right antiques worth preserving.

There's a need to record for future generations, in word and picture, the art and implements of the past...Too much of the past has been lost to our heritage simply because there were few historians who lent importance to the simple items in common usage; yet how they rejoice upon discovery of these everyday

"tools" in excavations, and how they bemoan the non-existence of manuals.
(Excerpt, P.1, Chapter 1, *The Collector's Encyclopedia of Hatpins and Hatpin Holders*, Lillian Baker. See Bibliography.)

As author of this definitive work about plastic jewelry of the twentieth century, I have tried to provide reading material that will educate, entertain, and give a feast for the eyes.

My book was written to satisfy one's curiosity about plastic jewelry, and I trust my work will compensate for the time it may take for readers to become educated on the subject.

If I have accomplished some of these aims, then I will feel justified by my intrusion into a reader's inquisitive mind and to his inner-eye's search for beauty so evident in plastic jewelry.

None of my efforts could succeed without the help and cooperation of those named under Acknowledgements. There are unnamed persons— readers of my other books. To these anonymous "fans," I conclude with two appropriate words that say it all...

Thank you!

Lillian Baker
Gardena, California
August 1991

Section I
Introduction

Unit II - Evaluating Plastic Jewelry: A Commentary on Pricing.

The retail current values in this book should be used only as a guide. The prices are not intended to set a market value, which certainly will vary from one section of the country to another and from one dealer to another.

Auction prices may well inflate prices and set an artificial evaluation of certain pieces. Auction prices often improperly gauge *retail values*.

Dealer prices vary greatly and are affected by demand and the nation's economy. Comparisons of east coast, west coast, and midwest prices prove this fact.

Prices differ widely when comparing domestic to the overseas marketplace. If a dealer has purchased fashionable plastic jewelry in either Great Britain or on the Continent, chances are the cost was higher and will result in a much elevated retail price stateside or in Canada.

A low-and-high price spread has been worked out for the benefit of the reader. Some Joseff-Hollywood pieces from the Joseff Archives have no price guide because the pieces are either unique, not for sale, or no true market value has been established by Mrs. Joan Castle Joseff.

Some pieces of sentiment simply do not carry a price tag despite the common assumption in some quarters that there are "offers that can't be refused."

The fact is that inheritance *is* valued by many people despite attempts by a few unethical dealers to "cut the ties that bind."

The reader is owed an explanation regarding the wide-spread differences in evaluating prices of one collection against another, including the pieces that are pictured from the author's collection. In this volume, I have relied heavily on collector-dealers in the field. Their prices reflect not only what they had to pay for specific pieces, but also their clientele, the sales area they cover, and whether they sell in shops or at shows. I believe readers will be interested in pricing differentials as related to their own collections and in future decisions regarding purchases of twentieth century fashionable plastic jewelry.

When values on the pieces shown in this book were decided upon, the final decision rested with the exhibitors of their collections. Some of the exhibitors were collectors while others were collectors and dealers. (Mr. Kenneth Jay Lane is a designer and distributor.) The author has based the values on pieces shown from her collection on research or on today's advertisements; shop, show, and auction prices; and the overall framework upon which prices are reached in the various marketplaces. Discussions on the subject of value guides brought interesting responses which are shared with readers.

Ginger Moro, collector and dealer, stated that the price guide for the pieces shown in this book from her vast collection, is based on twenty years of collecting in the United States and abroad.

"Considering the devastation of two World Wars," she states, "vintage European plastic jewelry is relatively rare and is priced accordingly. If French *Deco* pieces are more expensive here, it follows that American Bakelite fetches more in Europe. The supply is limited, but the demand continues to grow."

Therefore, when certain design pieces are limited in quantity, and the collectibility for such pieces is greater than ever, prices will rise with the competition for such items.

Christie Romero, owner of Christie's Treasures, is a collector-dealer-lecturer of vintage jewelry. Prices given for her pieces shown here are her estimates of values based on craftsmanship, condition, color, design, rarity, and collector demand. She notes sale prices at antique shops and shows in Southern California as well as taking into account regional market variables.

Milly Combs, an award-winning longtime collector of buttons and other antiques and collectibles, states with authority that Bakelite-type buttons, because of their current popularity, have increased in value consistently in the past half-decade. The embellished plastic buttons, combined with other materials, i.e. wood, metals, glass, etc., will bring higher prices than the simple designs. Subject matter will also influence price. Competition between button collectors and "Bakelite" collectors will influence some dealers at shows to *raise* prices. Due to the fragility of c.1870-1930 Celluloid buttons, there is a scarcity which of course will influence price structure.

Kenneth Jay Lane jewelry pricing relies not so much on the market demand or competition, but on set wholesale prices. Discontinued designs, or limited editions, will naturally bring revised collector evaluation.

Demand for specific pieces are often dictated by the uniqueness of the item, its rarity, its color and design, and whether the piece broadens or rounds out a particular collection.

So many factors enter into pricing that an author would do a disservice to readers by inflexibility. From day to day, there can be no set price(s), nor can one foretell demand or predict the marketplace. Because of these factors, readers are cautioned to use the printed price guide available with this publication, simply as a guide.

The price guide may also serve for ground-level insurance evaluations of pieces already in one's possession. In this regard, it is wise to photograph collectible pieces and enter reasonable values plus a full description on the back of each picture. Then store the photographs in a safety deposit box.

It must be emphasized that neither the Author nor the Publisher assumes responsiblity for any losses that might be incurred as a result of consulting the evaluations or price guide included in this publication or in any updated edition of this book. The Author and Publisher also disclaims responsiblity for the description of the types of plastic.

Further Disclaimer
Important note to the reader

Throughout this book, the terms "*Bakelite*" and "*Celluloid*" are, in many cases, accepted as generic terms to imply that the plastic is a thermoset product associated with Bakelite, or that the plastic is a thermoplastic product associated with Celluloid. Unless a piece of jewelry or a plastic accessory is actually tested for chemical content or analysis, it is next to impossible to positively provide the correct tradename of the manufacturer who supplied the plastic material to the producer of the finished product.

In pricing a piece of plastic fashionable jewelry, the author suggests that design, craftsmanship, coloration, and condition are of primary importance. Whether the piece is made of "Bakelite," "Catalin," "Tenite," "Celluloid," "Marblette" or "Beetle," is secondary in the opinion of the author.

To the "purist" collector of what is called "Bakelite" products, it may appear as if the author is a heretic merely because of an opinion expressed about plastic collectibles—especially jewelry of plastic materials. The author may reject a thesis or premise put forth by other colleagues. Yet one cannot deny documentation of the time (1935), the height of plastic jewelry manufacture which is today considered the most "collectible," and which fortifies the author's premise.

At the second plastics exhibition sponsored by *Modern Plastics* publishers, the exhibitors included both manufacturers and distributors of plastics to the jewelry trade.

In other words, only the plastic products and not the jewelry items, were supplied by the following: American Catalin Corporation; Auburn Button Works, Inc.; The Bakelite Corporation; Beetleware Corporation; Boonton Molding Corporation; Celluloid Corporation; Fiberloid Corporation; General Plastics, Inc.; Marblette Corporation; The Northern Industrial Chemical Co.; Resinox Corporation; The Siemon Co.; Tennessee Eastman Corporation; Toledo Synthetic Products, Inc.; and Waterbury Button Co.

According to *Modern Plastics*, each of these leading manufacturers and distributors adopted this creed and motto at the Spring (May 15, 1935) exhibition:

"Dedicated to demonstrating modern industry's solution of the practical, artistic and social needs of the average man, the exhibition will constitute in effect a review of the arts of modern civilization wherever they touch directly upon the life of the individual—from his toothbrush to his runabout airplane."

Overlooked in the above almost pontifical declaration, was the huge market for *women's* high fashion plastic jewelry and accessories.

To prove the adage, "actions speak louder than words," history reports that at the Rockefeller Center site of the exhibition, each of the above major makers of plastic products, included exhibits of jewelry and women's apparel accessories (such as buttons, clips, belt buckles and slides, pins, brooches, etc.). All types of phenol resins, cast phenolics, ureas, cellulose acetates, laminated plastics, pyroxylins, and caseins were shown and described in detail.

Now who is to say which of the products and from what manufacturer they were purchased by makers of jewelry? When one drives an automobile can one really tell what oil company supplied the fuel? Texaco, Standard Oil, Chevron—all of their ads would like you to believe there's a "tell tale" difference and that the driver will know and feel the difference after driving a tankful.

The analogy seems to fit the premise based on the above report which suggests that unless a piece of jewelry is MARKED, "Bakelite" or "Catalin" or "Celluloid" (or any trademarks cited in the article which is printed in Appendix A), it is virtually impossible to pinpoint the actual product used for jewelry collected today.

In Section I, Unit III, Fifty Thumbnail Sketches, there are instances where the jewelry shown is named by product-manufacturer. Several of the "sketches" report specific types of jewelry and what type of plastic product was used when first introduced in the 1930's. But these reports are a half-century or more past, and without identifying tags, labels or incised markings, a researcher would have to depend on archival materials, catalogues of the period, or the informative

but now defunct *Modern Plastics* magazine which served the industry throughout the exciting times until the war-clouds gathered in Europe.

At the risk of repeating the caution worded elsewhere in this chapter and throughout the book, buyers and collectors should not be as concerned with the product itself, but rather what was produced from the plastic product. What makes the piece collectible? Does it have artistic merit or is it simply exciting to own and to wear?

Even within the last decade, fashionable twentieth century plastic jewelry is sold by famous makers who keep the product and process used a closely guarded secret. Again, its the craftsmanship and design which should determine the value.

In this author's opinion, a jewelry piece is valueless if it doesn't cause that certain vibration within—the quickening of the pulse (or impulse). In other words, if it doesn't "move" you—move on and wait until a "must have" beckons. A piece that doesn't excite isn't a bargain *at any price*. But if it *does*, remember you always have a *plastic* card from the bank to fall back upon!

Happy hunting!

Section I
Introduction

Unit III - Fifty Thumbnail Sketches

An incredible bit of luck came my way when I resumed contact with Catherine Yronwode, an avid collector, dealer, and researcher of collectible plastics. She and Dean Mullaney founded The Society of Decorative Plastics in 1985, and published an informational newsletter with many photographs and illustrative material. Catherine, (or "Cat") shared editorial responsibility with Dean and they own a most impressive library and archives pertaining to plastics. Their collection of plastic articles, including jewelry, is extensive and could have provided enough variety of jewelry herein to cover the 1930-1940 era when thermoplastic and thermoset jewelry and fashion accessories were in their period of glory. I was fortunate to add a select few, shown on color plates 63 thru 66 inclusive.

The enthusiastic couple gladly shared boxes filled with bound copies of *Modern Plastics* magazine, first published in 1933. These definitive publications were excellent resource materials and provided accurate information about the progress in all fields of plastic uses and discoveries.

There was such a wealth of information, I decided to take voluminous notes and then boil these down to "thumbnail sketches" rather than try

to associate or tie them together although each is definitely related to the plastics industry.

Here, then, are some "sketchy" comments and excerpts garnered from the 1933-1938 issues of the now-defunct magazine, *Modern Plastics*.

Sketch #1 - The first annual exhibit of the plastics industry was held in the exhibit hall of the publisher Modern Plastics, located at 425 Fourth Avenue, New York City. All types of materials and products, including phenol resins, cast phenolics, ureas, cellulose acetates, laminated plastics, pyroxilyns and caseins were shown from November 15th through December 15th, 1934.

Sketch #2 - "Cast phenolics," wrote Herbert Chase, "are rightly classed as among the most beautiful of all plastic materials. In appearance, many of them resemble precious jewels, yet their moderate cost makes them available for a wide range of applications. The cast phenolics have gained a wide use in the manufacture of buttons, buckles and other dress ornaments, items of costume jewelry." (*Modern Plastics*, Nov. 1934, article: "Cast Phenolics—The Jewel-like Plastics." It should be noted that cast phenolics differ from the molding process which requires heavy presses employed for molding. Instead, the cast phenolics are cast into rods, tubes, sheets or special shapes without the use of heavy equipment and were therefore less expensive and more marketable. Because of the 1930's depression, it became necessary to produce inexpensive costume jewelry. President Franklin D. Roosevelt was elected in 1933, and promised through the NRA (National Recovery Act), a new regime that would bring prosperity to the depressed middle and lower classes. Gold had been retired from circulation; gangsters made headlines but these reports took back-page entries so that the devastating earthquake in Long Beach, California could be covered in detail. Adolf Hitler's rise to Leader-Chancellor in Germany, hardly rocked the nation as much as did gangster warfare, bootlegging and racketering, and nature's unheaval in the port city of Long Beach. Hitler's "havoc" would come less than a decade later and engulf the world. Plastics went to war and proved its worth tenfold. Plastic jewelry had to exit from center-stage until it was "cast" in a role after 1945.

Sketch #3 - Joseff of Hollywood designed and produced beautiful pieces of jewelry made of Tenite. Tennessee Eastman Corporation, subsidiary of Eastman Kodak Company, (Kingsport, Tenn.), insured its product called "Tenite" against chipping and breaking. In its November 1934 advertisement, it rightfully boasted that its "superior thermoplastic" known by its trademark "Tenite," was available in all colors, plain and variegated, and in all degrees of transparency from crystal clear to opaque. What we can learn from this advertisement is that Tenite cannot be chemically related to Bakelite because the latter is a thermo*set* plastic. Tenite is *not* thermoset and should not be confused with its "look-a-like" known as Bakelite.

Sketch #4 - Cast phenolics, unlike Celluloid, are non-flammable, odorless, and tasteless. As early as 1934, two-tone cast resinoid and cast transparent resinoid was utilized in making costume jewelry. At the *Modern Plastics* first annual plastics exhibit, as many as 25,000 plastic objects were displayed. By 1934, hardly two decades after plastics found its place in the "industrial revolution," plastics had changed from just a small group of products of comparatively limited application, to becoming a vital factor in almost every phase of manufacture.

Sketch #5 - *Modern Plastics* (December 1934 report about its first exhibit), listed what it called "an astonishing" collection of items all made of the up-and-coming material known as *plastic*. This list follows, but not until the reader's attention is drawn to the "astonishing" absence from this list of women's plastic jewelry, hat ornaments. and hatpins of the period. Exhibitors and sponsors who were leaders in the plastics field, are also printed, including companies which provided raw materials for plastic jewelry. The list is reprinted as reported, not alphabetically but altogether an amazing summary of ingenious applications of various man-

made plastics: gears, boxes, tank-balls, hair waving equipment, switches, distributor-heads, stove handles, displays, biscuit-cutters, measuring cups, salt-cellars, ash trays, picture frames, cream jars, powder jars, toaster bases, rheostats, cups, tumblers, radio dials, cigarette lighters, toys, dishware, closures, radio cabinets, match dispensers, vases, door knobs, escutcheon plates, kick plates, switch plates, soup plates, glasses, glass holders, eye-glass frames, dice, dresser sets, corrosion resisting equipment, heat resisting equipment, shock resisting equipment, signs, clocks, clock cases, clock parts, watches, pen stands, pens, pencils, fishing reels, fishing lures, paper mill equipment, bearings, pouring closures, soap dispensers, rayon spinning equipment, book racks, book covers, brush handles, saw handles, chisel handles, knife handles, tea strainers, coffee percolators, lamps, lamp shades, light sockets, statuary bases, barometers, artificial teeth, telephones, telephone stands, fans, combs, automobile fittings, refrigerator fittings, microphones, microscopes, cameras, razor handles, checkers, chess-men, buttons, toothbrush-handles, opera glasses, shoe heels, goggles, rotors, dictaphone parts, toilet seats, thermometers, lighting fixtures, pool-ball-tracks, electrical recordings, thimbles, pocketbook frames, desk pads, book ends, gear-shift knobs, compacts, coasters, wall surfaces, lighting enclosures, and translucent signs.

Although Celluloid and Bakelite have become generic terms for just about all thermoplastic and thermoset materials comprised of "meltable" and "perma-set" plastics, respectively, the following companies produced similar materials which have unfortunately not been recognized in their own right: American Catalin Corporation, Auburn Button Works, Inc., Beetleware Corporation, Gemloid Corporation, General Plastics, Inc., The Siemon Co., Tech-Art Plastics Co., and Tennessee Eastman Corporation. (The company names in some instances have been changed since 1934; in other instances, several companies were incorporated in a conglomerate and were thereby advanced by higher technology and financial investment for research purposes.)

Sketch #6 - Celluloid is a nitro-cellulose product. It is highly flammable whereas cellulose acetate is very slow burning. Cellulose acetate ranges in color from pure water white to inky black, and in almost any shade and degree of transparency to complete opacity. Many minerals and mineral structures can be duplicated, such as onyx, marble, agate and clear crystals of many kinds, as well as wood grains, ivory, shell, ebony, pearl, etc. Unlike a thermo-setting compound which changes chemically and permanently when molded, cellulose acetate is a thermoplastic substance which can hold its shape when molded but can then be softened simply by reheating the plastic. Cellulose acetate was widely used in the manufacture of combs, but these combs are often described as "Celluloid" when they are actually of the former substance.

Sketch #7 - Both American-born citizens and naturalized citizens were responsible for the pioneering and leadership of plastic products for which no other nation can boast. The United States outdistanced other nations with its invention and utilization of the nitro-cellulose and phenolic types of plastics. England followed America's lead with many innovations of plastics initiated by companies such as Insulators, Ltd., (London), and Birkby's, Ltd., (Liversedge, Yorkshire). A decorative product in England in 1935, was the hair ornament based on similar head decorations which were familiar sights in old Spain and pre-revolution Russia. Some of the modern plastics were excellent for this purpose. A head dress produced by Xylonite Company, Ltd., (London), was called "Bexoid," and was reportedly hand-carved from materials which were described as "non-flame celluloid." Presumably, the material would have been cellulose acetate, because "celluloid" is highly flammable. The head dress, however, boasted "paste diamonds" which were inlaid into the plastic, thereby giving the article effective distinction and decorative quality. The 1935 report stated that although the finished article was manufactured in England, the actual plastic materials were imported from Germany.

Sketch #8 - When world-famous designer, Raymond Loewy, was asked what he thought about the future of plastics, he replied that he didn't want to sound like "advertising," but that he was quite frankly prejudiced in favor of plastics. Loewy always took advantage of plastic materials whenever it was practical. Besides, he responded candidly, "It (plastic) is modern!" (January 1935 interview, *Modern Plastics*) Raymond Loewy opened his London office, Nov. 1935, with a full year's work already booked!

Sketch #9 - By January 1935, every major department and chain store had already well-established cosmetic, novelty, and jewelry counters. The *jewelry* was dominated by a wide variety of cast phenolic and pyroxylin items.

Pyroxylin plastics were earliest in the plastics field and ranked first in popularity for many years because it was one of the very few plastics that could be printed, lithographed, and readily dyed by the fabricator. It could easily be cemented to either itself or to other plastics. Pyroxlin was, therefore, a versatile plastic. It was sold under many names such as Celluloid, Pyralin, Amarith, and Fiberloid.

Pyroxylin (nitro-cellulose plastic) is a *true thermoplastic* material in that it becomes soft when heated and hard when cooled. It is a plastic that could be molded under compression, stretched, "blown," and produced into items without seams. Molded forms of this versatile plastic were accomplished by hydraulic presses that turned out a variety of forms of costume jewelry flooding the

1935 jewelry counters.

Combs and hair ornaments were made of Pyroxylin plastic which was cut to shape, and then the teeth of combs were slotted by machine.

Buckles, buttons and other decorative items for the clothing and millinery trade were either cut from sheet stock or from bar stock, the latter producing in special automatic machines a myriad of buckles, buttons as well as bulk-combs.

Pyroxylin plastic decomposes if subjected to strong acids or alkalis, and continuous contact with water could prove a disaster. Considering that Pyroxylin burned rapidly or explosively, it remains a mystery why it remained popular for so long. In some ways it was on a par or superior to other plastics which were not as tough or were easily bent and broken. Incredible as it may seem today, some cities required special fire-department permits for the manufacture of Pyroxylin, and special insurance underwriter requirements also had to be met. To avoid fire hazard and related expenses, manufacturers turned to the use of acetate in place of pyroxylin. The dangers and drain on finances associated with losses no doubt contributed to greater experimentation with plastic products. Such challenges resulted in non-flammable products and on to "space age" high tech plastics such as produced by today's Corning-ware, among others.

Sketch #10 - Colorful plastic jewelry was in high fashion during 1935, especially as costume accessories. A simple dress of neutral colors could be changed with a variety of choices in hats, bags, gloves, earrings, rings, necklaces, clips, bracelets, and belt buckles. All these items were made available over the counter by creative costume jewelry designers who provided sets of costume jewelry and accessories in every color. Cast phenolic costume jewelry in combinations with other materials such as wood, metal, rhinestones and ivory, enchanted buyers looking for a "brighter change" from the dark depression of the thirties.

In 1935, phenolic jewelry could be bought in retail stores from fifty cents to three dollars. The better known department stores catered to a clientele who could afford designer plastic jewelry which sold from $1.00 to $3.00. As advertised in 1935, "at these prices, women from all social strata could purchase sets or single items in colors that would harmonize with both daytime and evening dress."

It was 1935, and theatrical personage, Noel Coward, brought back the Regency period of dress with its lovely colors of dusty pink, mauve, light green, chartreuse, blue and white. Plastic jewelry was molded, cut, or carved with the favored feather motif, to be worn with the small Regency-style hats. Flower motifs to complement real flowers, corsages and *boutonnieres* were worn with the demure floor-length gowns.

New York's famed department stores were showplaces for plastic jewelry that featured deeply carved bracelets, clips, earrings, pins, rings, and belt buckles. Winter, 1935, showed fashionable colors which included dark brown, carnelian, green, and other color plastics that could harmonize with the simplicity of dress. Carved and uncarved black and brown plastic jewelry were mainstays of fashion accessories for years to come. However, in February 1935, the Celluloid Corporation achieved variegated color effects with its thermoplastic materials, ranging in an "infinity of colors to produce imitations of the most beautiful products of nature such as Ivory, Horn, Tortoiseshell, Mother-of-Pearl, Onyx, Quartz, Marble, Lapis Lazuli, Gemstones, Rare Woods, etc." These thermoplastics accepted tints to match or contrast the color of fabrics and leather, thus fabricators matched the colors of garments with the buttons, buckles, clasps, dress and millinery ornaments which were the important accessories of the year 1935.

Sketch #11 - Spring sales in 1935 included a renewal of popularity for cast phenolic materials combined with wood, wood and metal, metal and crystal, and other innovative conceptions. This "spring jewelry promotions" in the finest department stores, featured what was called *Bios Glace*, manufactured by D. Lisner and Company, (a name long remembered as a manufacturer of copyrighted design jewelry, marked "Lisner"). Lisner came out with an entirely new line of jewelry in 1935, doing away with metal rivets for fastening plastics to wood, or by the use of glue. A new combination was achieved by pouring the molten phenolic solution *over* the wood which had been previously placed in the mold. The transparent phenolic, when cold, was then polished. The resulting jewelry had the brilliance of crystal, and the transparent coating of cast phenolic acted like a magnifying glass, thus emphasizing the exquisite grain of the wood.

Although other manufacturers supplied Lord & Taylor, McCreery, Altman, Arnold Constable, Macy's and other fine stores with wood and metal combinations, Lisner's *Bois Glace* was unique, and the other plastic products sold for less and were really not competitive. Leo Glass, a manufacturer of costume jewelry for such New York outlets as Saks Fifth Avenue and Bonwit Teller, produced higher priced sophisticated plastic jewelry also using wood and cast phenolics. And since the clientele of these houses was younger and more "high style conscious" and less conservative, the pieces most in demand were the handsome larger pieces with high toned bright colors and material combinations. Some of these jewelry pieces are, of course, highly sought after by collectors of twentieth century fashionable plastic jewelry, and are worn by teenagers *and* senior citizens who are fortunate in finding such items while "on the hunt."

The intrinsic value of plastic jewelry plays a small part in the price. This was true in the 1930's as it is today. Ingenious designs in flexible bracelets, or a clever buckle or pin, geometric shapes of plastic combined with wood, metal, ivory or other materials, plus rarity of course, will influence price.

Sketch #12 - The importance of the plastic industry was recognized by the "new plastic section" printed for the first time in the *Thomas Register*, published by Thomas Publishing Company. For the first time, this publishing company advertised that manufacturers and fabricators of all plastic materials would appear in its relied-upon register used by industry.

Sketch #13 - Promotion by top department stores and manufacturers influenced saleability and desirability. Thousands of shapes and designs in infinite varieties were produced, thus keeping today's collectors on a continuous search for unique additions. The lovely thing about collecting these pieces is that they can be exhibited and fashionably worn.

Modern Plastics reported in 1935 that many beautiful effects were obtained by actually *combining* Bakelite, Catalin, or Marblette with other molded plastics such as ureas, phenolics, cellulose acetates, hard rubber, pyroxylin, wood and metal. Jewelry designers used one material as a base and another one or more types for sheer decorative effect.

Despite the popularity of the "new" pastel shades made available to a fashion-conscious society, about three-fourths of all molded parts in plastic jewelry and accessories were in black. Designing black plastics had many challenges. A flat black surface was dull until it was handcarved or cut to catch highlights. Catching and controlling these highlights was the plastic jewelry designer's real challenge. Pieces of black jewelry that achieved fine bas-relief sculpturing and shallow concave flutes, are shown on some of the black and white plates in this book. Naturally, these pieces with exceptionally fine detail are sought after as fashionable costume jewelry.

Sketch #14 - The year 1935 was a banner year for the synthetic resin industry of the United States which led the world as its largest producer and consumer of such plastics. The United States has maintained its lead today in the chemistry of synthetic resins, including "space age" plastics and synthetics.

By August 1938, Germany acted symbolically in noting the national importance of plastics by establishing a new Plastics Institute at Frankdor-on-Main, the principal center of Germany's chemical industry. The building was constructed near Frankfurt University, and was designed to provide laboratories and other rooms necessary for conducting scientific research work regarding plastics. The American Consulate General, reporting on Germany's extensive exhibits of plastics and chemicals held in Frankfurt (1937), stated it was the "most discussed section of the entire exposition." By this time, Hitler made Austria a German province—Japan, Italy, and Germany formed a triple alliance—the U.S. gunboat *Panay* was bombed by the Japanese in the Yangtze

River—all these happenings merely a prelude to the Act of War by the Axis nations.

Sketch #15 - Tweeds and "rough" fabrics were in fashion, Spring 1935, and thereby required new types of jewelry for the "sporting crowd." The newest craze was outdoor sports and "sports jewelry." Cast phenolics answered the problem caused by warm weather, metal jewelry, and human flesh blackened and stained by such a "mixture." Lighter in weight, colorful, and non-staining, the popularity of sports jewelry was advanced until over a million pieces sold on a yearly basis. Aside from the mass-produced types of plastic jewelry, there were rarer objects carved from Prystal and foreign or domestic plastic materials which required painstaking artistry and craftsmanship. Such dedication often produced plastic jewelry of rare beauty.

Rings, plain or intricate; bracelets, huge or tiny; bar pins, earrings, clips, buttons and buckles of identical pattern and color, were worn to emphasize sporting costumes.

A.D. Seidman, president of Ace Plastic Novelty Corporation, which made popular-priced sports jewelry exclusively for the jobbing trade, enjoyed much success in the plastics industry. "Cast phenolics," said Mr. Seidman, "are the ideal for fabricating sport jewelry because of rich and lasting colorings and their extremely light weight. Sport jewelry," he is quoted as saying during an interview, "because of the very purpose for which it is worn demands color and bulk without weight. It demands chic and smartness without flash. Rich opaques in the broadest range of delightful colors vie with an equally wide range of softest pastels and are splendidly balanced by lustrous blacks, whites, and clear phenolics to a completeness offered by no other material. Furthermore, they are odorless and non-porous so that they neither absorb perspiration, tarnish, nor change color."

"Another advantage of fabricating sport jewelry from cast phenolics is the number of matching pieces that can be included in the line. We make sets of bracelets, earrings, clips, finger rings, buckles and pins in matching colors and designs," concluded Mr. Seidman, "and if one cares to go that far, buttons and millinery ornaments may be secured in the same motif to complete an ensemble of extremely striking effect."

Sketch #16 - The above sketch mentioned Prystal plastic material. In May 1935, The American Catalin Corporation purchased the name and the United States' manufacturing rights covering Prystal. The material sold under the name PRYSTAL was a urea product of a waterclear nature, manufactured first by Nobel Francaise of Paris. This type of material was not only subject to limitations in applications but the most serious objection was its susceptibility to cracking and distortion under varying changes in temperature and atmospheric conditions.

Catalin purchased from Society Nobel Francaise of Paris, not only the U.S. registered trademarks covering

the name Prystal, but also the U.S. manufacturing rights under which this material was made. Prystal, as made by Catalin, was a cast phenolic resin having the same appearance as the former French Prystal, but was *much improved* in its physical characteristics. Catalin's Prystal was produced in larger varieties of shapes, sizes and colors.

One of the newest forms of this material produced by Catalin, was called "Star Dust." This form consisted of clear Prystal in which minute flakes of gold and silver were held in suspension, producing a unique luminous, brilliant and gem-like effect. Among some of the newer applications of Prystal as made by Catalin, is what D. Lisner produced as Bois Glace. Catalin's product also consisted of natural and rare woods imbedded in the clear plastic material.

Sketch #17 - Ruth Lampland, writer for *Modern Plastics* (June 1935 issue), stated that American Catalin Corporation's cast resins for jewelry were "the precious gem's only rival." This corporation pioneered the development of cast resins for jewelry and in less than seven years cast phenolic resins blossomed out of the laboratory to charm seven out of every ten women who wore costume jewelry. According to Lampland's calculation, by June 1935, 7 out of 10 women would be wearing jewelry of cast resins.

American Catalin corporation purchased the secret process in 1925 from a German company, including the manufacturing rights, of a material called Herolith. In 1932 they then purchased the cast resin patents of Dr. Fritz Pollak, an Austrian chemical "wizard," including thermo-setting phenol resins. Until then, there was only one place in the United States cast resins were known...Dr, Leo Baekeland, inventor of Bakelite. However, Baekeland's work was limited to his concentration on the successful product—Bakelite.

American Catalin Corporation envisioned the place cast resins would fill in American industry, and that vision paid off in their development and introduction of cast resins in the United States. By 1927, Catalin built its first plant at College Point Long Island, followed in 1930 by a larger and concededly the most modern plant of its kind, in Fords, New Jersey.

Catalin Corporation applied for the American patents on the secret processes which they had purchased abroad, and later purchased all the American patents formerly held by the London firm of Pollopas Limited.

By the early thirties, the company began selling and manufacturing Catalin in huge volumes. In the height of the depression, women were seeking jewelry that was both good-looking and inexpensive. The public was terribly money-conscious and with good reason. Through the lean depression era in the United States, the market for imitation jewels grew and grew. But fashion didn't want "fakes," they wanted a new material fashionable unto itself. Catalin and Prystal, beautiful in their own right, filled the bill dictated by forced frugality.

Catalin jewelry took the country by storm and for the first time a specific industry dictated fashion rather than vice versa. The Catalin and Prystal decorative ornaments became established merchandise in all the better stores in both town and country.

Sketch #18 - The power of advertising! In August 1935, just a few months after the announcement of Catalin's introduction of cast resin jewelry, (See Sketch #17), in the 34th Street windows of R.H. Macy & Co., New York, there appeared a display "telling customer how" cast resin jewelry was made.

There appeared rods and sheets and tubes of cast resins ingeniously arranged to show women and men how these colorful materials were fabricated. Several steps were shown in the exhibit from the material to the finished button, buckle, bracelet or pin. Different shapes of tubes were displayed including those used in the fabrication of both bracelets and buckles. These tubes of cast resin from which bracelets were made, resembled the old time Edison phonograph records standing on end. *Modern Plastics* magazine, (August 1935), reports in detail how effective this type of window display can be as a marketing device. The article states: "...to illustrate the process, was a tube with corrugated ribs ready to be sawn, and next to that were slices of the material showing the first operation, which gives a definite indication of the form the finished object will take. Then came examples of carving in the rough, followed finally by a splendid display of bracelets of many colors, some with inlay, all smoothly polished and glistening.

"Buckle tubes and rod stock were similarly shown. Buckle tubes in the form delivered to the fabricator have no great beauty, other than the natural beauty of the material itself. But when contrasted with the first crude slices, then etched and carved and polished, the wonder of the simplicity of it all makes its greatest impression."

The window display also showed examples of each step in the process of fabricating rod stock into pins, earrings, and buttons. By doing this, the "mystery" of plastic resin molding process was lifted somewhat.

The article went on to describe what must have been a most educational and unique exhibit for a department store to sponsor. Imagine a glorious array of color in sheets of resin in their final polishing mode!

"The background of the window was of soft, off-white fabric with a panel of pastel blue along the foreground of the floor," reported the article. One can imagine the delight in viewing plain sheets of cast resin of contrasting colors against such a background.

Captions on little cards explained each section of the exhibit. "To further dispel the mystery of cast resins, and to intrigue the imagination of those who witnessed the exhibit," the article continued to report, "plainly labeled bottles of chemicals which enter into their composition, formed the focal point of the display. There was a large bottle labeled

Liquid Marblette, another labeled *Formaldehyde*, and others of *Phenol Auramine*, and *Saframine*. No further secrets were divulged and there is little likelihood that those women who stood admiring the finished product would go home and try to roll their own. Nor is there any question that these women were impressed. It was probably the first opportunity many of them had ever had to learn even the fundamental nature of the material of which seventy percent of their costume jewelry is made."

All of the cast resins used in the R.H. Macy & Co. display, were Marblette, and the educational materials, accessories, and samples were furnished through the courtesy of the Marblette Corporation, Long Island, New York.

In response to those who question whether cast resins can be carved, according to the experts, cast resins can be carved. On decorative work, such as jewelry, where hair-line accuracy in the location of cuts is not essential, the carving tool is often guided by hand.

Sketch #19 - Although the Marblette Corporation furnished materials for the R.H. Macy & Co. display described in Sketch #18, the Marblette Corporation was competing with a new type of cast resins as advertised by Macy's competitor, John Wanamaker Department Store. The bold-face ad headlined: "Color Injection in New Catalin Crystal Jewelry! Bracelets—Earrings—Clips—Pins—Pairs of Clips. The color literally is injected. The crystal-clear jewelry is drilled, and the holes filled with gay Spring colors...yellow... green...blue...red, giving the effect of coral seen from a glass bottom boat!" After reading and studying the various advertisements about plastic jewelry, I'm convinced that Bakelite was *not used* in the colorful variety of Spring fashion jewelry which were advertised as "brightly colored." The majority of advertisements for Bakelite showed "earth" and "autumn" colors, and a prevalent use of ivory color, black, brown and shades of brown. Few truly "bright" classic colors which are highly collectible today were shown as "Bakelite." More often these colors were made in Catalin, Marblette, and some Beetle. Predominating the field of costume jewelry was Catalin.

Wanamaker's market report stated that costume jewelry of cast resins were estimated by a fashion authority as being used in 1935 for 70% of all summer jewelry. In 1934, winter jewelry consumed cast resin in such quantities that it was estimated that 30% of the plastic jewelry was made in cast resin. The use of cast resins for earrings, clips, pins, bracelets, necklaces, and other items of personal adornment "is now so widespread that it would seem that a point near saturation has been reached." However, Wanamaker's buyer predicted, rightfully so, that designers and manufacturers would "invent" a variety of applications for cast resin, and that the volume of this material used for costume jewelry would increase.

Sketch #20 - A German patent was taken out for

ornamentation of molded plastic articles, reported in *Modern Plastics*, April 1935. The patented process involved a new method that was both economical and with excellent results. It involved the impregnation of paper, fabric, metal foil or wire cloth (according to the nature of the molded article), with a synthetic resin. The patented material was applied to a desired pattern, then molded by heat and pressure which harden the resin and bond it firmly to the article to be decorated. This new method permitted a great variety of color and pattern effect.

The art of making high grade resins in top-grade transparency, invited the intrusion of never-before utilized ranges and purities of color effects. Improvements in the art of plastics permitted intricacies of pattern and design which enabled the designer of costume jewelry, and the maker, to offer an infinite variety of irresistibly attractive articles of comparatively small cost.

Bracelets, brooches, necklaces, charms, rings, eardrops, cuff links, hair ornaments and bar pins were reported among the many articles which were being made in the newest designs incorporating the German patent. Many of these articles are today described as "laminated plastics" which incorporate bits of fabric, colorful foils, wire cloth, etc. Although first introduced in 1935, experimentation with laminated layers of colorful resins brightened by impregnated materials, took place in France. After World War II, one of the better known success stories is the sought-after plastic jewelry signed, "Lea Stein, Paris," with several examples illustrated on the color plates in this book.

Sketch #21 - In 1935 the word "streamline" came into popular usage and was particularly ideal for plastics, because it gave items a cleaner, smoother look. During this same period, England was making bracelets from Leukon, which was a thermoplastic resin. Most manufacturers and designers were striving for curved contours in the use of opaque plastic because that kind of design would provide highlights in plastic. Transparent or translucent plastic materials depended on carvings and sharper corners to give a sense of texture or highlights achieved by curvatures.

Sketch #22 - In 1935, Corogram, Inc., created and patented "personality" buttons, pins, and belt buckles with "snap-in initials." The fancy belts helped promote the sale of robes, dresses, pajamas, millinery and coats. These sets of buttons, pins, and belt buckles were made in contrasting colors attainable by the use of urea plastics. The Associated Attleboro Manufacturing Company made the molds for these items for Paskon.

Sketch #23 - United-Carr Fastener Corp., makers of outstanding innovations in button-making, introduced in a preview showing at New York's Waldorf-Astoria, a variety of cast resin buttons and other items made of Catalin. All of these carved items were rendered by master craftsmen who relied on motifs suggested by outdoor sporting activities familiar to all in the 1935-1940 period. Most of the carved sets included bracelets, one or two clips, and buttons. The bracelets featured something *new*—double-hinge tips which allowed them to open sufficiently to slip over any size wrist without slipping off. This patented hinge was a departure in design from the familiar solid-ring "cuff" and "bangle." Some of the outdoor activity designs included horses, horseshoe motifs, serpents, or alligators coiled in repose, frogs, and florals. These latter designs were made in translucent plastics.

Sketch #24 - In October 1935, a French patent was taken out for unbreakable combs of treated vinyl chloride resin. The following month, D. Lisner & Co., importers of jewelry, reproduced Benvenuto Cellini 16th century boxes reproduced in cast resin. These boxes were adapted for cigarettes, while smaller such boxes became a compact, pill box, or one to carry saccharin. Lisner used plastic materials to recreate antique styles—mainly Catalin, a product also utilized by the famous Whiting & Davis manufacturing company, maker of many of today's collectible purses.

Sketch #25 - We usually think of The Gorham Company as makers of silver items, but in 1935 this company experimented with plastic cast moldings for cameos, buckles and novelty "Scottie" pins.

Sketch #26 - Miniature decorative flowers and earring buttons were molded for manufacturing jewelers by Synthetic Moulded Products, Inc., from stock molds of its own creation. The moldings were intricate and colorful and were styled to attract buyers who demanded inventories of such plastic costume jewelry.

Sketch #27 - In November 1935, an imposing history of the Bakelite Corporation from the birth of *exbyenzylmethylenglycolan-hydride* (meaning "resinoid"), appeared in the "Silver Anniversary" issue of *Bakelite Review*. The anniversary issue told of the invention of "Bakelite" in a humble laboratory at Yonkers, New York, and expanded the history to include the thousands of materials and the millions of uses of items manufactured in 1935 at its 125-acre plant in Bound Brook, New Jersey.

Sketch #28 - *Modern Plastics*, December 1935, paid tribute to Belle Kogan who designed the "polka dot" bracelets and earrings in two-color cast resinous jewelry. She was associated with her father in the jewelry business. Born in Russia, she came to the United States when she was only 4 years old. Belle Kogan studied in the famed jewelry center of Pforzheim (Germany) from 1930-31. Kogan's definition of "practical" was that any device which helped a manufacturer to sell more goods, could be defined as "practical"; she was one of the first in the jewelry industry to experiment with plastics. She designed plastic jewelry for Blefeld & Goodfriend who were jobbers for Woolworth's stores throughout USA. She also designed two sets of toiletware for

Celluloid Corporation, using Amerith, a translucent resin, and applied rhodium plated handles.

Sketch #29 - The fashion for Christmas 1935 plastic jewelry, was for Catalin and wood; cast resin plated with 24K gold "to make it non-tarnishable." Cast phenolic resins, with novel colors and combined with wood was novel, especially because the metal played a secondary role to the plastic resin. The jewelry was lightweight, colorful, and durable. That holiday season, D. Lisner & Co., combined Catalin beads and metal, forerunners of much of the plastic-metal combinations soon arriving from overseas.

Sketch #30 - *Modern Plastics*, February 19, 1936, announced the new Paris fashions in plastic jewelry and accessories by outstanding Parisiene couturiers such as: Schiaparelli, Vionnett, Vienne, and Hubert—the latter introducing "Jumbo," the elephant buckle with two elephants' heads in chocolate brown cast resin (American Catalin), with ivory tusks and eyes, to contrast with the basic brown color. From Paris designers came buttons, buckles, bag ornaments and trim, millinery ornaments, hair ornaments, jewelry, etc., some made of French plastics; others of American resins. Lilly Dache used plastic on hats worn at sporting events, the cocktail hour, and special dining chapeau decorated with plastic ornaments and trim. All were sold at I. Miller, Bloomingdale's and Saks Fifth Avenue.

Sketch #31 - In February 1936, Japan was using molded phenolic plastics for making Obi (sash) buckles. Japan was supplementing precious metals, jade, coral, porcelain, bone, and similar products, by incorporating plastic molding in two to three colors. This work closely imitated some of the work made in the United States. (In 1936, Japan produced only 50 cars a day!)

Sketch #32 - "Suit watches" were popularized in 1936, and sold as an eclat to be slipped into a breast pocket, or attached with a short leather cord to a bar pin. Some had a clip-type attachment for a dress or suit. Suits were made of sturdy tweeds, with huge buttons and buckles. Some of the "chunky" wooden buttons were covered with carved transparent plastic in the popular colors of red and butterscotch that went so well with such fabric. Also complementing tweeds, were the "man-sized" fob watches in red and green thermoset plastics.

Sketch #33 - Spring 1936 brought a flurry of exciting "fickle fashion"—faddish items such as a perfume fob of resin, with a transparent opening at the top. Dabs of cotton were tucked into small perforations in the back of the plastic fob, and a drop of favorite perfume was dabbed on the cotton floss.

Sketch #34 - Other fads c.1936, included plastic purses fitted with plastic combs, and for the first time molded plastic flowers were combined with gold metal links to create a "new look" in jewelry. By the summer of 1936, Cohn & Rosenberger, Inc., makers of hinged bracelets and carved buckles,

began to incorporate metal flowers on black plastic, and put the concoction on a large hinged cuff. Cahn & Company made transparent cast resin jewelry in a "linen weave" pattern. Geo. F. Berkander created boutonniere brooches to simulate varieties of flowers, then added stems and leaves of cellulose acetate, sprinkled with rhinestones. By summer, "Dude Rancher" cast resin pieces appeared in the shapes of six-shooter pins, 10-gallon Stetson pins, and various scarf pins all made of grey resin with bright red accents, such as a red band on the Stetson hat. Colorful belt buckles and buttons, in Bakelite cast resinoids were manufactured by Eureka Pearl Works, Inc., in July 1936.

Sketch #35 - The very first piece of Celluloid jewelry was made in the United States by George F. Berklander in 1906. He shaped and finished the piece of jewelry entirely by hand. According to his report, he was making his way home from work when he saw a toilet-set (dresser set) made of ivory color Celluloid in the window of Tilden & Thurber, a Providence R. I., leading jeweler. Berkander had previously made "French Ivory" combs from Celluloid. His company employed hundreds of craftsmen and craftswomen, and supplied millions of Celluloid and acetate plastic articles to department and chain stores throughout the United States. He remembered how metal bar pins tarnished, so he decided to try to make a bar pin by hand of plastic. He succeeded and thereby became the actual "pioneer of plastic jewelry." Berkander & Co. was responsible for 70% of all jewelry sold in 1936.

Sketch #36 - When George Berkander decided to market plastic jewelry for the first time, he convinced Miss Henrietta Graff, buyer for Berg Brothers (New York City), to place an order for three gross. Two days later, she ordered three more gross—7 or 8 times within hardly more than a week. Finally, she ordered 58 gross in one lot! Henry Siegal's Department Store, 6th Avenue, New York City, featured this plastic jewelry on only one counter. So successful was this move, that it wasn't long before the word spread to all other department stores where buyers begged for more. Most of the Celluloid bar pins sold for $1.00.

Sketch #37 - Cohn & Rosenberger, Inc. were one of the first manufacturers of the crystal clear, lightweight acrylic plastic jewelry known as Lucite, (Oct. 1938). Voges Manufacturing Co., stamped from sheet stock or cut from rods, Casein fabricated buttons which were non-flammable. Casein could be molded, turned, shaped, drilled, and sawed. Within a few years, both England and France would be at war (1914-1918 WWI), and the Casein plastic industry simply caved in. But prior to this tragic human event, the new plastics were gaining inroads, and contests were held to provide competition in the industry. Deauville Bags, Inc., received an Honorable Mention (Novelty category), for a clear Lucite frame for one of its purses (bags).

Sketch #38 - In November 1938, the Marlow

"Cosmetic Bracelet" of cast Bakelite resin, embossed with a metal band, opened when turned and revealed three receptacles holding a mirror, powder puff, and rouge.

Sketch #39 - Crystal-like Plexiglas, (soon to go to war), was exhibited by Röhm and Haas, at the Radio City Music Hall exhibit (May 1939). The plastic was made into a necklace of transparent, colorless, Plexiglas, which was much lighter in weight than were glass beads, and was unbreakable. Also exhibited by other manufacturers, were white cast resin bells, daisies, and dice, hung from cellulose acetate linked chains. Geo. F. Berkander Co., produced a "Donald Duck" pin, and a necklace comprised of a cluster of leaves on linked chain—all in plastic. The sporty pin-ons were made in a combination of cast resin, cellulose acetate, metal and cork.

Sketch #40 - A historical event occurred in August 1939: a George Gershwin Memorial Concert was held in Carnegie Hall, New York. Paul Whiteman, orchestra leader, introduced Al Gallodoro who played on a transparent Lucite clarinet (made by Pedler Co.), and achieved the special "reedy" tone adaptable for Gershwin's *Rhapsody in Blue*. The fad for Lucite fabricated pins in the shape of clarinets and other instruments prevailed.

Sketch #41 - Another simultaneous historical event occurred when a new "gemstone" named The Petrified Sunshine was cast in plastic. Costume jewelry cast in a multitude of shapes and forms in "gemstones," revolutionized the plastic costume jewelry industry. One of the first to feature the plastic "gemstone" was Milton & Brown, Co., Fifth Avenue, New York City. The producer: A. Knoedler Company, Lancaster, Pennsylvania, USA. The 1939 introduction of "gemstone" plastic jewelry, came hard on the heels of the 1936 "gold flecked jewelry" designed by Walter Heimler, from Catalin. Then in June 1937, it was "officially announced" that the costume jewelry industry was "a big-time industry" in the United States. To impress and convince other countries of America's advancement in this field, for the first time there were exhibitions in England to show American manufacturing moldings and their uses. The progress of plastic industries throughout the USA and on the continent, was told at this exhibit sponsored by England's Synplas Ltd.

Sketch #42 - The advances in plastic costume jewelry design were evident in 1937 when C.K. Castaing, (Stony Book, Long Island, New York), carved cacti and wheat designs on the *reverse side* of transparent plastic trays. These were sold by Georg Jensen Hand Made Silver, Inc., and the trays won third prize in "decorative" category, at the convention sponsored by *Modern Plastics* magazine. Castaing was, in his day, a famed sculptor-artist. This was the beginning of "reverse-carved" transparent plastic jewelry which is so collectible today.

Sketch #43 - In January 1937, the new year began with the introduction of "Moldite" by Ralph Manguso, of the Moldite Corporation. He began casting resins in rubber molds which could then produce very intricate purse handles of "ivory" cast resin, in a myriad of shapes and designs. A variety of shapes and designs of buttons in heavy bas-relief was also made possible by the use of these rubber molds.

Sketch #44 - The Vulcanized Fibre Co. provided the Bakelite Corporation with a semi-cured Phenalite which gave its product, Bakelite, reinforcement.

Sketch #45 - Dr.Otto Röhm, (Darmstadt, Germany), is mainly credited with the development of transparent acrylic resins in 1901, but it wasn't until 1931 that acrylic resins were made available in commercial quantities in the United States. (Readers who remember the cinema success, "Sabrina",[1] will recall the episode in which "transparent, strong, durable *plastic*" was introduced into the plot; and a hammock of plastic which could be "stretched like elastic," yet strong enough to hold a man, was made of the newest product—thermoplastic.

Sketch #46 - Fall 1937 fashions featured buttons, buckles, slides, pocketbook[2] trimmings, and other articles for which Casein plastics were used and supplied by duPont Chemical Corporation. At the same time, Catalin Corporation was boasting that its company was "the Gem of Modern Plastics," and showed "Catalin Buttons for Fall," including Arabian Sword shapes for both buttons and buckles.

Sketch #47 - Plastacele, a duPont Company product, was used predominately for costume jewelry featuring flowers in all colors and shapes.

Sketch #48 - Not to be outdone, Nixonite acetate for costume jewelry was offered in competition by the Nixon Nitration Works, Nixon, New Jersey (1937).

Sketch #49 - During that same Fall 1937, Celluloid Corporation was advertising injection molding with samples of Scotties, Ribbon pins, and other novelties accented with rhinestones.

Sketch #50 - Finally, Bakelite Corporation ran ads for its laminated plastics, but far and few of the "Bakelite" advertisements projected application of its plastics for jewelry.

[1] "Sabrina," with Humphrey Bogart, Audrey Hepburn, and William Holden, *Paramount Studios* release, 1954.

[2] "Pocketbook," adopted c.1937, was a more modern term than "purse" or "bag." The term "pocketbook" was probably used during the 1930's when women began to carry notepads, money, and other paper goods, besides combs and cosmetics. Women were entering the labor market in droves, perhaps driven by the depression and the need for income. Jobs for men were scarce while jobs "suitable for women" were opening up, i.e. secretaries, stenographers, receptionists, clerks, and so on. Women were also willing in those desperate times, to accept lower salaries. This unfortunately set a precedent which carried over even during periods of prosperity. However, in recent years, pay-scales for most jobs are non-discriminatory by either State or Federal law—or both. Because of this, one can see professional working women carrying "brief-cases" (not "pocket books"), similar to male counterpart. Modern women, oftentimes, carry with them what appear to be pieces of "luggage," "back-packs," or "body-bags" worn around the hips. The latter resembles the leather pouches or kits adopted by men so as to free both hands, making them "ready for combat against thieves or threats."

Section II

Includes:

An important explanatory note from the author to the reader, (below).

Full Color Plates with Captions

Black and White Photographs with Captions

Period Advertisements and Illustrations with Captions

An important explanatory note from the author to the reader.

The description and captioning for each piece of jewelry or accessory described in this book, have been prepared by the individual collector or collector/dealer.

The word "Bakelite" has, in many cases, been used as an umbrella term to cover a wide segment of manufactured articles of plastic jewelry and accessories which were made of thermoset phenolic resins.

The word "Celluloid" is commonly used herein to describe one of a variety of thermoplastic jewelry pieces and accessories manufactured from approximately 1900-1935. "Celluloid," after that period, could refer to a newer cellulose acetate which was not as flammable as was the earlier product.

Appendix A gives a fine breakdown of plastics, but for the purpose of easier association with this complex subject, the author has accepted the terms, "Bakelite" and "Celluloid," in common usage so as not to confuse the reader.

Plate #1

Location	Nomenclature	Circa	Description
Top to Bottom	Pins (4)	1960	Figural foxes in aqua, yellow, red, and violet. (Also made in colors: magenta, pink, light blue, black, white, navy, and pearlized plastic) Marked: "Lea Stein, Paris."
Center	Beads	1930	Multicolored, double-strand, American Bakelite.
Center, Top	Earrings (Clip)	1935	Carved Bakelite cherries. (Rare)
Center, L-R	Earrings (2/pr)	1930	Polka-dot & multi-color. (American)

In 1937, the New Jersey based E. I. duPont de Nemours & Co. Plastics Department, introduced Plastacele, a cellulose acetate plastic used for costume jewelry. At that time, duPont, ("Better things for better living—through chemistry"), had no less than six different plastic materials such as: Pyralin (used in some jewelry making), Phenalin, cast phenolic resin, and Lucite—both of the latter were experimented with by jewelry manufacturers and perfected in the production of popular fashionable costume jewelry.

DuPont's definition of *Plastics*: "man-made chemical combinations of nature's raw materials." Plastics are solid at ordinary temperatures, but when heated become soft and pliable. When molded under pressure, they take any desired shape and retain it.

In its May 1937 advertisement in *Modern Plastics*, the catchy line: A little cotton and a little vinegar can become this lovely bracelet!", is beautifully illustrated by a plastic cuff bracelet worn on a delicate wrist.

Note: The term "American Bakelite" is used generically to indicate that the type of plastic on a particular piece of jewelry is of a phenolic resin which is thermoset. The same notation applies to the general use of the term "Bakelite" as an overall generic term for thermoset plastic. Readers are directed to the chapter titled, Fifty Thumbnail Sketches, and Appendix A in this book.

Plate 1
Ginger Moro Collection

Plate #2

Location	Nomenclature	Circa	Description
Top, Row 1	Buckle	1930	Handpainted Celluloid. (French)
Row 2, L-R	Necklace	1930	Red & burgundy Bakelite beads with chrome.
	Necklace	1930	Red Bakelite with mesh chrome. (German)
	Necklace	1930	Carnelian color Bakelite with mesh chrome. (Belgium)
Center	Brooch	1930	Figural rooster with sterling silver accent. (American)

Next to the United States, Germany was the world's largest producer of synthetic resins. By 1937, 90% of Germany's synthetic resin production was of phenolic origin. Germany's interest and progress regarding pyroxlyin plastics steadily increased since 1929.

France had its growing plastics industries producing pyroxylin plastics from the turn of the century through 1934, when interest in synthetic resins rose considerably.

Meanwhile, plastics production in Great Britian spiraled upward, also competing with the United States' leadship in the field. However, by 1933, Great Britain's concentration on galalith and pyroxylin plastics made it a principle supplier of these earlier plastics.

By 1937, Czechoslovakia (not yet swallowed up by Nazi takeover), was making practically no pyroxylin plastic having replaced this highly flammable type of plastic with synthetic resins and other materials.

Because Japan was considered the "home of the camphor industry," and camphor being one of the ingredients required of pyroxylin, it was logical that Japan would be a significant producer. Japan's cheap labor prior to and from the turn-of-the-century, aided the plastics industry to grow considerably in contrast to the pyroxylin production in western countries. By 1934, Japan's firms were using synthetic phenolic resins for molded products used especially by household products industries.

None of the above nations seriously entered the competion for making plastic jewelry, against the United States.

Plate 2
Ginger Moro Collection

Plate #3

Location	Nomenclature	Circa	Description
Center	Necklace	1930	Celluloid raspberries with leaves. Rare. (American)
Row 1, L-R	Pin	1940	Figural bellhop with movable limbs. (French)
	Pin	1980	Figural sailor with movable limbs. (French) *Reproduction of c. 1930 pin.*
Row 2, L-R	Brooch	1980	Multi-color mask motif. (Italian) signed: "Missoni." (See Plate 6.)
	Pin	1980	Figural sailor with movable limbs. (French) *Reproduction of c. 1930 pin.*

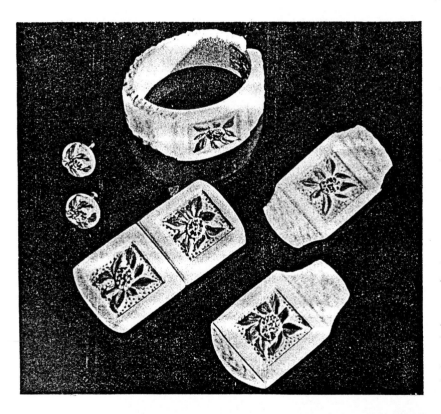

November 1937, Modern Plastics Magazine.

Bakelite Corporation announced that its new urea-formaldehyde molding compound was available in two colors—ivory and white. Other colors, they said, would be added to the line as demand necessitates.

However, cellulose acetate molding powder in twelve different colors was ready for commercial use, and special colors were offered upon request.

Bracelet, earrings, belt buckle, clip and pin, shown at left, were carved from milk-white cast resin and hand painted with a bright poinsettia motif.

Bottom illustration shows colorful pins, clips and buckles painted with the brilliance of tropical foliage. Typical scenes and figures were etched and carved from cast resin, and hand-painted with bright splashes of color. (Jewelry, c.1937, were from Ortho Plastics.)

Credit: Catherine Yronwode & Dean Mullaney Archives

Plate 3
Ginger Moro Collection

Plate #4

Location	Nomenclature	Circa	Description
Left to Right	Necklaces (6)	1955	Variations of setting, shapes of molded "stones," and endless styles of chains and clasps. All necklaces were sold with matching earrings, bracelets, and in many cases, brooches completed the parure.

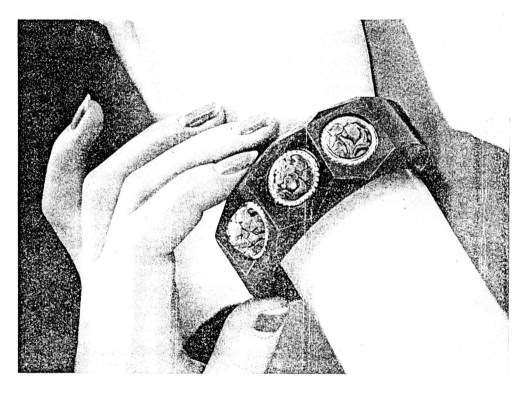

Credit: Catherine Yronwode and Dean Mullaney Archives

MAY 1937

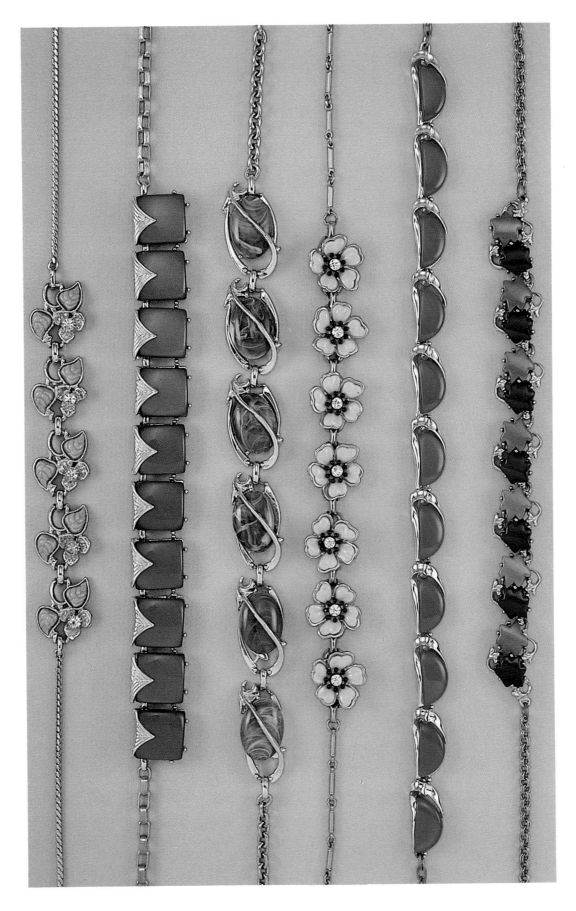

Plate 4
Author's Collection

Plate #5

Location	Nomenclature	Circa	Description
Top, L-R	Brooch	1930	Handpainted accents on carved Bakelite.
	Ring in box	1935	Laminated Celluloid ring box with large 1⅜"x¾" butterscotch color faceted Bakelite ring.
	Earrings	1970	Dark amber plastic oval drops, marked: "Trifari."
Center	Earrings	1935	Small button type, butterscotch color carved Bakelite.
Bottom, Left	Purse	1925	Beaded drawstring style with a Celluloid cover which slips up and down on silk cording.
Center, Right	Jewelry Box	1910	Celluloid, imitation "French Ivory," engraved "Lillian."
Bottom, Right	Bracelets (3)	1935	Butterscotch color carved Bakelite bangles.

Eve Main, fashion editor for *Modern Plastics* magazine, (December 1936), noted that jewelry manufacturers were "ringing in a new style note in costume jewelry with plastic rings for every occasion." The thermoset plastic product was Catalin, shown in "bulky" chunky carved florals to rectangular plaques of carved resin measuring from a full inch and larger. These novelty rings were fashionable with sports, dinner, or evening attire—just as long as they were unique and big. Although the ring shown on this plate is simply faceted, many of the period were imbedded with simulated rubies, sapphires and rhinestones.

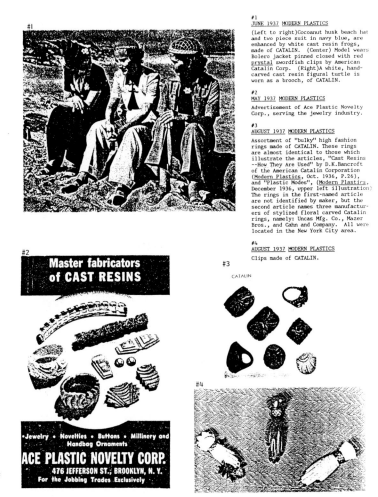

#1
JUNE 1937 MODERN PLASTICS
(Left to right)Cocoanut husk beach hat and two piece suit in navy blue, are enhanced by white cast resin frogs, made of CATALIN. (Center) Model wears Bolero jacket pinned closed with red prystal swordfish clips by American Catalin Corp. (Right)A white, hand-carved cast resin figural turtle is worn as a brooch, of CATALIN.

#2
MAY 1937 MODERN PLASTICS
Advertisement of Ace Plastic Novelty Corp., serving the jewelry industry.

#3
AUGUST 1937 MODERN PLASTICS
Assortment of "bulky" high fashion rings made of CATALIN. These rings are almost identical to those which illustrate the articles, "Cast Resins --How They Are Used" by D.K.Bancroft of the American Catalin Corporation (Modern Plastics, Oct. 1936, P.26), and "Plastic Modes", (Modern Plastics, December 1936, upper left illustration) The rings in the first-named article are not identified by maker, but the second article names three manufacturers of stylized floral carved Catalin rings, namely: Uncas Mfg. Co., Mazer Bros., and Cahn and Company. All were located in the New York City area.

#4
AUGUST 1937 MODERN PLASTICS
Clips made of CATALIN.

Master fabricators of CAST RESINS

•Jewelry • Novelties • Buttons • Millinery and Handbag Ornaments

ACE PLASTIC NOVELTY CORP.
476 JEFFERSON ST., BROOKLYN, N. Y.
For the Jobbing Trades Exclusively

CATALIN

Credit: Catherine Yronwode and Dean Mullaney Archives

Plate 5
Author's Collection

Plate #6

Location	Nomenclature	Circa	Description
Left, Top to Bottom	Earrings (2 pr.)	1980	Pair of red and a pair of green Bakelite with chrome. (Italian) Signed: "Missoni."
	Brooch	1980	Multi-color Bakelite mask, signed: "Missoni." (Italian) (See Plate 3.)
Center, Top to Bottom	Bracelet	1980	Large Bakelite cuff, signed: "Missoni." (Italian)
	Bracelet (3)	1950	Laminated, carved Celluloid. (French)
	Bracelet (3)	1950	Red, white, and blue Bakelite and brass. (French)
	Bracelet (3)	1950	Laminated carved Celluloid. (French)
Right, Top to Bottom	Bracelet	1930	Large Bakelite cuff, buckle design with sailor motif. (American)
	Bracelet	1940	Carved Bakelite, butterscotch color.
	Bracelet (8)	1950-1970	Extendable elastic, laminated Celluloid. (French)

COSMETIC BRACELET

Complete with Powder, Rouge, Lipstick, 3 Puffs and 2 Mirrors cleverly hidden within the bracelet. A turn of the gold-decorated band transforms this unique bracelet into a complete make-up kit. Ultra-smart! $2.20 Postpaid complete with 9 extra refills. Tax paid! Exclusive with the

HOUSE OF GIFTS

Box 2008-T2, Miami Beach, Fla.

Credit: Roselyn Gerson Archives
Town & Country magazine ad, 1942.

The "cosmetic bracelet" pictured in this advertisement is also shown as Fig. 139 #11, in Roselyn Gerson's definitive work, Ladies' Compacts of the Nineteenth and Twentieth Centuries, (Wallace-Homestead Book Company, Radnor, Pennsylvania, 1989).

It is described as: Marlow Co. "Parisienne" plastic cosmetic bracelet complete with compartments for powder rouge, lipstick, 3 puffs and 2 mirrors. A turn of the gold-decorated metal band transforms this unique bracelet into a complete make-up kit. Available in several different colors, c. 1940's.

Two more plastic compacts are shown in the above-referenced book by Gerson, as follows:

Fig. 139 #9 - Black plastic compact/bracelet set with rhinestones, grosgrain band, c.1920's.

Fig. 140 #4 - black plastic vanity case with rhinestone geometric design on lid; front opens to reveal mirror, powder and rouge compartments; back contains coin pocket; black carrying cord with lipstick concealed in tassel, c.1920's.

Eve Main, writing editorially for Modern Plastics, (1934), said that "the desire for personal adornment is the foundation upon which has been built one of the oldest and most important industries—the making of jewelry." Another industry which has become deeply involved in the adornment of women in a rather superficial way, is the cosmetic industry which has become in the past and present a companion which complements the wearing of jewelry. The need for make-up created compacts.

Plate 6
Ginger Moro Collection

Plate #7

Location	Nomenclature	Circa	Description
Top to Bottom			
Row 1, L-R	Earrings (clip)	1935	Red plastic set with rhinestones. Button shape.
	Clip	1935	Red Bakelite daisy with yellow center.
	Clip (pr.)	1935	Carved green Bakelite with original sales tag. (Matching buckle not shown)
Row 2, L-R	Clip (pr.)	1935	Red Bakelite with chrome rectangular grid.
	Clip (pr.)	1930	Red Bakelite and chrome, *Deco* design.
Row 3	Hat Ornament	1930	Brown plastic with rhinestones, *Deco* design.
Row 4, L-R	Clips (Dress)	1935	Deeply carved green Bakelite.
	Set: Buckle & Clip	1930	Green & light amber color carved Bakelite.
	Clips (pr.)	1930	Brown carved Bakelite, floral design. (Original card not shown, which reads: "Latest Novelty Twin Clips.")
Row 5, L-R	Clip	1930	Red carved Bakelite flower.
	Clip	1930	Long, red carved Bakelite floral design.
	Buckle	1930	Round, carved, dark amber color Bakelite, one-piece with hasp.
	Clips (pr.)	1930	*Deco* design, laminated wood and red Bakelite.

Credit: Catherine Yronwode & Dean Mullaney Archives

Transparent and translucent buttons are made of Bakelite resinoid. Pictured are buttons made by Iowa Pearl Button Company.

Plate 7
Christie Romero Collection

Plate #8

Location	Nomenclature	Circa	Description
Top	Necklace	1930	*Art Moderne* geometric. (American) Celluloid.
Center	Pin	1950	Figural vintage automobile. Laminated plastic. Marked: "Lea Stein, Paris."
Center, L-R	Bracelet	1980	Bakelite polka-dot cuff, signed: "Missoni." (Italian)
	Bracelets (2)	1940-1950	Plastic bangles, (French).
Bottom	Pins (2)	1960	Celluloid figural foxes, available in green, yellow, black, white, red and violet. Marked: "Lea Stein, Paris." (Company out of business in late 1970's.)
Bottom, Center	Bracelet	1935	Snake motif, bangle, "French Ivory" color Celluloid.

In describing "Ivory-Like Materials," author and collector Godfrey Harris cautions us that "with the creation of plastic materials, a blizzard of imitation ivory material began to appear."

He writes:

The first synthetic plastics, in fact, were created specifically in the hope that they would become a worthy substitute for genuine elephant ivory. They not only proved to be just that, but early plastics such as celluloid were soon adopted for much wider uses as well. Thomas Alva Edison, for one, considered celluloid a better material for his new phonograph records than wax and he later used celluloid for the film required to show the first motion pictures.

After Celluloid's first appearance in 1868, other wholly synthetic plastics were brought to market. Each, in turn, was developed to become a more acceptable substitute for ivory than Celluloid. As a result, these other plastics appeared with a wondrous collection of trade and popular names such as Ivorine, Eburine, Bakelite, Fiberlite, faux ivory, French ivory, Ivorie Parisienne, vegetable ivory, and Celluloid ivory.

(From The Fascination of Ivory, see bibliography.)

Plate 8
Ginger Moro Collection

41

Plate #9

Location	Nomenclature	Circa	Description
Top	Back comb	1925	Intricately designed Celluloid with a multitude of rhinestones. *Art Nouveau* design, "French Ivory" color.
Bottom, Left	Hair Ornaments	1935	Plastic and Lucite combination with rhinestone accents. Hinged. Approximately 8" overall. (Author's Collection)
Bottom, Right	Comb	1925	Exceptionally large amber color Celluloid with pave set rhinestones. A comparison with the hair ornaments, will give an idea of proportion.

Readers are referred to *Sketch #9* found in chapter titled, Fifty Thumbnail Sketches.

For further information specifically about various types of combs, please see Baker's *100 Years of Collectible Jewelry* (listed in the bibliography), wherein four full-color plates showing a gorgeous assortment of Stella Tarr's combs can be studied and enjoyed.

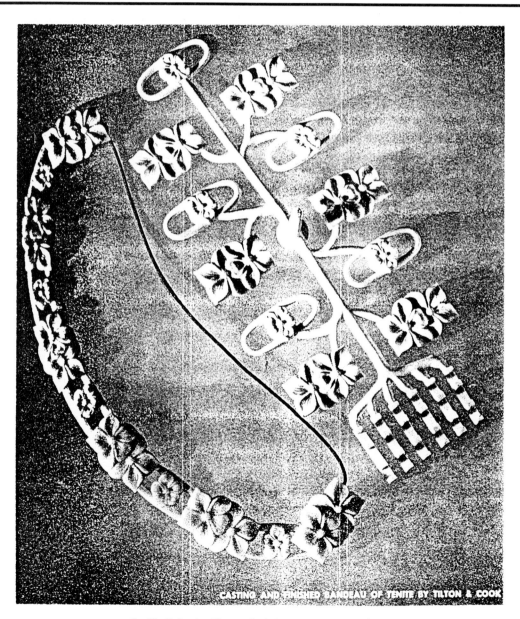

Credit: Catherine Yronwode & Dean Mullaney Archives

Plate 9
Stella Tarr Collection, unless otherwise noted

Plate #10

Location	Nomenclature	Circa	Description
Top to Bottom			
Row 1	Buckle	1935	2-piece Bakelite and metal, designed as a "buckle within a buckle." Unique.
Row 2	Set: Buckle and Clips	1935	2-piece buckle, pair of clips of translucent Bakelite with applied metallic flowers.
Row 3	Bracelet	1935	Reverse-carved, light amber color and black Bakelite with round links.
Row 4	Buckle	1935	Large 2-piece plastic figural pair of elephants.
Row 5, L-R	Brooch	1935	Large, dark amber color Bakelite Maltese cross.
	Brooch	1930	Maroon (reddish chestnut color) Bakelite, fob type, *Deco* design.
	Clips (Dress)	1935	Pair of carved amber color Bakelite.
Row 6, L-R	Pin	1935	Tortoise color Bakelite and yellow metal, figural sword.
	Pin	1935	Black Bakelite and chrome figural sword.

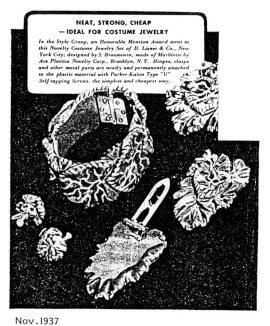

NEAT, STRONG, CHEAP
— IDEAL FOR COSTUME JEWELRY

In the Style Group, an Honorable Mention Award went to this Novelty Costume Jewelry Set of D. Lisner & Co., New York City; designed by S. Braunstein; made of Marblette by Ace Plastics Novelty Corp., Brooklyn, N.Y. Hinges, clasps and other metal parts are neatly and permanently attached to the plastic material with Parker-Kalon Type "U" Self-tapping Screws, the simplest and cheapest way.

Nov. 1937

PARKER-KALON *Modern* **FASTENING**

TYPE "Z" HEX CAP A HARDENED SELF-TAPPING SCREW FOR EVERY KIND OF ASSEMBLY

Credit: Catherine Yronwode & Dean Mullaney Archives

Costume Jewelry fashioned by Ace Plastic Novelty Company.

C. 1937

Credit: Catherine Yronwode & Dean Mullaney Archives

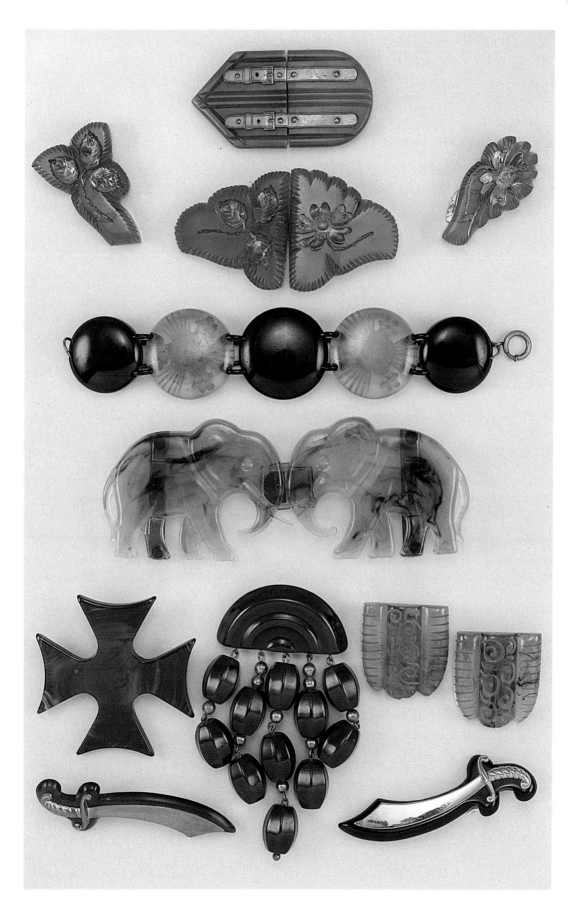

Plate 10
Christie Romero Collection

Plate #11

Location	Nomenclature	Circa	Description
Top to Bottom	Belt	1935	Butterscotch Bakelite and red plastic.
	Buckle	1930	Carved butterscotch color and black Bakelite. (American)
	Buckle	1920	Handpainted Celluloid, fruit motif.
Row 4, L-R	Buckle	1930	Coral color Bakelite, carved. (American)
	Buckle	1935	Green, butterscotch, orange and brown Bakelite. (American)

Much of Celluloid was handpainted. But in May 1937, Celluloid Corporation, (established 1872), registered a trademark as the sole producer of Lumarith which, according to its advertisement was a Celluloid product which gave thermoplastics its own "color and character." The May 1937 advertisement in *Modern Plastics* , magazine is quite revealing:

> *"More and more each day, modern manufacturers are becoming color-conscious. In almost every field of industry, they are striving to give their products the sales advantages that only color can bring."*

The "new era plastic," named by Celluloid Corporation, Lumarith, offered to the plastic world of jewelry the brilliant hues of reds, the yellows, the blues, the violets, and the subtle in-betweens.

The boon to the jewelry trade was the infinite variety of color combinations, including translucent and transparent tones, plus the mottled and variegated effects.

According to the experts, Lumarith was not only strong, resilient and colorful, but it was also odorless, tasteless, and non-flammable. Unlike the early Celluloid, it could be carved, cemented to other materials, die-formed, embossed, laminated, machined, molded, printed, pleated, scored, stiched, stretched, swaged, or even hand-shaped.

Without chemical analysis, it's almost impossible to tell if a plastic piece is made of Bakelite, Catalin, or Lumarith. We can be certain of one thing: it is *plastic*, man-made, and colorfully exciting.

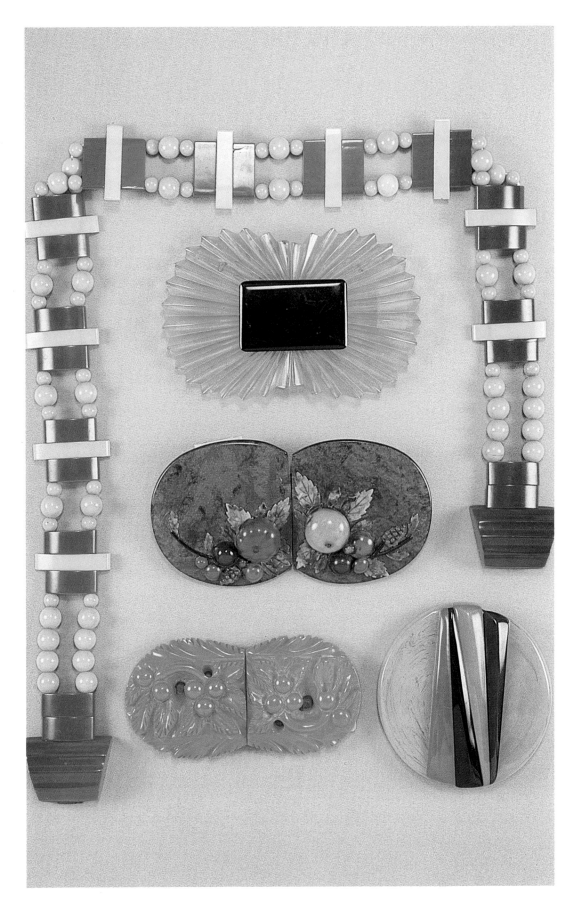

Plate 11
Ginger Moro Collection

Plate #12

Location	Nomenclature	Circa	Description
Left to Right	Hatpin Holder	1920	Figural handpainted celluloid "French Ivory." Weighted bottom.
	Hatpin Holder	1925	Celluloid with geometric design influenced by *Deco* period.
Bottom	Tiara	1920	Amber color Celluloid, handpainted design silver overlay, studded with rhinestones.
Top, Left	Hatpins (3)	1915-1925	Varied configurations of designs, combined with metal accents and rhinestones.
Top, Right	Hatpins (2)	1915-1925	Free form Celluloid and rare figural bug, partially molded Celluloid and cut plastic.
Center, Bottom	Hatpins (3)	1915-1925	Influence of Egyptian design, following the discovery of "Valley of the Kings" and King Tut's tomb. Molded Celluloid and free-form plastic "slices." Button-shaped hatpin is bezel-set into a metal backing which is attached with a tubular finding to the pin stem. The center free-form hatpin shows a tubular or socket jeweler's finding used to properly attach ornamental heads to pin-stems.

After the invention of the pin-making machine, (1832), the pin became a common commodity and the *Spectator* called the pin a mere "trifle." Yet prior to the invention which so many take for granted—pin-making—people were taxed to pay for the Queen's pins, and the penalty for stealing hand-made pins was hanging! Pins were so valuable they were bequeathed in wills and could only be purchased on New Year's Day. So came the term "pin money." Yet after pins became plentiful, it was indeed common to hear such phrases as "I don't care a pin for her." Shakespeare's Prince Hamlet said he didn't set his life at a "pin's fee." But then a Prince could afford what a pauper could not.

Plate 12
Author's Collection

Plate #13

Location	Nomenclature	Circa	Description
Center	Pendant/Necklace	1925	Bakelite and brass, with Bakelite beads. Egyptian influence in design factor. (Dorothy Buhrman Collection)
Top, L-R	Brooch	1935	Stylized scarab. Bakelite and brass. Signed: "Jeanne."
	Brooch	1930	Frame is reverse and obverse carved Bakelite, with molded plastic cameo. Large piece.
	Brooch	1930	Figural bird of wood, carved Lucite and brass beading.
Center	Brooch	1925	Large carved Bakelite scarab.
	Button	1930	Bakelite and Brass, *Deco* design.
Bottom, Left	Pendant	1925	Laminated Celluloid with applied brass Egyptian design.
	Pendant	1930	Marbleized molded Celluloid, handpainted, with applied Celluloid accents.
Bottom, Right	Set: Hatpin and Hat Ornament	1920	Handpainted molded Celluloid heads, Egyptian motif. Molded and threaded "nib" on end of hat ornament. (Rare set)

Credit: Catherine Yronwode & Dean Mullaney Archives

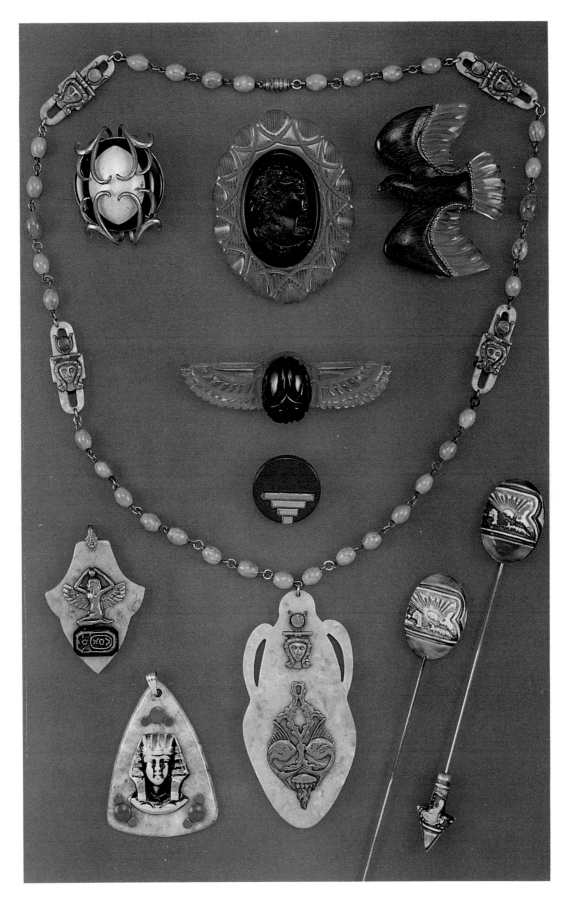

Plate 13
Author's Collection unless otherwise noted.

Plate #14

Location	Nomenclature	Circa	Description
Top to Bottom	Necklace	1920	Linked "end of day" amber color Celluloid. (English)
	Necklace	1935	Celluloid link chain, with Bakelite fruit pattern in mixed colors. (Rare)
	Necklace	1925	Green link plastic chain with flower basket design drops.
	Necklace	1935	Bakelite cherries on Celluloid chain. (Rare)

JET REPRODUCED

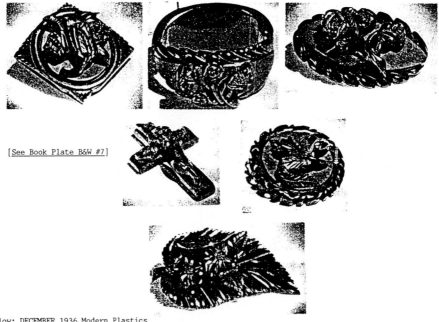

[See Book Plate B&W #7]

Below: <u>DECEMBER 1936 Modern Plastics</u>

DECORATING WITH LIQUID METAL

by BISSELL BROOKE

American Catalin Corp.

Explaining a new process of pouring metal decoration in the form of inlays into cast resin materials which have been fabricated to shape but not finished

Credit: Catherine Yronwode & Dean Mullaney Archives. April 1938—*Modern Plastics* Magazine.

Plate 14
Ginger Moro Collection

Plate #15

Location	Nomenclature	Circa	Description
Row 1, L-R	Clips (Dress)	1930	Pair of carved Bakelite.
	Pin	1930	Lime color plastic.
	Brooch	1950	Plastic with prong-set rhinestones.
	Earrings	1950	Lemon color plastic. (Thermoset)
Row 2, L-R	Set: Earrings and Bracelet	1950	Lemon color plastic. (Thermoset)
	Brooch	1960-1970	Unique design, with combination of Lucite, plastic, and glass. Marked: "W. Germany."
	Earrings	1950	Thermoset plastic set in rhodium.
Row 3	Bracelet	1960	Marbled Lucite set in white metal.
Row 4	Bracelet	1960	"Neon" orange color linked plastic with metal backing.
Row 5	Bracelet	1960-1970	Avocado green color linked thermoset plastic. Marked: "Charel."
Bottom	Earrings	1935	Molded transluscent autumn colors in thermoset plastic. Marked: "Lisner."

Costume jewelry of Tenite by Tilton-Cook Company, (1937)

Credit: Catherine Yronwode & Dean Mullaney Archives

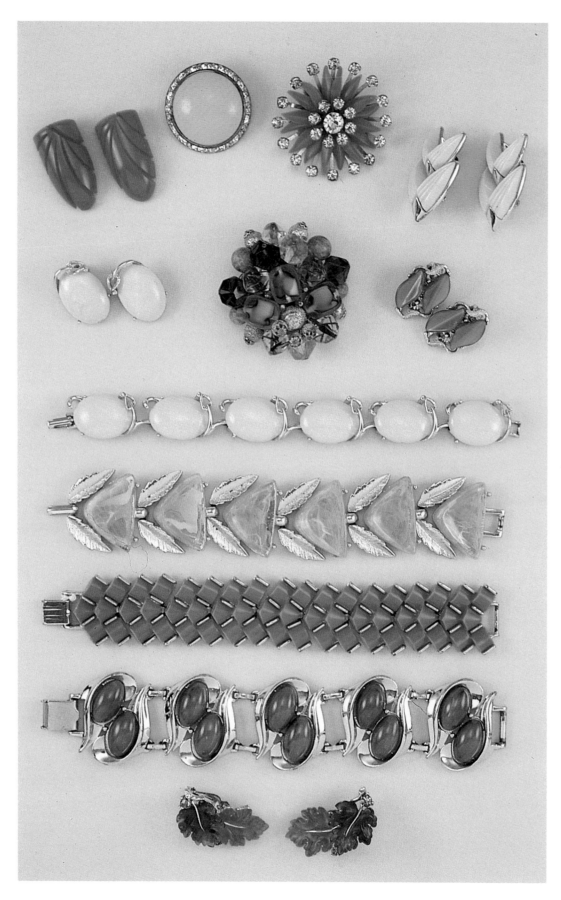

Plate 15
Author's Collection

Plate #16

Location	Nomenclature	Circa	Description
Top, L-R	Pin	1960	Laminated plastic, figural bellhop. Marked: "Lea Stein, Paris." (Dorothy Buhrman Collection)
	Brooch	1960	Turquoise thermoset plastic "gemstones" with emerald color glass stones. Marked: "Sarah Coventry."
	Pin	1960	Figural sailor, Celluloid. Marked: "Lea Stein, Paris." (Dorothy Buhrman Collection)
Center, L-R	Brooch	1975	Figural stylized leopard. Enameled, thermoset plastic, and pave set rhinestones. Marked: "KJL."
	Brooch	1960-1970	Libra sign (scales), enamel, ivory color thermoset plastic and turquoise color round plastic beads. Marked: "DiNicola."
Center	Set: Earrings and Bracelet	1960	Clip earrings. Thermoset molded plastic. Marked: "BSK."
Bottom, L-R	Combs (3)	1940	Amber color Celluloid.
	Set/3 Buttons	1935	Celluloid figural top hats. Unique.

The Waterbury Button Co., Plastic Division (Est. 1812), Waterbury, CT, manufactured a variety of buttons, and in 1935 advertised buttons combining metal and plastics. During the year, nitro-cellulose became restricted in use for buttons because the less expensive plastics, such as cast phenolics were more economical.

However, molded phenolics in light colors were avoided because light colors were hard to match for sets of buttons, so darker colors were made extensively for sweaters, trousers, work shirts, windbreakers, lumber jackets, and on suits and overcoats.

Ureas plastic molded buttons were available in light translucent shades which gave depth and intensity of color that was not as apt to fade.

Cast phenolics were replacing horn, vegetable ivory, and nut-shells previously used in making buttons.

Plate 16
Author's Collection unless otherwise noted.

Plate #17

Location	Nomenclature	Circa	Description
Top to Bottom			
Row 1	Buckle	1935	2-piece, beige and taupe plastic, *Deco* design.
Row 2	Set: Buckle and Buttons	1935	Dark green plastic with unique mechanism on the buckle, in the form of a "twist-and-turn" locking device. Matching buttons, Made in Czechoslovakia.
Row 3, L-R	Buttons	1935	Thermoplastic "bunch-of-bananas" design.
	Buckle	1935	2-piece dark blue plastic with clip-type clasp.
	Set: 6 Buttons	1935	Plastic figurals: belt, hat, gloves, handkerchief, purse and shoe. Miniatures.
Row 4, L-R	Belt	1920	Black & butterscotch colors, Celluloid with black Celluloid link chain.
	Set: Buckle & Buttons	1935	Celluloid figural footballs. (Rare)

Pins, clips, buckles and millinery ornaments were usually designed on paper, then tracings of these concepts were made into patterns which were then fastened to a flat sheet of cast phenolic and sawed out with jig-saws to give them their outline.

Holes were drilled into the finished design for insertion of pins or other decorative metals which had to be done by hand. Before adding the actual pinning device or decorative metals, the plastic substance, fully sawed and cut, was tumbled in big revolving wooden drums filled with sawdust. The pieces were tumbled ever so slowly until they were perfectly smooth. After the desired texture was at hand, the final insertion of metals and pinning devices completed the item.

George A. Lippincott Company, (Philadelphia, PA), made buttons exclusively of Catalin.

Ivorycraft Company, (Long Island City, NY), and Colonial Kolonite Company, (Chicago, IL), were also known for favoring Catalin as *the* plastic product for jewelry items, buttons, and dress ornaments.

Fancy buttons required handcarving and other skilled operations. A second method of producing buttons was by molding. In such work the molding phenolics chiefly used were: Bakelite, Durez, Resinox, Textolite and Makalot. The urea plastics included Beetle, Plaskon and Unyte. Some furfural* resins were used as well as cellulose acetate, such as Lumarith, Masuron, and Tenite, but the latter were employed to a limited extent in the 1935-1940 era.

Molded buttons were less expensive to produce and in some respects were superior to the Casein or Galalith.

*furfural — a chemical distillation comprised of bran, sugar, wood and other compounds which resulted in a colorless oily liquid resin.

Plate 17
Christie Romero Collection

Plate #18

Location	Nomenclature	Circa	Description
Full Plate	Assorted Buttons	1920-1940	Bakelite type buttons have become very popular and increased in value since the 1980's. These buttons are usually thick thermoset plastics which can be enhanced by ornamentation. These embellishments can be of metal, glass, or applied molded plastics. Designs range from *Art Nouveau* to *Art Deco*, but conventional designs are more dominant. Egyptian and Oriental motifs prevailed in the early 1920's. Bakelite buttons of the 1930's and 1940's varied in sizes and designs, and many were enhanced by hand carving or combined materials. The hand work is represented by clever inlay designs.

"There's no limit to the inventiveness and imagination of button makers and surely, Grandmother's button box never boasted such a conglomeration of unusual colors, shapes and sizes from which to choose. Book-shaped brown cast resin buttons have a checked gold metal panel on the top; big round translucent balls are intricately carved; deep ridges appear on flat round buttons available in all colors; scalloped edge, gold flecked cast resin buttons have opaque brown spots for decoration...round black cast resin buttons are mounted with red plastic letters to spell out a name or initial for gals who like to be labeled."

(From "Plastic Modes" by Eve Main, Dec. 1936, *Modern Plastics*, courtesy Catherine Yronwode and Dean Mullaney Archives.)

During this same period of inventiveness, American Catalin Corporation introduced an exclusive process of metal inlay, in which metal was embedded in plastic buttons. This development was announced by the Birnbaum Novelty Company, makers of Catalin accessories. This was a new process of pouring metal decoration in the form of inlays into cast resin materials already fabricated. This innovation followed three years of experimentation and affected the styling of all plastic accessories, including buttons and other dress ornaments.

Plate 18
Milly Combs Collection

Plate #19

Location	Nomenclature	Circa	Description
Top to Bottom	Purse	1930	Black leather with carved Bakelite elephants. (English)
	Purse	1930	Black leather with Bakelite handle. (English)
	Purse	1930	Green leather with Bakelite handles. (English)
	Purse	1930	Silk with carved Bakelite crocodiles.

Cast resin "bag" tops—the term applied to ladies' purses—became varied by 1937. Styles were featured deeply carved, 7¾" long and ⁵⁄₁₆" thick to ¾" thickness. Transparent tortoiseshell designs, or clear resins were molded by specialty manufacturers who offered a wide variety of cast resin bag tops in a myriad of colors and designs. Maize, a very pale yellow color, proved to be excellent for contrast in deeply carved pieces, and complemented the most popular colors for bags, brown and black.

"Celluloid, Bakelite, and Fiberlite, with their characteristic light grain stripes, all have a strong superficial resemblance to real ivory. Only the general uniformity of their overall color and the perfectly parallel pattern of the grain markings, suggest that they are not. Nevertheless, many pieces made with this material are now approaching an age of 100 or so years. As such, they have become legitimate antiques in their own right, are eminently collectible, and are beginning to command prices that reflect their age, their special history, and their own intrinsic value." *Godfrey Harris*. (See bibliography.)

Tennessee Eastman Corporation, (Subsidiary of the Eastman Kodak Co.), Kingsport, Tennessee reported in its c.1935 advertisements that prior to its suitable plastic product, Tenite, only tedious time-consuming hand carving could produce bags or purse handles of intricate designs made possible by a molding process. Colorful Tenite handles could be molded complete in just eighteen seconds "to retail for the first time at only twenty-five cents." Tenite was made of cellulose acetate which had more durability than the earlier celluloids and was "tough and practically unbreakable."

Still competing with the newer products were plastic frames for handbags styled by William Wilder, Inc., New York City, which won an honorable mention for the uniquely designed handbag entered into a competition for innovative uses of plastic. Wilder used thermoplastic Celluloid, (a cellulose nitrate material made by the Celluloid Corp., New York City.)

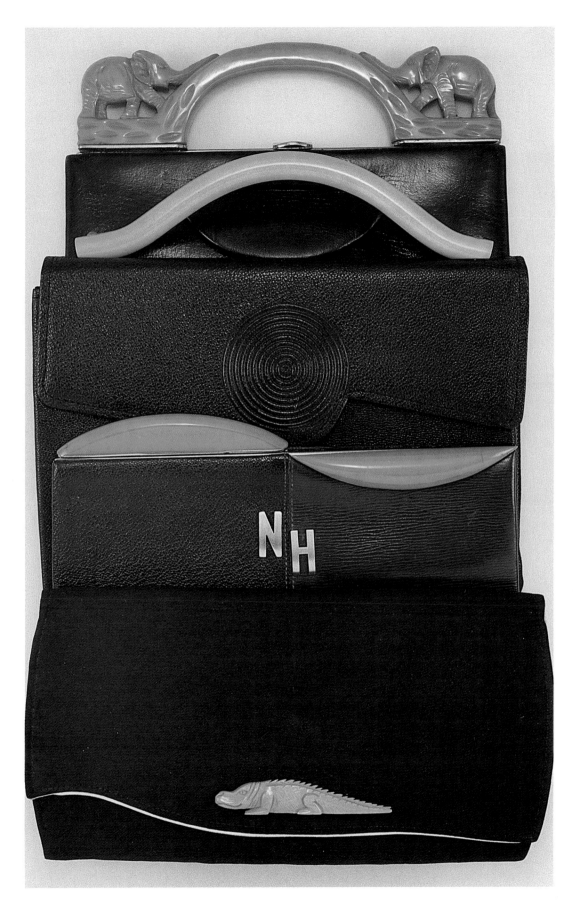

Plate 19
Ginger Moro Collection

Plate #20

Location	Nomenclature	Circa	Description
Top, L-R	Bracelet	1935	Translucent red, faceted Bakelite bangle.
	Bracelet	1935	Pearlized white Lucite bangle.
	Bracelet	1935	1" wide, green pearlized thin Lucite bangle.
Center, L-R	Bracelet	1935	⅞" dark green pearlized Lucite bangle (thick material).
	Bracelet	1960	Large magenta color Lucite free-form bangle.
	Bracelet	1935	Pearlized white Lucite saucer-shape bangle.
Bottom L-R	Bracelet	1935	Large, red unpolished surface machine cuts, made in a swirl pattern.
	Bracelet	1935	Large diameter white Lucite bangle set with large rhinestones.
	Bracelet	1935	Teal blue pearlized Lucite bangle (thin material.)

Credit: Catherine Yronwode and Dean Mullaney Archives

Plate 20
Christie Romero Collection

Plate #21

Location	Nomenclature	Circa	Description
Top to Bottom Row 1, L-R	Earrings (clip)	1950	Large button-shape green Lucite with green rhinestones.
	Buckle	1930	One piece, carved Bakelite in two-tone light and dark butterscotch colors, set with rhinestones.
Row 2	Bracelet	1950	Red Lucite, square-linked.
Row 3, L-R	Necklace	1970	Round and square clear Lucite beads with label (not shown) marked: "Encore."
	Pin	1935	Fob type, dark red and clear laminated Lucite, heart-shaped.
	Pin	1935	Fob type, light red and clear Lucite, heart-shaped.
Row 4, L-R	Earrings	1935	Dangle type, painted red and black on Bakelite amber colored balls.
	Earrings	1935	Large tear-drop, red Lucite.
	Earrings	1960	Large hoop-shaped, pearlized white Lucite.

MARBLETTE *wins* JUDGES' AWARD *in the* STYLE PLASTIC JEWELRY GROUP

Whatever the competition, whatever the industry—Marblette proves a winner!

Now Marblette joins hands with Ace Plastic Novelty Corporation, progressive leaders in the plastic jewelry field, to accept the Judges' Award for the attractive pieces illustrated.

For Real Marblette is the ideal cast phenolic resin, jewel like in its brilliant tone, texture and colorings, most practical in its ease and flexibility of fabrication.

Our specialized personnel stands ready to co-operate to aid you solve your plastic problems.

Informative literature on request

1937 Modern Plastics** advertisement placed by **The Marblette Corporation, Long Island City, New York.

Credit: Catherine Yronwode & Dean Mullaney Archives

Plate 21
Christie Romero Collection

Plate #22

Location	Nomenclature	Circa	Description
Top , L-R	Bracelet	1935	Deeply carved, butterscotch color, floral rose motif, bangle.
	Bracelet	1935	Wide oval Bakelite bangle, marbled rust color.
	Bracelet	1935	Pale yellow, cut through to black, Bakelite bangle.
Center, L-R	Bracelet	1950	Dark amber color Bakelite bangle with round copper inserts.
	Bracelet	1935	Dark butterscotch color Bakelite "twist" bangle with heavy metal overlay. (Rare)
	Bracelet	1960	Brown plastic, square outershaped bangle with inlaid wood. Indian designs.
Bottom, L-R	Bracelet	1935	Variation of a "polka-dot" ivory color Bakelite bangle with raised faceted "French Jet" glass ornaments. (Rare)
	Bracelet	1935	Red Bakelite "twist" bangle, combined with metal. (Rare)
	Bracelet	1935	Maroon Bakelite bangle with chrome band.
	Bracelet	1935	Ivory color Bakelite bangle with alternating red spacers.

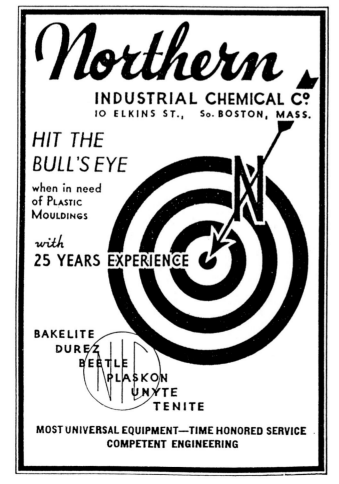

Modern Plastics, *1937.*

Plate 22
Christie Romero Collection

Plate #23

Location	Nomenclature	Circa	Description
Top to Bottom Row 1, L-R	Brooch	1935	Large red, carved Bakelite figural flower.
	Pin	1930	Black and red Bakelite, *Deco* motif. (Buttons and chains added)
	Brooch	1935	Large carved red Bakelite figural flower.
Row 2	Necklace	1930	Orange color Bakelite and wood. *Deco* style.
Row 3	Bracelet	1935	Seven charms, Bakelite fruit and leaves, linked to a yellow metal chain.
Row 4, L-R	Earrings	1940	Large, hoop-shape, red Bakelite.
	Pin	1935	Red Bakelite arrow-shaped pin with hole for a pendant. (Missing pendant drop.)
	Pin	1940	Blue plastic name pin, "Helen."
	Earrings	1940	Black and yellow plastic with concentric hoops.
Row 5, L-R	Earrings	1935	Flat-cut, long, triangular deep yellow drops.
	Earrings	1930	Black and yellow laminated Bakelite dangles. *Deco* design.
	Earrings	1940	Red plastic tassel type.
	Earrings	1935	Large, heavy, orange color Bakelite, triangular shaped drop.

Link bracelets with charms dangling from each link became the rage in the 1900's, and then reappeared in popularity in the 1930's. The charms were represented by hearts and clover, etc., and during the age of plastics took on just about any shape, such as fruits or animal figurals. The links were often of Celluloid whereas the charms could be made of Catalin or Bakelite or another thermoset plastic.

Plate 23
Christie Romero Collection

Plate #24

Location	Nomenclature	Circa	Description
Left, Top to Bottom	Bracelet	1935	Bakelite bangle with harlequin motif accented with rhinestones. (Scarce)
	Bracelet	1935	Heavy, wide, dark green Bakelite bangle with rope-twist pattern.
	Bracelet	1920	Handpainted Celluloid bangle, paisley pattern.
	Bracelet	1920	Handpainted Celluloid bangle, over-all floral motifs.
	Bracelet	1920	Handpainted Celluloid, narrow bangle, with applied molded plastic Egyptian style heads.
	Bracelet	1920	Carved Celluloid bangle with handpainted metallic colors of gold and orange.
	Bracelet	1920	Carved Celluloid bangle, handpainted in mustard, green, and black colors.
Right Top to Bottom	Bracelet	1935	Tortoise color plastic wrap-around, stretch-carved figural fish pattern with rhinestone eyes.
	Bracelet (3)(Left)	1935	Narrow, faceted Bakelite bangles.
	Bracelet (Center)	1935	Narrow, green Bakelite bangle, quilted pattern.
	Bracelet (Right)	1920	Scalloped ivory color Celluloid bangle with handpainted roses.
	Bracelet	1935	Dark amber Bakelite backed with laminated wood. Expandable elastic.
	Bracelet (Left)	1935	Dark blue saucer-shape Bakelite bangle.
	Bracelet (Right)	1970	Layered Bakelite, yellow carved to black, saucer-shaped bangle, signed: "Diane von Furstenberg."

Plate 24
Christie Romero Collection

Plate #25

Location	Nomenclature	Circa	Description
Top, Row 1, L-R	Earrings	1935	Large Bakelite egg-shaped.
	Pin	1935	Dangling Bakelite cherries with leaves.
	Bracelet	1935	Heavy faceted Bakelite, expandable elastic.
Row 2, L-R	Pin	1935	Red Bakelite heart-shaped with dangling berries (slight imperfection).
	Key Chain	1935	Green molded plastic figural squirrel (slight flaw).
	Bracelet	1935	Red Bakelite and metallic chain, with metallic rider on horse. (rare)
Row 3, L-R	Bracelet	1960	Shaped plastic with expandable elastic.
	Bracelet	1950	Bakelite, expandable elastic with metallic spacers.
Row 4, L-R	Pin	1935	Bakelite, wood log pattern, with dangling cherries. (Imperfect)
	Ring	1935-1950	Marbled, carved Bakelite.
	Ring	1935	Large, carved Bakelite, daisy pattern.

Plate 25
Christie Romero Collection

Plate #26

Location	Nomenclature	Circa	Description
Left Top to Bottom			
Top Row, L-R	Rings (3) (Left)	1935	Light butterscotch stretch-carved Bakelite.
	Ring (Center)	1935	Rectangular carved Bakelite.
	Ring (Right)	1935	Rectangular carved Bakelite.
Bottom Row, L-R	Rings (3) (Left)	1935-1950	Bakelite dome-shaped.
	Ring (Center)	1935-1950	Translucent, faceted Bakelite.
	Ring (Right)	1935-1950	Faceted Bakelite.
Left Top to Bottom	Bracelet	1935	Heavy, carved Bakelite, hinged bangle, philo leaf motif.
	Bracelet	1935	Dark butterscotch color, carved Bakelite, oval shaped, and pierced bangle.
	Bracelet	1935	Black and butterscotch Bakelite with brass studs.
	Bracelet	1935	Very wide cuff, carved open-work front, Bakelite, hinged.
Right Top to Bottom	Bracelet	1935-1950	Plastic cuff with large faceted rhinestones, each circled by small rhinestones.
	Bracelet	1935	Light yellow Bakelite, hinged with a cross-hatch design in front.
	Pin	1935	Ceramic figural bull's head with applied green Lucite horns and a genuine fur forelock.
	Brooch	1935	Carved and handpainted Bakelite sombrero accented with Bakelite beads. (Rare)
	Bracelet	1960	Hinged plastic, accented by a combination of aurora borealis sets and rhinestones.
	Bracelet	1935-1950	Wrap-around hinged plastic, highlighted with rhinestones.

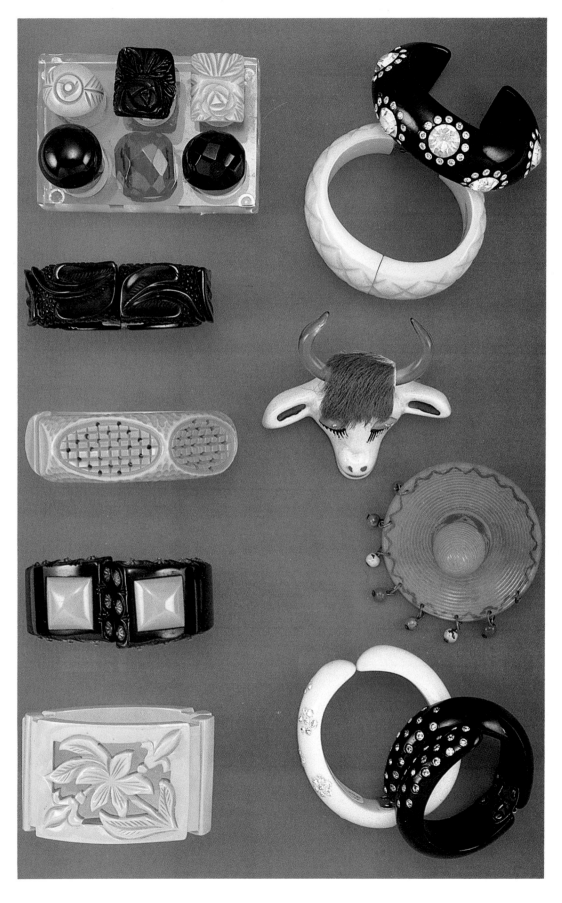

Plate 26
Christie Romero Collection

Plate #27

Location	Nomenclature	Circa	Description
Row 1, L-R	Pin	1930	Black Sambo, fashioned after period "crib toys." (American) Rare.
	Bracelet	1960	Bakelite, wood, and gilded brass. Marked: "Kenneth Lane."
	Bracelet	1930	Multi-color Bakelite elastic stretch. (American)
Row 2, L-R	Set: Clip and Bracelet	1930	Coral color carved Bakelite.
Row 3, L-R	Bracelet	1930	Multi-color Bakelite elastic stretch.
	Bracelet	1935	Linked Bakelite.
Bottom signed:	Eyeglasses	1950	Frames of Celluloid and rhinestones, "Schiapparelli."

Credit: Catherine Yronwode & Dean Mullaney Archives

Manufacturers of costume jewelry are big consumers of cast resin. Examples made of Phenalin may be seen in this illustration. (Modern Plastics 1937.)

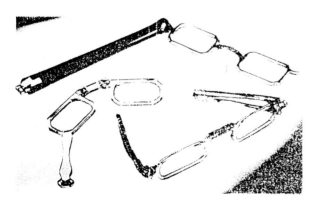

Credit: Catherine Yronwode & Dean Mullaney Archives

Pink and "crystal" Celluloid frames of ultra-modern design, (1934), from Celluloid Corp. and Optical Products Co.

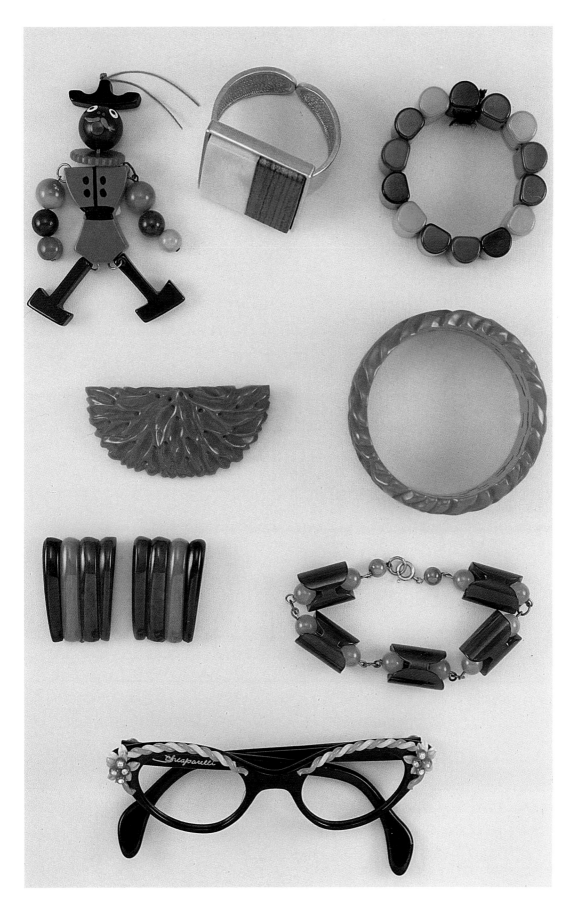

Plate 27
Ginger Moro Collection

Plate #28

Location	Nomenclature	Circa	Description
Top Row, L-R	Bracelets (4)	1940	Dimpled Bakelite cuffs. (American) Colors: Ivory, mustard, butterscotch, and persimmon.
Center, L-R	Bracelet (6)	1950-1970	Large cuffs. Translucent, laminated Celluloid with inserts of lace (French, c.1950-1970), and one reverse carved translucent plastic c.1930 (American).
Bottom, L-R	Bracelets (8)	1950	Three large multi-colored layered cuffs (French), and four American polka-dots, c.1935. One reverse carved translucent plastic, c.1930.

Bracelets have been popular since time immemorial. We see in this publication jointed wide-cuffed bracelets and unjointed bangle-types, the latter often given in friendship. Adjustable bracelets were worn by both ladies and infants and had an adjustable "expando" mechanism. With the discovery of the "Valley of the Kings," Egyptian motifs were very much in vogue in all types of jewelry, including bracelets. Some of the most eloquent were designed during the *Art Deco* period.

From 1850 to 1910, the "stiff band" or cuff bracelet was preferred and measured from 1" to 2" wide. High relief and much intricately carved florals or lamination became popular from 1925 right up to the present time.

Plate 28
Ginger Moro Collection

Plate #29

Location	Nomenclature	Circa	Description
Top, L-R	Brooch	1930	Ivory color plastic, "Headhunter" design, with brass dangles. Marked: "Joseff-Hollywood." (See B-5.)
	Brooch	1930	Same as above except for black Tenite plastic. (See B-12.)
	Earrings	1950	Tenite, thermoplastic. Marked: "Joseff."
Center	Set: Necklace and earrings	1930	Tenite (by Eastman Tennessee Co.), thermoplastic. Marked: "Joseff-Hollywood." Tenite is a patented plastic compound used by various jewelry manufacturers to shape and color faux gems and gemstones.
	Brooch	1950	Celluloid. Marked: "Joseff" (script lettering).

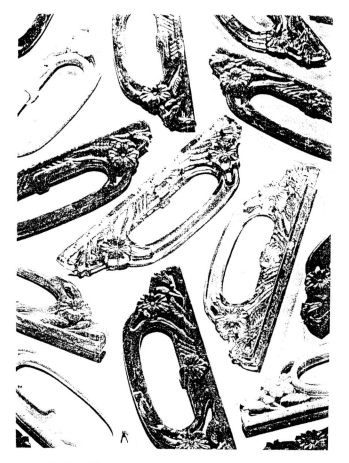

Purse (or bag) handles, molded (not hand-carved), made of colorful, lustrous Tenite. Tenite was made of "practically unbreakable" Eastman Corporation cellulose acetate (c.1935).

Credit: Catherine Yronwode & Dean Mullaney Archives

Plate 29
Ginger Moro Collection

Plate #30

Location	Nomenclature	Circa	Description
Full Plate	Set: Belt Buckle, 3 Buttons, Necklace, Earrings with posts.	1930	This parure of Bakelite ranges in colors of butterscotch, carmel, red and brown. These are colors usually associated with patented Bakelite.

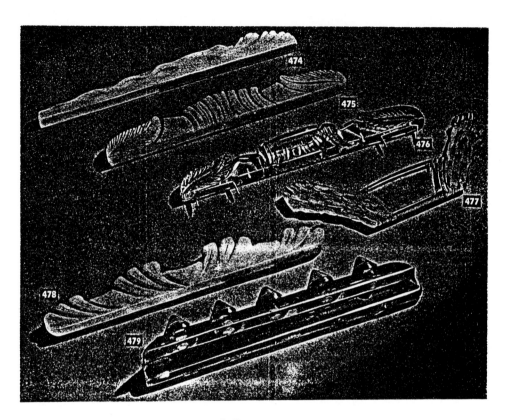

CAST RESIN BAG TOPS

These bag tops are not molded but are stock items made from cast resins and are available in a wide variety of colors and designs. Interested executives should write on business letterhead to obtain the manufacturer's name.

474. Tapered white bag top, deeply carved. 7³/₄ in. long and ⁵/₁₆ in. thick

475. Maize colored top 7 in. long and ³/₄ in. thick with carved center and ends

476. Transparent top with attachment clamps and opening for strap handle, 7¹/₁₆ in. long and ⁵/₁₆ in. thick

477. Ends of this transparent bag top are carved but unpolished, giving a ground-glass effect. 6 in. overall, 3 in. at top and ⁵/₁₆ in. thick

478. Maize top, 7 in. long and ³/₄ in. thick. Deeply carved

479. Transparent top, tortoise shell pattern, with five turned knobs as decoration. 7 in. long, it is cut from ³/₄ in. stock, one half of which is cut with a ³/₈ in. rabbet

Address all inquiries to Stock Mold Department, Modern Plastics, 425 Fourth Avenue, N. Y. C. All molders are invited to send samples from stock molds to appear on this page as space permits.

40 MODERN PLASTICS
MAY 1937

Credit: Catherine Yronwode and Dean Mullaney Archives

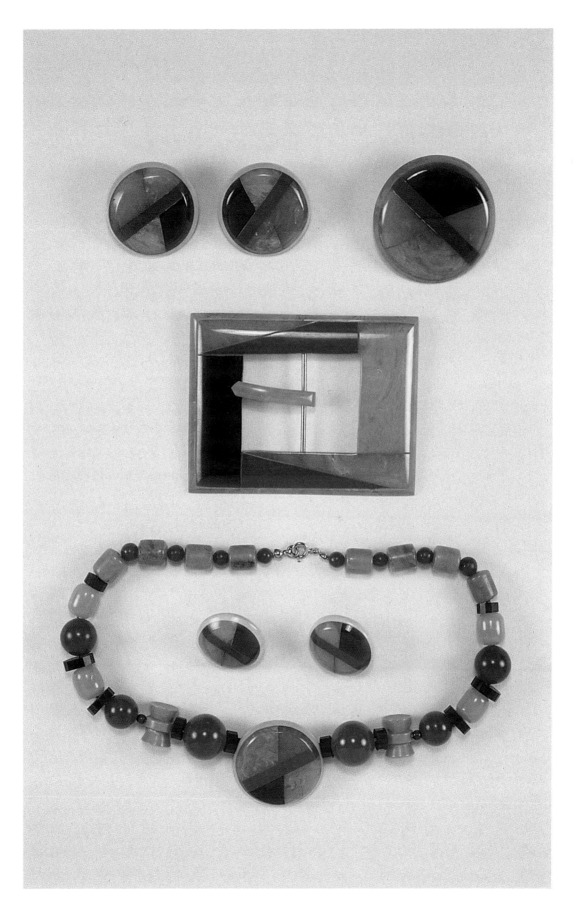

Plate 30
Ginger Moro Collection

Plate #31

Location	Nomenclature	Circa	Description
Top	Bracelets (2)	1930	Figural frogs, red and green Bakelite. (French)
	Pins or clips (4)	1930	Small figural frogs in assorted colors. Carved Bakelite. (French)
	Pin (1)	1930	Large figural frog. Coral color carved Bakelite. (French)
Center, Row 3	Pendant	1950	"Sardines in a Can." Chrome and Bakelite. Signed:"Hattie Carnegie." (American)
Bottom, L-R	Pins (2)	1950	Laminated Celluloid, stylized broad shouldered female, fashioned after actress Joan Crawford. Marked: "Lea Stein, Paris."
Center, Row 4	Pin	1950	*Moderne* design influence. Woman's profile with ruffle. Celluloid. Marked: "Lea Stein, Paris."
Bottom Row, Center	Pin	1950	Vintage auto. Celluloid. Marked: "Lea Stein, Paris."
Bottom Row, Left	Set: Pin and Earrings	1950	Figural ram's head, with ram's horn design earrings, highly stylized. Bakelite with rhinestones and gold overlay accents. Marked: "Hattie Carnegie." (American)

Plate 31
Ginger Moro Collection

Plate #32

Location	Nomenclature	Circa	Description
Top to Bottom	Necklace	1930	Turquoise and blue color plastic with chrome beads. (French)
	Necklace	1930	Chrome and red Bakelite with rhinestones. (French)
	Necklace	1930	Jade green color Bakelite with chrome. (German, Bauhaus influence)
	Necklace	1930	Robin egg color blue with bow. (German, Bauhaus)
	Necklace	1930	Carved red Bakelite and chrome. (French)

The "new" Bauhaus had taken American art circles by storm, and in November 1937, the Association of Arts and Industries was begun in Chicago, Illinois.

At Harvard University, Dr. Walter Gropius, professor of architecture on campus, brought his influence to his classroom. Professor Gropius was the founder of the world famous art university, The Bauhaus, in Dessau, and brought his teachings to the United States.

New schools dedicated to the principle of Bauhaus design, were enthusiastically supported in the United States and abroad, and teachers of the "new culture" were heartily welcomed. Among them came painters and designers who had trained at The Bauhaus university, such as Prof. L. Maholy-Nagy who had an international following.

In effect, Bauhaus simplicity is shown in jewelry design, and most emphatically in Raymond Loewy's 1938 designs for the "Broadway Limited" of the Pennsylvania Railroad Service. As industrial designer and consultant to the Pennsylvania Railroad Company, he collaborated with them in re-designing railroad cars and elite Pullman cars on the railroad service between the major cities of New York, Philadelphia, and Chicago. Loewy incorporated Bauhaus clean, simple lines in his design, and substituted the modern plastics for "rattling" metals both on the exterior and interior of the railroad cars.

His post-WWII designs for the Studebaker cars showed his continued interest in Bauhaus, and his automotive design influence can be readily seen in all modern vehicles.

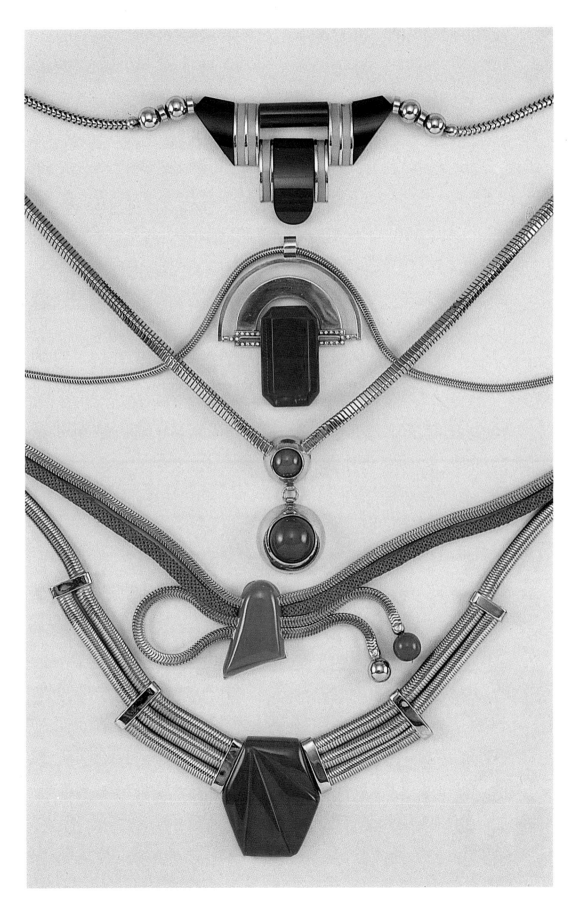

Plate 32
Ginger Moro Collection

Plate #33

Location	Nomenclature	Circa	Description
Row 1, L-R	Pin	1930	Figural horse. Bakelite accented with glass eye and metal chain. (American)
	Pin	1930	Tyrolean hat of Bakelite. (American)
	Pin	1930	Figural bird in flight, with glass eye. Bakelite. (American)
Row 2, Center	Pin	1930	Figural hat of carved Bakelite, with straw flowers. Butterscotch color. (American)
Row 3, L-R	Scarfpin and Brooch Combination	1930	Olive green Bakelite.
	Brooch	1950	Laminated Celluloid with faux tiger-eye coloring. Marked: "Lea Stein, Paris."
	Pin	1954	Figural rooster of red, black, and yellow Bakelite. Marked; "Hattie Carnegie."
Row 4, L-R	Pin	1930	Figural parrot's head of chrome and Bakelite. (French)
	Brooch	1930	Figural sword, Bakelite with brass chains. (American)

The yellow scarf worn by the model with a brown riding habit—appropriately named, "The Plainsman" (sold at R.H. Macy & Co., 1937), is held in place by a carved pin of cast resin, shaped like a horse's head. (Plastic from Catalin Corp.) Buttons, in the shape of Chessmen were of cast resin, and came in red, green, black, and brown. Carved plastic heads, horse's head motifs, were made in graduated sizes as buttons or clips, and black or colored cast resin became the background for a white horse.

Credit: Catherine Yronwode & Dean Mullaney Archives

Plate 33
Ginger Moro Collection

Plate #34

Location	Nomenclature	Circa	Description
Row 1, L-R	Buckle	1938	Celluloid with Patent #2108905, dated, 1938. (American) (*Author's Collection*)
	Pin	1935	Celluloid cockatoo with red faceted stones. (*Christie Romero Collection*)
	Hairpin	1930	Celluloid in "French Ivory." (*Author's Collection*)
Row 2	Necklace	1935	Celluloid flower-buds on link chain. (*Christie Romero Collection*)
Row 3	Necklace	1970	Thermoplastic. (*Author's Collection*)
Row 4	Necklace	1950	Pink Celluloid floral necklace on link chain. (*Ginger Moro Collection*)

Plate 34
Credits as indicated.

Plate #35

Location	Nomenclature	Circa	Description
Top, L-R	Hatpins	1920-1935	Assorted thermoplastics, including one pair of royal blue and one red Catalin (thermoset) plastic in *moderne* shapes. Bright yellow hatpin has handpainted elongated "polka-dots" of royal blue color. The tall hatpin (center), has an applied modern porcelain transfer portrait (c.1980), pasted on an authentic c.1925 thermoset Catalin hatpin head.
Bottom	Brooch	1989	Thermoset plastic face painted to resemble fine porcelain. Brooch is displayed on a modern Lucite watch stand. Miniature black glass hatpin is actually a very small dressmaker's marking pin, c.1910.

Hatpins V. Hat Pins

It has been long settled among researchers and historians reporting on jewelry and jewelled accessories—including international writers of high repute—that when referring to a woman's pinning device, the item is correctly spelled hatpin, (one word).

All modern encyclopedic reference books show *hat pin* and *hatpin*, and the differences are clearly made between the two "collectibles."

Since language is the great communicator for educational purposes and understanding, an agreed upon term makes understanding and communication simpler. As the author of the first and only worldwide definitive encyclopedic work on the subject of hatpins and hatpin holders, it was my responsibility to devise the proper nomenclature and terms relative to the subject, and I enjoyed world-wide acceptance of same.

When referring to a woman's pinning device, it's not only archaic to use the out-moded term "hat pin," but such use confuses readers of advertisements, particularly if the ad does not have a photo or graphic illustration. However, there's no doubt whatsoever as to the meaning or description of *hatpin*—the one word properly used to describe the strictly feminine use of the functional, decorative, historical, and political piece of jewelry known as a *hatpin*.

Simply stated, a *hatpin* is a device to anchor a hat upon the hair and head of women.

Historically speaking, men did not wear hat "pins." Rather they wore hat badges or *enseigne*, which was a type of ornament worn on the hat or cap of prominent men. Thus, when one man approached another, he could observe by this badge of "station," who was subservient and thereby tip the hat first, or await the salute of the other. This mode and manner still exists in many countries and is particularly observed in the military.

Originally, a badge was worn by knights to mark or distinguish them and to provide heraldic cognizance. Men could be recognized by what was worn on the head as to his "station" in life, i.e., butcher, baker, shepherd, painter, Cardinal, Pope, Bishop, King, and so forth. "Green Berets" were adopted as Military head gear, accentuated by a special badge. Theses badges were functional for identification and were quite decorative. More recently, both men and women collect *hat pins* from the Olympics, souvenirs of travel (especially the wide variety of colorful pins with feather and brush accents offered in Austria and Switzerland for Alpine sport hats.)

Newly found clubs for collectors of souvenir *hat pins* make it even more essential to separate the actual *period hatpin* (1865-1925) from the pins that were never used as "anchors" or pinning devices.

Plate 35
Author's Collection

Plate #36

Location	Nomenclature	Circa	Description
Top and Bottom	Earrings (5 pr.)	1940	Bakelite and chrome, for pierced ears. (French)
Center	Pendant	1960	Interchangeable pendant in three carved Bakelite colors, with chain. (In original box, not shown). Marked: "Christian Dior."

FROM HOURS to MINUTES

by EVE MAIN

MAY 1937

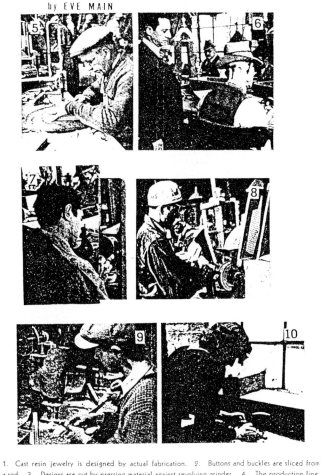

1. Cast resin jewelry is designed by actual fabrication. 2. Buttons and buckles are sliced from a rod. 3. Designs are cut by pressing material against revolving grinder. 4. The production line. 5. A number of thicknesses are jigsawed at one time. 6. Machine carving a buckle. 7. A bracelet. 8. Polishing the edges roughened by cutting. 9. Beads are pierced for stringing on a foot-treadle machine. 10. Sorting and sizing beads which have been turned and polished

In the beginning the jeweler's art was a tedious task which modern materials and methods have made comparatively rapid and simple

***Modern Plastics*, May 1937**
Credit: Catherine Yronwode and Dean Mullaney Archives

Plate 36
Ginger Moro Collection

Plate #37

Location	Nomenclature	Circa	Description
Top to Bottom	Cigarette Cases (4)	1930	Varied plain and mottled Celluloid with applied clasps designed as a freeform human hand. (French)
	Pin	1935	Laminated Celluloid figural elephant.
	Pin	1935	Laminated Celluloid figural panther.

Credit: Catherine Yronwode & Dean Mullaney Archives

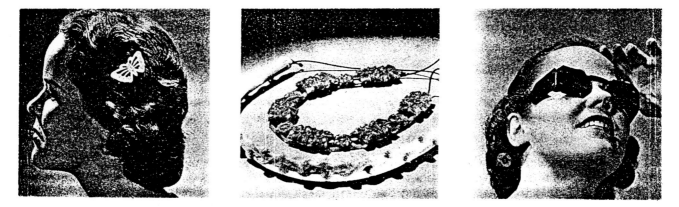

Buckles and buttons for wash dresses adopted floral motifs to harmonize with some of the hair ornaments. An exquisite white butterfly barrette perched cockily over the ear manages to look ethereal while admirably doing its job of holding hair in place. Flexible links between blossoms characterize a pale green bandeau, and a yellow bandeau sprouts tiny flowers and leaves. (Injection molded of cellulose acetate by Tilton Cook.) The above were featured in the popular department store, McCreery's, August 1937.

Plate 37
Ginger Moro Collection

Plate #38

Location	Nomenclature	Circa	Description
Left to Right	Set: Necklace, Bracelet, and 2 pairs of earrings.	1930	Bakelite. (American) Earrings can be interlocked for dangle effect. Bakelite beads can extend the length of the necklace to popular longer drape or fall.

Oct. 1937, Buttons & Buckles in every color and effect are virtually unbreakable.

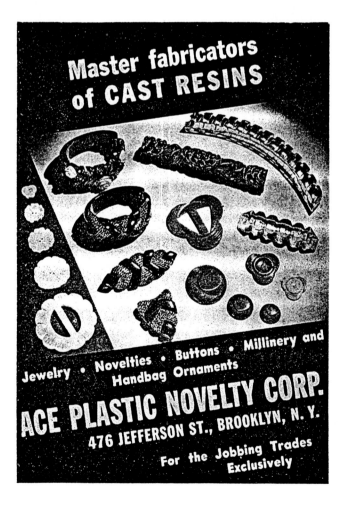

Oct. 1937, Modern Plastics advertisements.

Credit: Catherine Yronwode & Dean Mullaney Archives

Plate 38
Ginger Moro Collection

Plate #39

Location	Nomenclature	Circa	Description
Top	Watches (2)	1960	Made in Switzerland for the American trade. Lucite faces with plastic wristbands.
Top, Left	Bracelets (2)	1935	Snake motif bangle in fuchsia color, and a pearlized Celluloid.
Center	Watches (3)	1960	Swiss mechanism, exported for the American trade. Lucite cases with plastic wristbands.
Bottom	Pin	1935	Reverse carved Lucite. (Obverse side is shown on this plate. See Plate 50 for back carving.)

JUNE 1937

1 MOISTURE RESISTANT
2 TRANSPARENT
3 FLEXIBLE
4 UNBREAKABLE
5 RESISTANT TO CHEMICALS
6 LIGHTWEIGHT
7 RESISTANT TO OXIDATION
8 CAN BE WORKED OR TOOLED

Du Pont announces an amazing new plastic

HERE is the finest plastic modern chemistry has yet developed! It is "Lucite"* methyl methacrylate plastic, formerly known as "Pontalite."

"Lucite" is crystal-clear. You can read news-print through a thick block of it. Only half as heavy as common glass, it is flexible, non-shattering, strong and durable. Sunlight doesn't affect it and neither do most chemicals; it absorbs very little moisture; can be worked or tooled in practically any fashion.

It can be made in all colors and in the most delicate translucent, transparent, opaque and pastel shades.

"Lucite" is now available as a molding powder, and will soon be available in sheets, rods, and tubes.

The tremendous interest already shown by designers and manufacturers is convincing evidence of the place "Lucite" will fill in industrial and decorative design.

"Lucite" is the newest of du Pont's

fine plastics. Du Pont's leadership in chemistry and chemical research has made possible the development of no less than *six* different plastics. And research is developing more.

We will gladly show you how du Pont Plastics can be profitably used in *your* business, or send you more complete information about them. E. I. du Pont de Nemours & Co., Inc., Plastics Department—Industrial Division, Arlington, New Jersey.

"Lucite" is du Pont's registered trademark for its methyl methacrylate plastic, formerly known as "Pontalite."

(See B4)
Credit: Catherine Yronwode & Dean Mullaney Archives

PLASTICS

Plate 39
Ginger Moro Collection

Plate #40

Location	Nomenclature	Circa	Description
Top, Left	Brooch	1960	Thermoset plastic and rhodium.
Top, Right	Necklace	1950	Turquoise color thermoset plastic, combined with wood and painted cork.
Center	Set: Bracelet and Earrings	1950	Thermoset plastic oval shaped bracelet in unusual turquoise color, set with rhinestones. Earrings are button clip.
Bottom	Set: Necklace and Bracelet	1950	Molded plastic set in rhodium. Extension chain is comprised of glass beads. Rhinestone highlights. Marked: "Lisner."
Bottom, Center	Brooch	1965	Plastic imitation of turquoise gemstone. Molded thermoset plastic combined with glass beads. Convertible hook on back so pin can be worn as a pendant on a chain. Marked: "Sarah Coventry."

Plate 40
Author's Collection

Plate #41

Location	Nomenclature	Circa	Description
Top, L-R	Hair Ornament	1910-1940	Simulated tortoise with applied gold leaf. Signed: "Auguste Bonaz." (See Plates B-19 & B-20.)
	Hair Comb	1935	Gilded brass inset with rhinestones. Tortoise color plastic, (Galalith or American Casein).
	Barrettes (pr)	1910-1940	Geometric design, plastic with gold overleaf. Signed: "Auguste Bonaz." (See Plates B-19 & B-20.)
	Pin w/Pendant	1930	Bakelite with applied gold leaf. Signed: "Auguste Bonaz." Bonaz patented his gold leaf on plastic process. (See Plates B-19 & B-20)
Center	Hair Ornament	1920	Simulated tortoise shell in plastic, with gold leaf. Signed: "Auguste Bonaz." (See above.)
Bottom, L-R	Hair Ornament	1920	(See above.)
	Barrettes (pr)	1920	Bakelite with gold leaf trim. (On original card, not shown.) Signed: "Auguste Bonaz."
	Hair Ornament	1920	Simulated tortoiseshell with applied gold leaf. Signed: "Auguste Bonaz." (See Plates B-19 & B-20.)

In the United States, gold inlaying of Celluloid, Catalin, Tenite and similar plastic materials was accomplished in 1935 by the use of rolled gold leaf. The machines, tools, dies, molds, and other necessary manufacturing devices were provided by the Standard Tool Co., Leominster, MA.

Ginger Moro was kind enough to translate a report from the 1987 catalog from the factory in D'Oyonnax, France, describing a recent exhibition which included some unique pieces by Auguste Bonaz:

"This collection, known as the most complete and beautiful in all Europe was acquired by The Museum of Combs with State aid under the Department of Cultural Development (1984).

"The collection is comprised of an exceptional ensemble of combs, pins, boxes, and decorative panels made of celluloid from 1900 to 1930, roughly. It represents all of the models of The Auguste Bonaz line, as well as one-of-a-kind prototypes created especially for stands at exhibitions where *The Maison Bonaz* participated, (for example, *Exposition des Arts Decoratifs*, Paris, 1925, a seminal exhibition where all the major countries of the world and their designers exhibited).

"*The Maison Bonaz* was one of the most important producers of handmade combs in France from 1880-1940.

"Along with this collection, The Museum of Combs has gathered numerous machinist documents, photographs, and press books of publicity from 1900-1940, as well as a beautiful collection of bound fashion magazines of the period.

"The inventory of collections of the museum is actually being collated by Mme. Agnes Bruno of the Ethnological Department and should be finished by the end of 1987." (*Ginger Moro Archives*)

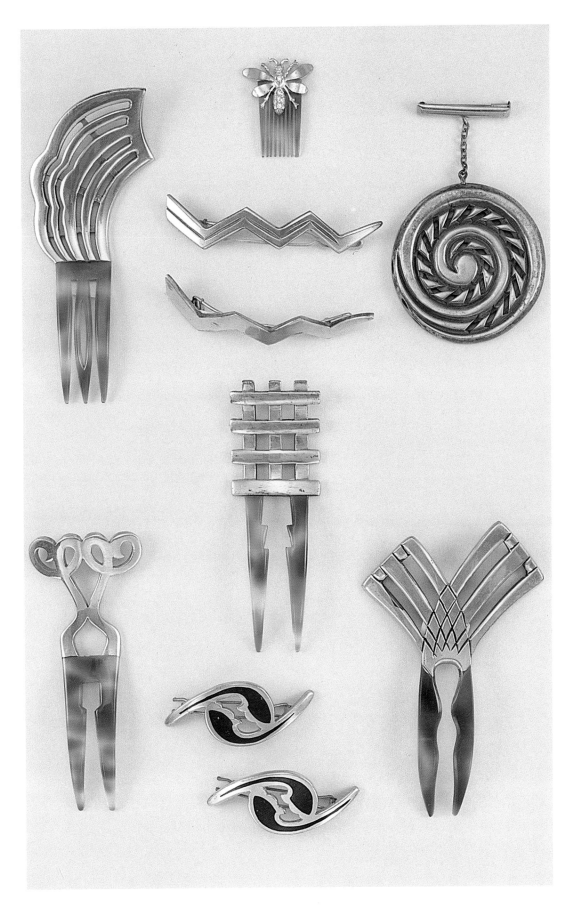

Plate 41
Ginger Moro Collection

Plate #42

Location	Nomenclature	Circa	Description
Row 1, L-R	Pin	1935	Butterscotch color Bakelite figural head of horse with metal studs and chain.
	Buckle	1921	Plastic with initial "D," enhanced by rhinestones. Marked with 1921 patent date.
	Pin	1935	Green Bakelite, carved figural Scottie dog.
Row 2	Shoe Buckles	1950	Thermoset plastic, marked "Tip Toe Pats. Pend." Dutch-style design for popular fabric-topped shoes. (*Author's Collection*)
Row 3, L-R	Pin	1935	Carved red Bakelite figural parrot with handpainted beak.
	Scarf Slide	1938	Molded Celluloid, woman's hand with hand-painted red nails. Marked: "1938 Patent"
	Pin	1930	Ivory color Celluloid figural fox with blue rhinestones.
Row 4, L-R	Pin	1935	Molded plastic woman's hand design accented with a ring and bracelet inset with rhinestones.
	Brooch	1935	Butterscotch color Bakelite mounting for a black molded cameo. Yellow metal frame.
	Pin	1935	Stretch-carved purple color Lucite figural bird with a rhinestone eye.
Row 5, L-R	Pin	1935	Reverse carved and tinted Lucite, head of horse with handpainted eye.
	Earrings	1980	Thermoplastic molded earrings with a mold mark at top. (*Author's Collection*)
	Pin	1935	Butterscotch color carved Bakelite Scotties with inset eyes.

Modern Plastics, (August 1937) describes and pictures "diminutive hands of carved Catalin in many colors which are clipped on the lapels of a summer suit. The hands have black or red fingernails and wear painted bracelets."

Cohn & Rosenberger manufactured small clips and pins in the shape of bulldog heads, full figural Scotties, singly or in pairs. These were called in 1930's, "kennel" jewelry, and this series came hard upon the popular production by this same manufacturer of swordfish, porgies, bass, and several breeds of familiar pets.

All of these shapes of pins and larger brooches were available over the counter in a considerable range of colors including jade green, navy, olive green, tortoise, black, white, red and blue. The figurals sold retail for 50¢ each in the depression years of the 1930's.

Plate 42
Christie Romero Collection unless otherwise noted.

Plate #43

Location	Nomenclature	Circa	Description
Top to Bottom	Hatpins (10)	1915-1925	Thermoplastic variety of molded, twisted, cut, and blown Celluloid-types of hatpins. Egyptian design influence visual in the bottom row, as well as Deco design. There is seemingly an endless variation of plastic hatpins with many produced in imitation "French Ivory" plastic.

When women took to wearing hats instead of bonnets, the term *hat pin* had a derogatory meaning. That is, women could wear "pins" but not badges. There were a few exceptions when a Queen, for instance, could wear her "badge of office," and to this day, England's Queen Elizabeth wears hers on her hat or on a ribbon.

Research has proven that *"hat"* pins (c.1850-1910), was the name begrudgingly assigned to women's pinning devices needed to keep the bonnet or chapeau atop the hair and head.

With the cutting of bonnet strings, women found "emancipation." But men reserved hats and badges. Women with no "station" in society were delegated to wearing a "pin" such as a hat*pin* and hair*pins*. Women wore "hat ornaments," not "badges."

Eventually, "hat pin" was hyphenated, (hat-pin), and finally evolved into the accepted spelling—hatpin—which first appeared in Webster's *New International Dictionary of English Language* (1918).

The *Encyclopedia Britannica* never mentioned the hatpin as a woman's pinning device until 1975, when it adopted the one-word usage and definition as provided in Baker's encyclopedia.

Harold Newman's *An Illustrated Dictionary of Jewelry*, (Thames and Hudson, Ltd., 1981), recognized the need for a specific term for describing the item used to secure a lady's hat upon hair and head, "used especially from Victorian times until c.1940." Thus, Newman makes the distinction between a "hatpin," a "badge," and a "hat pin."

Plate 43
Author's Collection

Plate #44

Location	Nomenclature	Circa	Description
Full Plate	Hatpins	1985-1990	Assorted "New Vogue" mottled and pearlized plastics and Lucite, signed: "Rex." With a resurgence of interest in feminine head-covering, such as turbans, beach-hats, sport hats, and design millinery, hat ornaments and hatpins which served either a decorative or functional use, came back into vogue. One of the first to recognize the new market was designer and maker, Rex Franz. He studied the "old fashioned" way of attaching the ornamental head to the pin-stem and devised and improvised modern jewelers' findings and stainless steel shanks. So that the trade and potential buyers would recognize the "New Vogue" hatpins from older vintage production, Mr. Franz punch-marks each pin-stem on his products: "Rex." Some of the "New Vogue" hatpins utilize 1935-1950 beads. Others are one-of-a-kind improvisations. Most of the "Rex" hatpins are sold by milliners or in specialized boutiques.

Plate 44
Rex Franz Collection

Plate #45

Location	Nomenclature	Circa	Description
Top	Bracelets (2)	1935	Carved Bakelite bangles, 1" wide, in apricot and butterscotch colors.
Center	Bracelet, watch combo.	1940	*Faux* malachite thermoset plastic wide cuff, with 17 Jewel "Royal Dynasty" watch. Unique.
	Bracelet	1930	Carved green color Bakelite, 1" cuff (shown side view).
Bottom, L-R	Bracelet	1930	Reddish brown, deeply carved Bakelite.
	Bracelet	1970	Thermoset, concave polka-dot type.
	Bracelet	1930	Carved and pierced custard color Bakelite.
Left	Bracelet	1935	Linked translucent thermoset plastic.
Top, Center	Fur Clip	1970	Sheet plastic imitation of natural dyed leather, combined with gilded brass. Marked: "Judith Leiber."
Top, Left	Hatpin	1925	Handpainted Celluloid.
	Hatpin	1925	Ram's horn, "French Ivory," molded Celluloid, seamed.
	Hatpin	1925	Painted, molded Celluloid with seam covered by plastic strip. Iridescent colors.
Center	Earrings	1950	Molded thermoset, clip type.
Right	Earrings	1935	Marbled Bakelite, button-shaped, with screw-on type.
Center, Left	Brooch	1950-1960	Laminated Celluloid. Marked: "Lea Stein, Paris."

Plate 45
Author's Collection

Plate #46

Location	Nomenclature	Circa	Description
Full Plate	Set: Necklace, Bracelet and Earrings	1950	Each piece is marked: "Miriam Haskell" (American). Unique combination of Lucite and Austrian crystals. Necklace is primarily crystal beads. The bracelet and earrings have a good proportion of crystal-color Lucite so that there is less weight to the large drop-earrings. A most impressive parure of highly collectible Haskell jewelry.

Miriam Haskell's jewelry was first produced more than a half century ago in a little shop on West 57th Street, New York City. Her unique jewelry was an instant success, so much so, Miss Haskell was able to move her enterprise to "the Avenue" — Fifth Avenue, New York —beginning with one upper floor at 392 Fifth Avenue. Her business thrived and she expanded until the design and manufacture of her ever-popular jewelry took several floors of that building from 1933 until the late sixties.

Her interest in jewelry began when she was proprietor of a gift shop in the exclusive McAlpin Hotel located in New York's 1920's posh Herald Square. *Miriam Haskell* jewelry has been produced consistently as high fashion costume jewelry since 1924. A shrewd and talented businesswoman, Miss Haskell was one of the first jewelry designers to recognize the advantage of combining plastic—lightweight material—with other units, thus making her costume jewelry more comfortable to wear. Her artistic background served her well and she incorporated this talent in designing her jewelry. Her ideas and sketches were produced in complete designs by a young genius, Frank Hess, who designed exclusively for Miriam Haskell. It was a lifelong association which continued even after she sold out her jewelry company to her younger brother, Joseph Haskell, in the early 1950's.

Haskell Jewels, Ltd., has been producing the internationally respected name of Miriam Haskell jewelry in what has remained a totally self-contained, privately owned company. Mr. Sanford G. Moss, President, was the sole owner and only the third proprietor of the company until he retired a few years ago when the company was taken over by a new owner. Miriam Haskell jewelry is still being made and sold in fine department stores, through catalogues and specialty shops. Although some of the early 1925-1930 jewelry was only tagged, her jewelry from the late 1930's on will have the familiar trademark of an oval escutcheon on the underside of the piece, plainly stamped: Miriam Haskell. The trademark has remained the same under four ownerships.

For an in-depth biography of Miriam Haskell, refer to the author's book, *50 Years of Collectible Fashion Jewelry: 1925-1975*, listed in the Bibliography.

Part of a seven piece ensemble from Miriam Haskell, c.1934, featuring plastic beads attached with gold wires. The set included a necklace, two bracelets, earrings, a pair of clips and a brooch. (Modern Plastics magazine.)

Credit: Catherine Yronwode & Dean Mullaney Archives

Plate 46
Ginger Moro Collection

Plate #47

Location	Nomenclature	Circa	Description
Top to Bottom	Set: Necklace, Earrings, and Bracelet	1950-1960	Combined thermoset plastic, with resin clasp, glass beads, and gold electroplated metallic beads. Marked: "Hobé." Bracelet expands on wired frame. Clip-type earrings.
Top to Bottom	Hat Ornaments	1920-1935	Assorted variations of Celluloid, resin, Lucite and thermoset plastics, accented with metal or rhinestones. All have threaded "nibs" or point-protectors. Hat ornaments are not hatpins inasmuch as they were not used as pinning devices but were strictly ornamental. Hat ornaments differ from hatpins because they were not "anchors" to keep a hat pinned to the hair and head. However, hat ornaments were sometimes used to pin a ribbon or flower to the headband or crown, or to secure the ends of a wrapped turban. Silken scarfs or feathers were fastened in like manner. A classic style hat could thereby be transformed to suit a costume or occasion.

Plate 47
Author's Collection

Plate #48

Location	Nomenclature	Circa	Description
Full Plate	Buttons	1925-1940	Award-winning Bakelite buttons shown properly mounted on a card, glassed and framed.

Plastic materials were well represented at the National Notion and Novelty Exhibit, held at the Hotel Pennsylvania, New York City, February 7-12, 1937.

Included in the Spring lines of various button manufacturers were a galaxy of bright colored plastic buttons and ornaments in the shape of tailored bows, hooks and eyes, fruits and vegetables, butterflies, birds, fish, twisted rope, leaves, circus clowns, drums and many other variations.

Symbolizing the importance of plastic buttons for Spring and Summer dresses, one showroom was decorated with a flower shaped button, four feet in diameter, fashioned from red Pyralin, and huge Catalin buttons carved into unusual shapes. (Reported in *Modern Plastics*, 1937.)

Plate 48
Milly Combs Collection

Plate #49

Location	Nomenclature	Circa	Description
Left to Right	Pendant/Necklace	1935	Bakelite and metal with carved Celluloid beads. Egyptian motif.
	Pendant/Necklace	1920	Celluloid and metal, Egyptian motif. Beads are strung on a black silk ribbon.
Center	Necklace	1935	Bakelite with molded glass images of Pharohs. Yellow metal chain.
Top, Right	Hat Ornament	1930	Celluloid, with an exceptionally short pin-stem. Probably an appropriate ornament for fastening a wrap-around turban. (*Author's Collection*)
Center	Clip	1925	Large tri-color carved Bakelite dress clip, *Deco* design.
Bottom, L-R	Hatpin	1920	Papyrus design, molded and handpainted Celluloid. (*Author's Collection*)
	Hatpin	1925	Brass scarab enhanced by handpainted molded Celluloid "King Tut." Note how the jewelers tubular and ball-shaped findings anchor the ornamental head to the pin stem. (Rare hatpin) (*Author's Collection*)
	Hatpin	1925	Brass "King Tut" anchored to a heavy resin mounting. (Rare) All three hatpins shown have the authentic types of jewelers findings which properly cover the hole into which a pin-stem is inserted, thus attaching the head of a hatpin to the pin-stem. (*Author's Collection*)

Plate 49
Christie Romero Collection unless otherwise noted

123

Plate #50

Location	Nomenclature	Circa	Description
Top, L-R	Pin	1930	Reverse carved Lucite. (See obverse side on Plate 39.)
	Rings (6)	1950	Assorted thermoset plastic and Lucite, some imbedded with insects.
Bottom, L-R	Earrings	1950	Designer earrings by "Coppola e Toppo."
	Pin	1960-1970	Laminated plastic on wood with imbedded sea shells and sea urchin, etc. (*Author's Collection*)

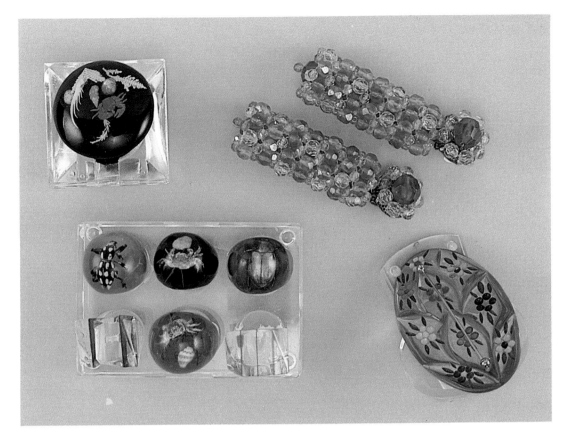

Plate 50
Ginger Moro Collection unless otherwise noted.

Plate #51

Location	Nomenclature	Circa	Description
Top, L-R	Necklace	1970-1980	Laminated plastic combined with pulverized gemstones, and carved cinnabar. (Unique clasp is Pat. 3427691 c.1970.)
	Cufflinks	1950	Lucite imbedded with abalone chips, set in goldtone metal.
	Bracelet	1950	Bakelite and gilded brass, marked: "Ciner." (American) (*Ginger Moro Collection*)

Plate 51
Author's Collection

Plate #52

Location	Nomenclature	Circa	Description
Top to Bottom	Necklace & Earrings	1965	Lucite incorporated with thermoplastic beads. Marked: "W. Germany."
Top, Center	Earrings	1960	Hoop style, clip-type, plastic combined with goldtone metal.

By 1937, the race for prominence in the plastics field was in dead earnest. The United States had, until then, been the undisputed leader in the field. The Celluloid Corporation, sole producer of Celluloid, Lumarith and Protectoid, rightfully and correctly advertised, "John Hyatt produced Celluloid when plastic couldn't be made."

The "new year," 1938, was celebrated by Celluloid Corporation's bold, *moderne* graphics which illustrated the company's program of forging ahead with newer and better ideas derived from its *first* plastic, *Celluloid*. True to its slogan, "Limitation is a fighting word," it compared its pursuit of creating, refining, and exploration into new chemical formulas, with "limitations" imposed on the unimaginative.

"...Columbus sailed half-way around a *flat* globe. The Wright brothers soared high in the air—when only birds could fly. John Hyatt produced Celluloid when a plastic couldn't be made."

When the challenge arose to create a man-made plastic substance that would have *unlimited* use in exploring the "new world" of *outer* space, the oldtime plastics companies picked up the gauntlet and met the test. And Uncle Sam sent a man to the moon because of *modern plastics*.

Along the way of unlimited exploration, came such products we take much for granted such as microwave cookware, computerware, and all kinds of newer plastics for the jewelry trade.

Lumarith, the "new era plastic" of 1938, introduced almost an unlimited color range. It was a plastic that could be carved, cemented to other material, die-formed, die-cast, embossed, laminated, machined, molded, pleated, printed, scored, stitched, stretched, swaged and even hand-shaped. *Lumarith* was Cellulose acetate which was produced by "the Grand-daddy of them all," the plastics division, Celluloid Corporation, (established in 1872).

By the 1950's, the plastics industry's exploration without "limitations," gave us "space-age" phenolic resins which were quickly adapted to many uses by jewelry designers and manufacturers.

Plate 52
Author's Collection

Plate #53

Location	Nomenclature	Circa	Description
Top, Left	Pin	1965	Thermoplastic, figural boy on a skateboard. Marked: "Lea Stein, Paris."
Center	Pin	1965	Unique design of a man's vest on a hanger. Marked: "Lea Stein, Paris."
Right	Pin	1940	Thermoset painted plastic combined with a wooden hand-painted sombrero.
Center, Left	Bracelet	1935	Thermoset plastic, lapis-blue unusual color, cuff. (*Author's Collection*)
Right	Brooch	1970	Thermoset bezel-mounted scarab with rhinestones and enamel. Egyptian motif. Signed: "KJL" (*Author's Collection*)
Bottom	Necklace	1980	Molded thermoset plastic set with crystal eyes. (*Kenneth Jay Lane Archives*)

Plate 53
Christie Romero Collection unless otherwise noted.

Plate #54

Location	Nomenclature	Circa	Description
Top, Left	Earrings	1990	Thermoset *faux* jade plastic disc set with *faux* coral cabochons. Original card (not shown), read: "Couture Collection."
Top, Right	Pin	1990	Flying Pegasus of thermoplastic *faux* jade, with channel-set rhinestones in wings. Marked: "Kenneth Jay Lane."
Center, Left	Pendant with Chain	1965	Thermoset *faux* jade. Marked: "KJL" on small disc.
Bottom, Left	Necklace	1970-1980	*Faux* jade, coral, jet and pearls. Molded thermoset plastic. Marked: "Kenneth Jay Lane."
Center, Right	Bracelet	1960-1990	Large thermoset plastic, simulating jade cuff, is combined with rhodium and rhinestones. Cuff is fitted with clasp, marked: "KJL."
Bottom, Right	Brooch	1960-1990	*Faux* jade and onyx made of thermoset plastics, set with rhinestones. Marked: "KJL." Depending on the design factor, Kenneth Jay Lane jewelry pieces may be marked: "KJL", or "Kenneth Lane" (omitting "Jay") or "Kenneth Jay Lane." Marking is usually with an applied disc. In England, the mark is "Ken Lane."

Harper's Bazaar, (March 1991), shows a lovely model wearing *KJL* jewelry of *faux* jade and rhinestones as described on this color plate. The bracelet was first introduced as fashionable in the 1960's, and true to form, Kenneth Jay Lane's jewelry is *not seasonal*. (See KJL's biographical notes captioned with *Plate B-21*.) The advertisement in *Bazaar* is from *Henri Bendel, New York*, a longtime top-rated fashion salon.

Plate 54
Author's Collection

Plate #55

Location	Nomenclature	Circa	Description
Top	Bracelet	1991	Clear thermoset plastic with channel or pave set rhinestones. Clasped cuff.
Center	Necklace	1990	Coral color thermoset molded plastic coin motifs.
Bottom	Beads	1970	Triple strand "carved"—actually molded—*faux* coral beads, with jet black separators set with rhinestones.

Much to Kenneth Jay Lane's credit, is his attribution to designers who came before him, such as the late David Webb, Cellini, Jacques Cartier, and unnamed designers whose works appear in the auction catalogues published by Christie's and Sotheby's. He can probably attribute much of his success to the fact that he consistently supervised every stage of the production of his jewelry, from designing, to the molding or casting, to the coloration, and to the comfortable fitting which makes his jewelry easy to wear.

Such dedication and the affordable prices for such tantalizing pieces answers to the continuing popularity of KJL designer jewelry. It easily explains his 4,000+ pieces ranging in prices from $25-650, made available from his stock at Trump Tower (New York.)

Because many of his signature pieces would be exceptionally heavy if made of glass or natural elements, Mr. Lane substitutes plastic, and then returns to his very early use of rhinestone "diamonds" to complement the other material.

Plate 55
Kenneth Jay Lane Archives

Plate #56

Location	Nomenclature	Circa	Description
Top to Bottom	Necklace	1980	Approximately 20" long, this extraordinary piece is comprised of thermoset plastic *faux* coral and various tones of amber color "chips." Large rounds of thermoset plastic are accentuated by large design-stamped gold electroplated separators. High fashion jewelry.
Center	Necklace	1970	Clear thermoset plastic with *faux* jade and onyx stones of ingenious plastic. "Jet" is channel-set with rhinestones. Overall length, including sparkling crystal clear plastic beads, measures 20".

Plate 56
Kenneth Jay Lane Archives

Plate #57

Location	Nomenclature	Circa	Description
Top, Left	Earrings	1970-1990	Clear thermoset plastic with rhinestones. Clip-type. Marked: "K.J.L."
Top, Right	Pendant with Chain	1960	Egyptian motif of gold electroplate, mounted on a large slab of *faux* ivory made of thermoset plastic. Marked: "K.J.L."
Bottom, Center	Earrings	1990	"Angel Skin" color, molded plastic. Marked: "K.J.L."
Center	Necklace	1960-1990	"Angel Skin" floral design. (See clip-type earrings, above.) Marked: "K.J.L."

Plate 57
Author's Collection

Plate #58

Location	Nomenclature	Circa	Description
Top	Bracelet	1990	Exceptionally large cuff of *faux* lavender jade made of molded thermoset plastic. Hinged mechanism.
Bottom	Necklace	1970	*Faux* emerald and ruby gems made of thermoset plastics. Ethnic design from India.

An Interview with Kenneth Jay Lane
by Davida Baron
co-publisher & co-founder of
Vintage Fashion & Costume Jewelry Newsletter/Club
P.O. Box 265, Glen Oaks, NY 11004
(reprinted with permission from Volume 1, No. 2, April, 1991 Newsletter)

An Interview with Kenneth Jay Lane:

Kenneth Jay Lane can be said to be one of today's favorite jewelry designers. Already collectible, Kenneth Jay Lane jewelry reflects his unconventional rules in designing some of the most magnificent jewelry and the belief in his own creativity which sets his work apart from everyone else. His name will be included with the great jewelry designers of the century.

When asked if he started out to be a designer of jewelry, his answer was, "No," although he did major in advertising design at the Rhode Island School of Design. This explains his unusually high aptitude for marketing his merchandise. It is one thing to have a beautiful product, it's another to project that beauty to others. Famous people like Elizabeth Taylor, Audrey Hepburn, the late Gloria Swanson, Roz Russell and Diane Vreeland have all been adorned by his jewelry.

In fact, he arrived at the KJL trademark, in 1963 while working for Genesco for whom he designed shoes. While doing shoes for Arnold Scaasi's collection, he designed outrageous earrings set with rhinestones. "I made six pairs of earrings and they sold in Bonwit Tellers within three minutes. The New York Times wrote a story on me and within a month, my KJL Collection was selling in every store on Fifth Avenue in New York City."

After his success with Bonwit Tellers, Saks Fifth Avenue approached him and requested that he design an exclusive collection for them which he signed "Kenneth Jay Lane." The trademark "Kenneth Jay Lane" was sold in Saks Fifth Avenue and "KJL" was sold everywhere else.

Today his trademarks still include "KJL," "Kenneth Jay Lane", "KJL by Kenneth Lane," and "Kenneth Lane for Avon." His earring cards carry the name "Kenneth Jay Lane Couture collection" as opposed to "KJL" because he likes the distinction.

About two years ago he did design a line for the Home Shopping Club from Florida. These pieces did not have his trademark, but did have a "Kenneth Jay Lane" box.

In the near future, Mr. Lane may be designing another collection for QVC Shopping Channel and may even venture into Telemarketing Synchronauts, better known as "informmercials."

Although not a collector of vintage costume jewelry himself, his admiration for past jewelry designers include Nettie Rosenstein, Hattie Carnegie, Mazer and Boucher. When asked how old a piece of costume jewelry had to be in order to be considered vintage, his answer was, "I would say 20 years. If a piece of costume jewelry can survive 20 years of wear, then you know the quality and craftsmanship is there."

He finds designing jewelry as exciting today as the first day he stepped into the world of fashion.

All his designs are his own and his pride shows in each and every piece. Mr. Lane was once asked why he did not design real jewelry, whereupon he replied, "Because I'm lazy and if I dropped an emerald, I don't want to be bothered by picking it up."

At the same time he feels, "There are many women who wear real jewelry who also opt to wear costume jewelry because it's good for travelling, it makes them feel young, it's fun and it's a change. A woman may buy a wonderful dress, but she wouldn't wear that same wonderful dress all the time."

His showroom is not as glamorous as his shops. It's a place to do business, and designing jewelry is serious business. He has a stone setter, one bead stringer, and of course, one designer, himself. He does not believe in proteges since they usually leave to start their own jewelry business and market knock-offs, and why should anyone settle for less than the best. His elegant shops are located in London, Paris, Vienna, The Trump Tower in New York City, The Taj Mahal in Atlantic City, Rodeo Drive and South Coast Plaza in Costa Mesa, California.

Mr. Lane does confess that there are times when some of his jewelry does escape his famous signature, but a picture of it can be sent to his showroom for confirmation, along with a stamped, self-addressed envelope. At one time, he did have little metal tags attached to the necklace, but aesthetically it just didn't look right. "It's hard to sell a necklace if there's a little metal thing sticking out of it. It's annoying...and it's not very chic."

As for the jewelry that's being made today, he does consider Carolee clever, as well as being a good merchandiser. Wendy Gell is another designer he admires. But, all in all, he really does not keep up with the competition since his concentration is more into his own world of designing jewelry, shoes, scarves, belts, hair ornaments, and sunglasses. Another project in the near future may be a new collection of table top glassware. He designed porcelain jewelry for Royal Worcester. He has also designed jewelry for Orrefors.

As for meeting Mr. Lane, it was definitely a pleasure for us. He is a tall, distinguishable gentleman, dressed to suit the title of "America's Best Dressed" and talented enough to accentuate a woman's beauty through jewelry. His love for his craft is shown in every piece he designs and will continue to grow in the hearts of all who love costume jewelry. We thank you, Mr. Lane, for giving us this

Plate 58
Kenneth Jay Lane Archives

Plate #59

Location	Nomenclature	Circa	Description
Left	Bracelet	1960	Thermoset "free form" *moderne* design influence. Marked: "KJL"
Right	Earrings	1980	Star motif, thermoset plastic clip-type. Marked: "KJL."

Plate 59
Author's Collection

Plate #60

Location	Nomenclature	Circa	Description
Top, Left & Center	Earrings (on card) & Necklace	1940	Wheat and leaf design in Tenite thermoplastic.
Top, Right	Pin	1940	Faux ivory made of Tenite thermoplastic. Head is modeled after actor Tyrone Power.
Bottom, Center	Brooch	1940	Variation of popular wheat pattern in *faux* ivory.
Bottom	Necklace	1940	Wheat and flower pattern in ivory color Tenite plastic. Also available in turquoise color. All pieces on this Plate are marked: "Joseff-Hollywood."

Plate 60
Joseff of Hollywood Archives

Plate #61

Location	Nomenclature	Circa	Description
Row 1, Left	Brooch	1940	Large "Seacutter" design, with three Tenite thermoplastic pear-shaped molded sets combined with a scroll design in brass. Worn by actress Virginia Bruce.
Row 1, Right	Brooch	1940	"Seacutter" with one turquoise color pear-shaped drop molded from Tenite.
Row 2, Left	Brooch	1940	*Lei No Ka Oe*, 6-petal brooch worn by actresses Ann Sheridan and Joy Hodges. Tenite, a tradename for Tennessee Eastman Company's thermoplastic, was used extensively by Joseff of Hollywood for his molded plastic pieces.
Row 2, Right	Bracelet	1940	"Seacutter," exceptionally large, hinged cuff, with one pear-shape molded set.
Row 3, Left	Bracelets (2)	1940	Pair of linked bracelets made with Tenite molded plastic in leaf design. Tenite, manufactured by Tennessee Eastman Company, was a thermoplastic used for other products besides jewelry. The company is a subsidiary of Eastman Kodak Company.
Row 3, Center	Brooch	1940	Variations of the center designs for the 6-petaled flower shown above.
Row 3, Right	Brooch	1940	"Seacutter" design with two molded pear-shaped plastic sets.
Bottom	Brooch	1940	Large wheat pattern with molded plastic leaves. (Also available in lavender and ivory colors.) All of the jewelry on this Plate are marked: "Joseff-Hollywood," and were loaned by courtesy of Joan Castle Joseff, wife of the late famed jewelry designer and manufacturer.

Plate 61
Joseff of Hollywood Archives

Plate #62

Location	Nomenclature	Circa	Description
Top	Brooches (3)	1940	Variations of gilded brass centers (stamen) for 5 and 6 petaled *Lei No Ka Oe,* Hawaiian flowers. Available in many assorted colors as well as in black and white.
Center	Earrings	1940	Green color floral to match above flower design. Shown on original card.
Center	Bracelet	1940	Green petals on goldtone linked chain. Worn by actress Jean Parker.
Bottom, Left	Brooches (2)	1940	Variations of the above.
Bottom, Right	Brooch	1940	Different design of the popular wheat motif. Worn by actresses Gail Patrick and Lucille Ball.

Plate 62
Joseff of Hollywood Archives

Plate #63

Location	Nomenclature	Circa	Description
Row 1, Left	Clips	1936-1941	Carved "apple-juice clear," (originally, water-clear), and red Catalin stylized floral.
Row 1, Center	Bar Pin	1936-1941	Amber, orange, light green, brown & ivory color Catalin "Triangles on bar."
Row 1, Right	Clip	1936-1941	Laminated and carved ivory and black Catalin thermoset plastic. "Floral geometric."
Row 2, Left	Bar Pin	1936-1941	Carved black and ivory Catalin, "*Deco* bow tie."
Row 2, Center	Pin	1936-1941	Carved ivory and black Catalin "Sunburst."
Row 2, Right	Bar Pin	1936-1941	Amber, orange, light green and brown Catalin, "Discs in a Row." Also made in red, ivory, burgundy and black combinations.
Row 3, Left	Clip	1936-1941	Laminated (inlaid) and carved amber and dark green Catalin, "Six Fingers."
Row 3, Center	Clip	1936-1941	Carved black and ivory Catalin, "*Deco* Flat Triangle."
Row 3, Right	Clip	1936-1941	Carved ivory and black Catalin, "Comb Style."
Row 4, Left	Clip	1936-1941	Brown and ivory Catalin, "Three Rod."
Row 4, Center	Clip	1936-1941	Carved brown and olive-drab, (the latter color associated with WWII army fatigues which is a yellow-green), Catalin, "Two Curves."
Row 4, Right	Clip	1936-1941	Red and ivory Catalin, "Three Rod." Non-autumn colors, such as shown on this clip, will demand higher prices.
Row 5, Left	Clip	1936-1941	Carved ivory, green, and orange Catalin "Floral Swirl."
Row 5, Center	Clip	1936-1941	Carved black and ivory Catalin "Fan-stepped *Deco*."
Row 5, Right	Clip	1936-1941	Carved ivory and green Catalin. "Zig-Zag Deco."

Note: The name of each piece in quotation marks was appropriately assigned by Catherine Yronwode, recognized authority on plastics.

Plate 63
Catherine Yronwode and Dean Mullaney Collection

Plate #64

Location	Nomenclature	Circa	Description
Row 1, Left	Dress Clip	1936-1939	Carved green Catalin leaf-shape with rhinestones. If this clip was available in a red color, price would be higher.
Row 1, Center	Dress Clip	1936-1939	Carved brown and orange Catalin set with aluminum. Price would be higher if in bright yellow or white.
Row 1, Right	Dress Clip	1936-1940	Carved brown and green bar-shaped Catalin set into metal with rhinestones.
Row 2, Left	Dress Clip	1936-1940	Carved amber color Catalin set in brass.
Row 2, Right	Dress Clip	1936-1939	Four laminated layers of carved burgundy Catalin set with aluminum ball-studs. Price would be higher if the varied layers were of bright colors instead of monochrome.
Row 3	Set: Dress Clips and Belt Buckle	1920	Green casein triangles set into metal with rhinestone accents. *Art Deco* influence.
Row 4, Left	Bar Pin	1936-1939	Carved amber color Catalin capped with alumium balls.
Row 4, Center	Belt Buckle	1920	Orange casein triangles set into metal with rhinestones.
Row 4, Right	Bar Pin	1936-1940	Carved red Catalin fitted over aluminum rod. Catalin is a thermoset plastic while casein is a meltable and bendable thermoplastic product. As with Celluloid and Bakelite, Catalin is a registered tradename. Catalin was sold exclusively by the American Catalin Company, New York.

Plate 64
Catherine Yronwode and Dean Mullaney Collection

Plate #65

Location	Nomenclature	Circa	Description
Row 1, Left	Pin	1936-1941	Carved deep navy blue turtle on ivory scallop shell, Catalin plastic.
Row 1, Right	Scarf Clasp	1937	Carved black Catalin "Kissing Horses," made by Nat Levy & Co., Inc. "Scarf or tie clasp which consists of facing heads affixed by tiny springs to the plastic bar pin. The heads may be lifted and the scarf tucked under, where the heads springing back into place hold it securely." ("Equestrian," Eve Main, *Modern Plastics*, September 1937.)
Row 2, Left	Pin	1936-1941	Carved red Catalin cherries. Being reproduced in 1991 in a media called "plastic clay."
Row 2, Center	Bracelet	1936-1941	Carved deep navy blue catalin, hinged, with carved ivory Catalin swordfish with glass eye.
Row 2, Right	Pin	1936-1941	Carved black Catalin sailfish with painted eyes.
Row 3, Left	Pin	1936-1941	Carved ivory Catalin full figural goldfish with glass eye.
Row 3, Right	Pin	1936-1941	Carved amber and translucent rust-brown Catalin Arabic dagger with brass findings.
Row 4, Left	Pin	1936-1941	Carved yellow Catalin with handpainted details.
Row 4, Center	Belt Buckle	1936-1941	Carved red Catalin with handpainted details.
Row 4, Right	Pin	1936-1941	Carved amber color Catalin figural fruit (pear), with a green felt fabric stem.

Catherine Yronwode explains that "seaside" or "beach" jewelry was written about extensively by Eve Main, (*Modern Plastics*, June 1937), in an article titled *Seashore Suavities*. "Beach jewelry" was a term sometimes used to designate white Catalin jewelry with seaside or waterfowl motifs. (Much of Catalin white has now turned to shades of ivory.) Another category of "beach jewelry" had nautical motifs, such as anchors, pilot wheels, boats, and oars. Nautical jewelry usually came in brighter colors than did the motifs of fish or wildfowl designs.

Plate 65
Catherine Yronwode and Dean Mullaney Collection

Plate #66

Location	Nomenclature	Circa	Description
Row 1, Left	Pin	1937	Carved amber color Catalin, profile of horse with glass eye. Mounted on a disc suspended from carved Catalin riding boot.
Row 1, Center	Pin	1937	Carved amber color with rust-brown "resin wash," full frontal face and head with glass eye and metal bridle.
Row 1, Right	Pin	1936-1941	Carved amber color Catalin, with glass eye, black painted details and brass findings.
Row 2, Left	Pin	1936-1941	Carved amber color Catalin profile with glass eye, painted details and brass findings. "Arabian" horse.
Row 2, Center	Pin	1937	Carved amber color with rust-brown "resin wash" Catalin figural horse with glass eye, suspended from carved Catalin riding crop.
Row 2, Right	Pin	1937	Carved amber color with rust-brown "resin wash" Catalin horse with glass eye and metal bridle.
Row 3, Left	Pin	1936-1941	Carved ivory Catalin, full figural giraffe with painted details.
Row 3, Center	Pin	1936-1941	Carved ivory Catalin eagle with painted details and rhinestone eye.
Row 3, Right	Pin	1936-1941	Carved ivory Catalin pigeon in flight, with rhinestone eye.
Row 4, Center	Pin	1936-1941	Carved amber color Catalin and Rosewood, laminated before carving, "Duck in Flight." Figural duck has a glass eye.

Plate 66
Catherine Yronwode and Dean Mullaney Collection

Plate #B-1

Location	Nomenclature	Circa	Description
Row 1	Pin	1935	Figural stylized cricket, carved Bakelite. (French)
Row 2, L-R	Bar Pin	1935	Black and White Bakelite.
	Bracelet	1935	Polka-dot bangle (American)
	Bracelet	1935	Carved Bakelite bangle.
Row 3, L-R	Pin	1930	Celluloid figural cat. (French)
	Bracelet	1935	Bakelite with beads. (American)
	Ring	1930	Small "pinkie" finger ring, Celluloid. (*Author's Collection*)
Row 4, L-R	Pin	1935	Laminated Celluloid "Bow Tie." (French)
	Earrings	1965	Bakelite, marked: "Yves Laurent."

Several rules-of-thumb to tell ivory from man-made plastics that have the *appearance* of natural elephant and walrus ivory, are carefully outlined in Godfrey Harris' chapter, "Understand Ivory." (See bibliography.) He cites the importance of examining for *uniformity* of grain, a sure give-a-way. He offers hints regarding *texture, color,* and *testing,* etc.

Serious collectors are urged to study the works of other authors who specialize in or are experts on specifiic phases involving the use of plastics as substitutes for other materials.

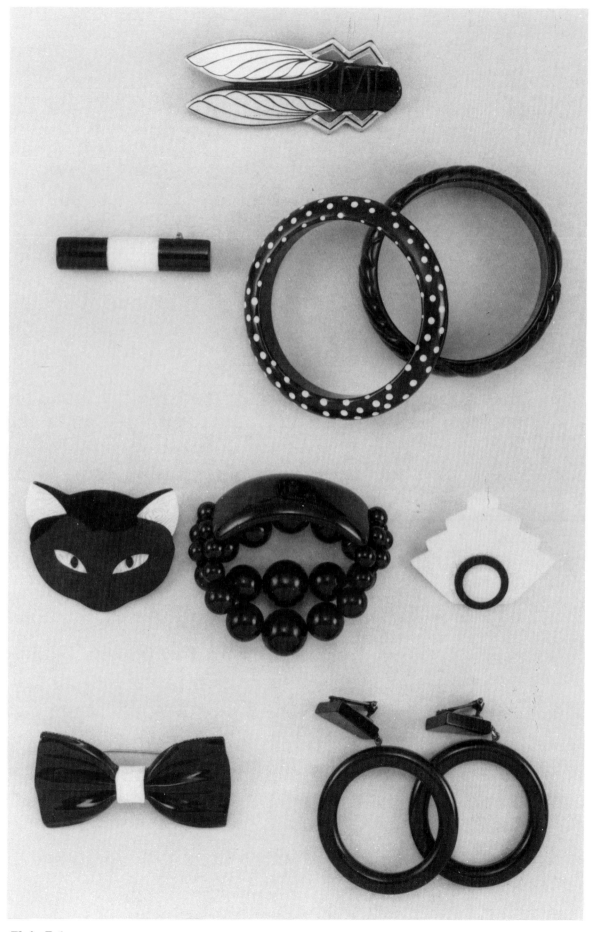

Plate B-1
Ginger Moro Collection unless otherwise noted.

Plate #B-2

Location	Nomenclature	Circa	Description
Left to Right	Necklaces (5)	1950-1975	Assorted white "space-age" phenolic thermoset plastics and resins manufactured for the jewelry trade by several companies. Note the assortment of extension chains in size of links and designs. Most of these necklaces had matching pieces, including brooches, bracelets and earrings.

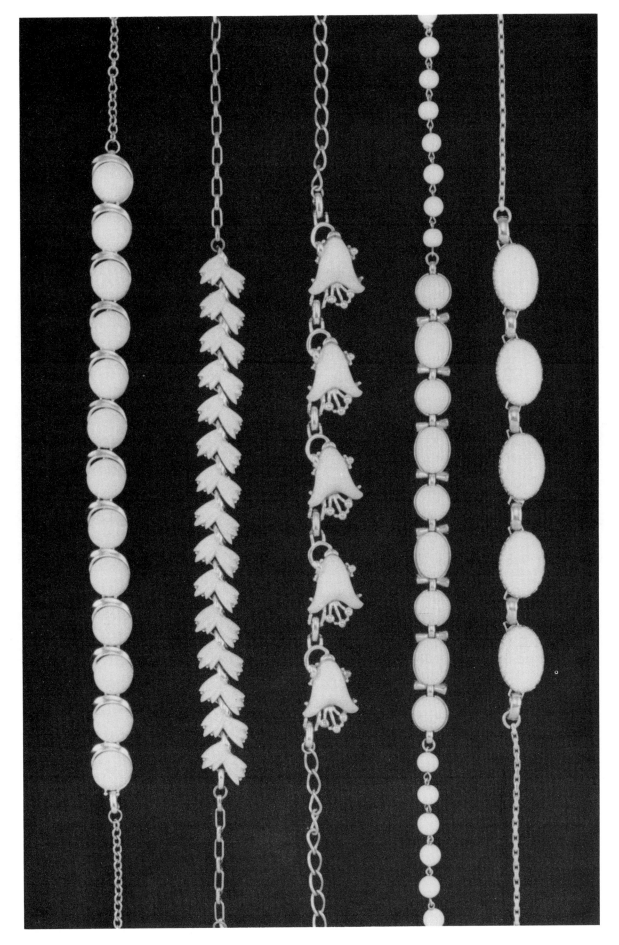

Plate B-2
Author's Collection

Plate #B-3

Location	Nomenclature	Circa	Description
Row 1	Earrings	1955	White thermoset plastic set in patented "goldtone" by Emmons (Newark, New York), a company that originated the jewelry "party plan" called "Emmons Fashion Shows." Each piece of jewelry was given a name. This was called, "All Seasons Favorite" and was a best-seller for many years.
Row 2	Bracelet	1955	Same as above. Earrings and bracelet match the necklace shown on Plate B-2.
Row 3	Bracelet	1965	Lucite and pearlized white plastic and rhodium.
Row 4, L-R	Earrings	1950	Plastic, rhodium and rhinestones, clip type. Molded fuchsia flower. Earrings match necklace shown on Plate B-2.
	Pin/Locket	1970	Fleur de Lis pin with suspended locket. Pastry shell design rim, rhinestones, and a plastic cameo.
	Earrings	1950	Clip type, marked "Trifari."
Row 5	Bracelet	1960	Molded thermoset plastic links with metallic backing of patented "Goldtone." Marked: "Emmons."
Row 6, L-R	Earrings	1950	White molded thermoset plastic and rhinestones, drop earrings marked: "Lisner."
	Earrings	1960	Molded plastic flowers with rhinestone centers. Screw-type, button style.

D. Lisner & Co., New York City, was one of the earlier innovators of costume jewelry made of plastic. In the early 1930's, it won an honorable mention for its "Novelty Costume Jewelry Set in Autumn Leaves design." The plastic used was Marblette, a cast resin manufactured by the Marblette Corp., Long Island City, and fabricated by Ace Plastic Novelty Corp., Brooklyn, N.Y., with screw fittings by Parker-Kalon Corp., New York City. S. Braunstein designed the set for the Lisner Company. It therefore becomes apparent how difficult and sometimes impossible to attribute pieces correctly without actual factory records.

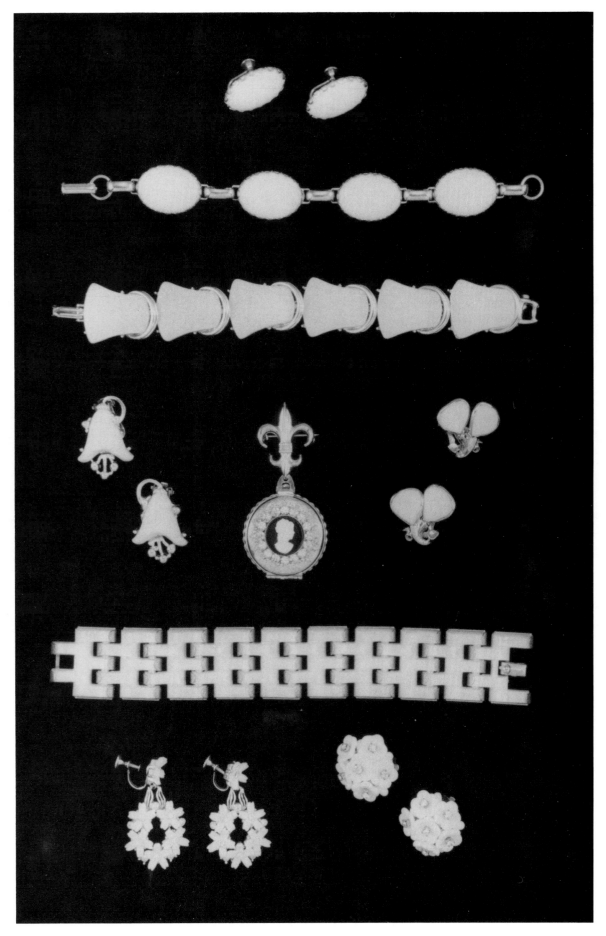

Plate B-3
Author's Collection

Plate #B-4

Location	Nomenclature	Circa	Description
Full Plate	Buttons	1935	Assorted Lucite Buttons

June, 1937, and du Pont announced in big, bold, black letters "an amazing new plastic." It was Lucite (a registered trademark), that was formerly known as "Pontalite."

"Lucite is crystal clear," boasted the advertisement, and *"you can read news-print through a thick block of it...Sunlight doesn't affect it and neither do most chemicals...."*

We usually think of Lucite as being made as a clear plastic product, but in reality, it was made in all colors and in delicate translucent, transparent, opaque and pastel shades.

When first introduced in 1937, it was a plastic product available only as a molding powder but eventually it was produced in sheets, rods, and tubes which enabled designers and manufacturers to adopt a wide field of endeavor in making costume jewelry.

Buttons were a "natural" for Lucite as this plate clearly illustrates. Perhaps a few reasons for the popularity of Lucite buttons was its moisture resistance, and because it was unbreakable and lightweight. These were desirable qualities for any buttons because of early laundering methods and easy care.

Plate B-4
Milly Combs Collection

Plate #B-5

Location	Nomenclature	Circa	Description
Row 1	Brooch	1935	Heavily carved black Bakelite.
Row 2	Bracelet	1935	Black Bakelite linked with metal chain and snap clasp.
Row 3, L-R	Earrings	1935	Carved and painted Lucite with rhinestones. Button-style with clip.
	Pin	1935	Black Bakelite ship's wheel design.
	Pin	1935	Black plastic with rhinestones. "Free form" design.
	Earrings	1930	Black plastic with rhinestones set in *Deco* pattern, button-clip style.
Row 4, L-R	Slides (2)	1925	Black plastic with rhinestone accents. Egyptian heads.
	Bracelet	1935	Black Bakelite rope-twist designed bangle.
	Pin	1935	Faceted black Bakelite, heart-shaped.
Row 5, L-R	Brooch	1935	Large carved black Bakelite figural flower.
	Pin	1935	Black Bakelite shaped like a woman's riding boot.
	Pin	1935	Carved black Bakelite, figural butterfly.
Row 6	Bracelet	1935	Black Bakelite, carved flowers and plain polished plastic with brass links.

Plate B-5
Christie Romero Collection

Plate #B-6

Location	Nomenclature	Circa	Description
Top	Necklace	1930	Cobalt color Bakelite with chrome. (German *Bauhaus*) The theme of *Bauhaus*, simply put, was "less design is better," which was a protest against gothic Victorian "configurations of the *more* the better." Simplicity, and clean lines were the epitome of *Bauhaus* design.
Top, Center	Pin	1960	Laminated Celluloid. Marked: "Lea Stein, Paris."
Center, Left	Bracelet	1930	Red Bakelite and chrome. (French)
Center, Right	Bracelet	1930	Red plastic and chrome. (French)
Bottom	Necklace	1930	Cobalt blue Bakelite and chrome. (German *Bauhaus*)
Bottom, Center	Brroch	1940-1950	Black Bakelite and chrome. (French)

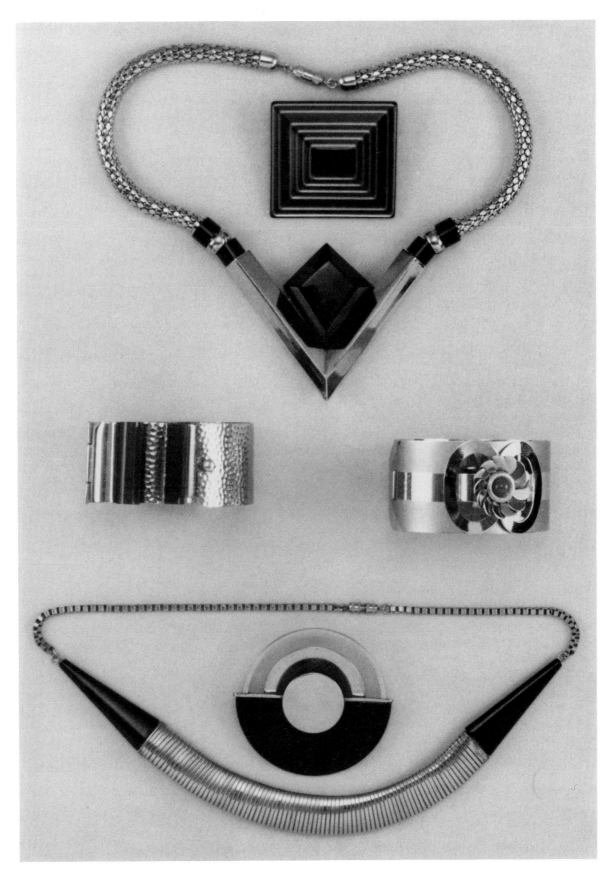

Plate B-6
Ginger Moro Collection

Plate #B-7

Location	Nomenclature	Circa	Description
Row 1, Left	Buckle	1935	Large 2-piece black Bakelite, carved leaf motif.
Row 1, Right	Clips	1930	Pair of large dress clips in black Bakelite.
Row 2, L-R	Bracelet	1935	Unusual belt-strap pattern in black Bakelite.
	Buckle	1930	Black plastic, 2-piece daisy pattern.
	Clips	1930	Carved black Bakelite, acorn pattern.
Row 3	Necklace	1925	Black Bakelite half-round beads, *Deco* style.
Row 3 Center	Hat or Cravat Pin	1939	Black thermoplastic *Deco* style 1939 New York World's Fair symbol.
Row 4, L-R	Buckle	1935	Pierced and carved 2-piece black Bakelite.
	Bracelet	1935	Narrow, carved black Bakelite bangle.
	Bracelet	1935	Oval shape, rope-twist pattern, black Bakelite.

An interesting article appeared in *Modern Plastics* (April 1938), concerning the reproduction in plastic of *Whitby Jet*. Captions for the photographs described the pieces as "sandblasted Catalin, a cast phenolic resin, with highly polished contrasting relief sections which has supplemented the Whitby jet of our grandmother's day. These currently popular designs are created by D. Lisner and Company."

Nature's jet is "mineral in the next stage of petrifaction to coal which is commonly found at Whitby, England, from which place it derives its name," the article stated. It continued with information of interest to collectors *today*, just as it was in *1938*, to wit:

"... the trend toward heavy costume jewelry is being revived and manufacturers turn to jet for inspiration. In their search for a material which would be more lasting and could be more easily handled and carved, they turned naturally to synthetic resins which they found durable, and not only suitable to be carved by hand but which carve into more unusual effects. The plastic jewelry is lighter, too, not such a burden to wear.

"Cast resin which can be sandblasted for a dull finish or polished to a high luster together with the advantages of easy fabrication and light weight, proved to be a satisfactory material.

"Modern fashions (1938) dictate slim, more attractive lines and the museum pieces which have been copied in plastics have been refined to meet these tastes. Black being popular for women's wear, and ecclesiastical design being currently modish, permitted these effective reproductions of Whitby jet pieces to be quickly accepted by the fastidious.

"Exquistely carved Gothic crosses with dull finish surmounted by polished floral designs with clips and brooches to match have been fashioned of black resin by the Alesite Company at one-eighth the cost of genuine jet. The intricate engravings and striking design of the jewelry well becomes the simple unrelieved black dresses which are predicted for Spring." (*Modern Plastics*, April 1938, courtesy Catherine Yronwode and Dean Mullaney Archives).

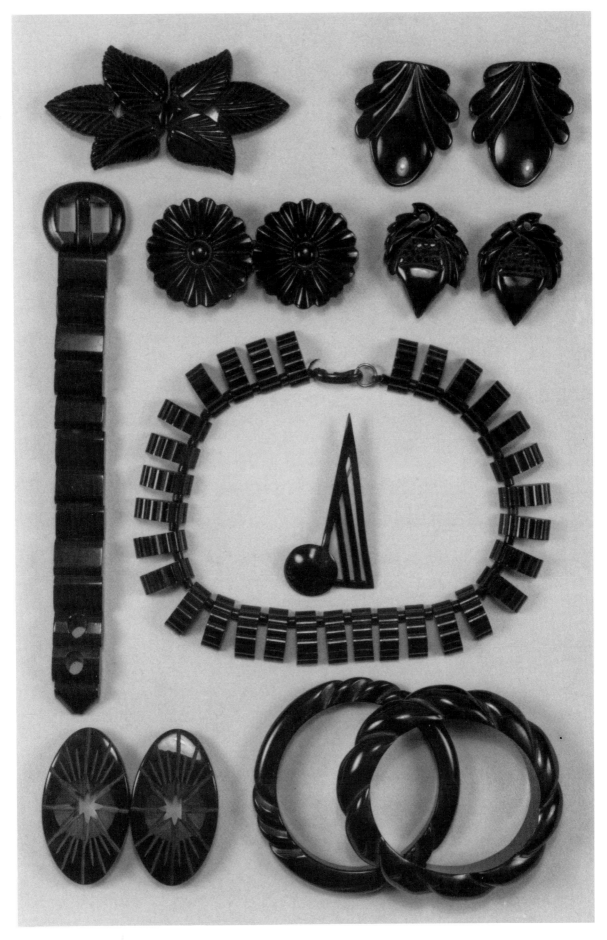

Plate B-7
Christie Romero Collection

Plate #B-8

Location	Nomenclature	Circa	Description
Row 1	*Lorngnette*	1950-1960	Thermoset plastic frame embellished with aurora borealis stones, with magnifing lenses.
Row 2, Left	Bracelet	1945-1950	Hinged black thermoset plastic set with large rhinestones.
Row 2, Right	Earrings	1935-1940	Black Bakelite studded with rhinestones, clip type.
Row 3	Hatpins (6)	1985-1990	Assorted plastic, thermoset, and Lucite ornamental heads. Punch-mark: "Rex."
Row 4	Evening Purse	1925	Carved and handpainted Celluloid with stones. Silk lining and snap closure. *Deco* influence.

Plate B-8
Author's Collection

Plate #B-9

Location	Nomenclature	Circa	Description
Row 1	Watch Fobs (3)	1930	Design variations in black Bakelite and chrome.
Row 2	Bracelet	1930	Red Bakelite and chrome. (French)
Row 3	Necklace	1930	Black Bakelite and chrome with large beads. (German *Bauhaus*)
Row 3, Center	Brooch	1935	Chrome with pink Bakelite. (French)
Row 4	Brooch	1935	Carved Bakelite and chrome. (French)

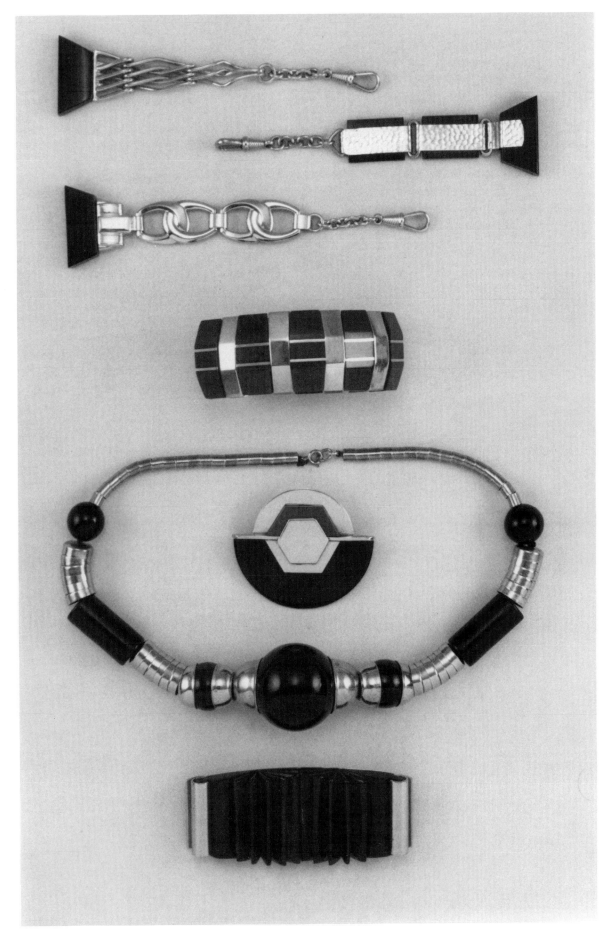

Plate B-9
Ginger Moro Collection

Plate #B-10

Location	Nomenclature	Circa	Description
Top	Brooch	1940	Molded Tenite cameo mounted in gold metal frame. Worn by actress Anita Louise.
Center	Brooch	1940	Antique type frame with molded Tenite cameo. Worn by actress Olivia de Havilland.
Bottom	Necklace	1940	Shown in black and white. (See Plate 62.) Tenite petals on link chain. Worn by actress Jean Parker. Available in several colors and black and white. (Also see Plate B-11.) Tenite is a thermoplastic manufactured by Tennessee Eastman Co., subsidiary of Eastman Kodak, located in Kingsport, Tennessee.

Plate B-10
Joseff of Hollywood Archives

Plate #B-11

Location	Nomenclature	Circa	Description
Row 1	Brooch	1940	Oversize plastic and chrome scroll pattern. Pear-shape Tenite plastic. (See Plate 61.) Worn by actress Virginia Bruce.
Row 2	Bracelet	1940	Link chain with petal drops. (See Plate 62.)
Row 3, L-R	Brooch	1940	Five and six petal Hawaiian blossom, *Lei No Ka Oe*, showing variations in metallic centers and coloration. (See Plates 29, 61, and 62.) Worn by actresses Ann Sheridan and Joy Hodges. Brooches were available in seasonal colors as well as in black and white.
Row 4	Earrings	1940	Matching earrings, shown on original card, for above brooches. (See Plate 62.)

Plate B-11
Joseff of Hollywood Archives

Plate #B-12

Location	Nomenclature	Circa	Description
Full Plate	Photo by Tennessee Eastman.		Unidentified model wearing "Headhunter" brooch. (See Plate B-18 and Plate 29.)

Plate B-12
Joseff of Hollywood Archives

Plate #B-13

Location	Nomenclature	Circa	Description
Photo by Tennessee Eastman.		1940	Parure, necklace, earrings, and brooch. Available in seasonal colors. Tenite thermoplastic pear-shape and scroll design. Necklace was worn by actress Carol Lombard. The brooch was worn by actress Constance Bennett.

Plate B-13
Joseff of Hollywood Archives

Plate #14

Location	Nomenclature	Circa	Description
Photo by Tennessee Eastman.		1940	Wheat spray design necklaces, brooches and bracelets made in Tenite, a thermoplastic manufactured by Tennessee Eastman Co., Kingsport, Tennessee. (Subsidiary of Eastman Kodak). Jewelry was worn by actresses Gail Patrick and Lucille Ball. Various colors of these designs are shown on Plates 60 and 62.

Plate B-14
Joseff of Hollywood Archives

Plate #B-15

Location	Nomenclature	Circa	Description
Photo by Tennessee Eastman.		1940	Variations of blossoms made of a thermoplastic product called Tenite. (See Plate 29 and Plate B-11.)

Plate B-15
Joseff of Hollywood Archives

Plate #B-16

Location	Nomenclature	Circa	Description
Top, Left	Brooch	1960-1990	Black thermoset plastic and rhodium set with rhinestones. Marked: "KJL."
Bottom, Left	Ring	1960-1990	*Art Deco* to *Moderne*, these design influences are still alive and well. The ring is shown in Lucite ring box. Large "size-all" shank, can be adjusted. Ring is made of thermoset plastic *faux* onyx channel-set with rhinestones. Rhodium mounting. Marked: "KJL."
Center, Right	Bracelet	1991	Clear thermoset plastic combined with black enamel on metalic gold frame. Clasp type wide cuff. Marked: "KJL."

Kenneth Jay Lane, could be the subject of a most fascinating biography. A self-made man who wisely recognized opportunity when it knocked—and it knocked several times in his early career—Lane took advantage of every experience offered to him.

He began designer experience working for Genesco, a conglomerate of well-known names such as Tiffany, Bonwit Teller, and I. Miller. The latter is identified with high-fashion *shoes*, for which Lane's designs were exemplied.

Meanwhile, he collaborated in jewelry design with his friend, Arnold Scassi, a fashion designer in his own right. During the 1960's Lane introduced into the Scassi's Collection, rhinestone clip accents for Scassi's shoes. Eventually, matching accessories such as earrings, buttons, brooches, and hair ornaments were introduced

The landmark year for Kenneth Jay Lane was in the 1960's, when he went into high gear designing, making, and distributing KJL jewelry to Fifth Avenue shops catering to fashion-conscious clientele.

The popularity of Lane's jewelry took leaps and bounds when First Lady Barbara Bush wore the triple-strand *faux* pearls created by KJL and now called, "The Inauguration Pearls," (1989).

Plate B-16
Author's Collection

Plate #B-17

Location	Nomenclature	Circa	Description
Row 1, Left	Brooch	1940	Thermoplastic (Tennessee Eastman's Tenite). *Lei No Ka Oe*, 6-petal brooch. (See Plate 61.)
Row 1, Right	Brooch	1940	Metallic gold, set with molded thermoplastic Tenite.
Row 2, Center	Brooch	1940	Exceptionally large, carved leaf.
Row 3, Center	Bracelet	1940	Linked with molded plastic leaf design. (See Plate 61.) Matching necklace is shown on Plate B-10.
Row 4, Left	Brooch	1940	Pear-shape plastic available in seasonal colors with metallic scroll pattern. Worn by Constance Bennett. (See Plate 61.)
Row 4, Right	Brooch	1940	Same as above except for the variation of flower's center (stamen). (See Plate 61.)

Plate B-17
Joseff of Hollywood Archives

Plate #B-18

Location	Nomenclature	Circa	Description
Photo by Tennessee Eastman.		1940	"Headhunters" brooch, once worn by actress Kay Francis. Plate B-12 is *not* Kay Francis but a professional model. Molded brooch of Tenite. (See Plate B-12 and Plate 29.)

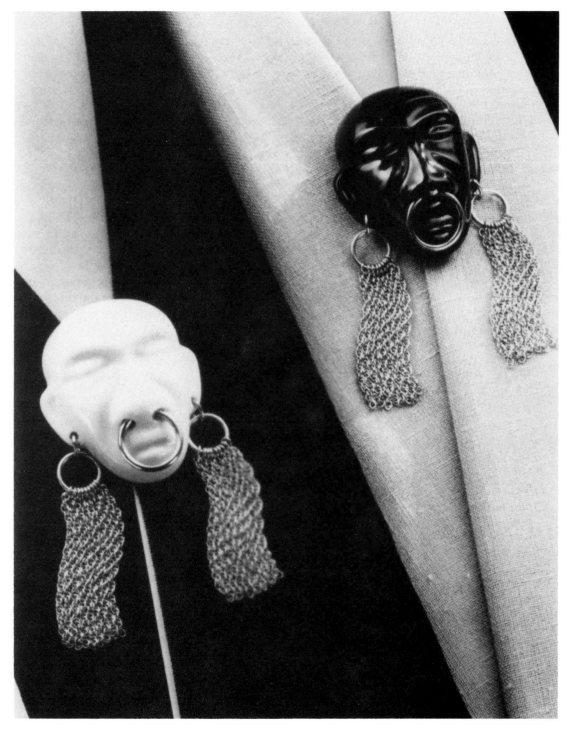

Plate B-18
Joseff of Hollywood Archives

Plate #B-19

Location	Nomenclature	Circa	Description
December 1933 publication,			L'ILLUSTRATION' (Paris). Advertisement, Auguste Bonaz. (See Plate 41.)

Auguste Bonaz made hair combs of gold leaf and marcasites from the turn-of-the-century into the early 1920's. However, when the famous style-setting Chanel bobbed her hair, hair fashions changed almost overnight. Hair combs, for utilitarian purposes became obsolete, although some were worn as a decorative accent.

Because of the above, Bonaz turned to creating his acclaimed barrettes (shown on Plate 41).

In the 1930's, Bonaz worked in "Bakelite" and Galalith (which in English translates to the same type of product known as casein.) Casein was one of the earliest plastics to replace natural materials and there was an extensive use of it until by 1935 superior types of plastic took its place.

In Europe, casein was known mostly as Galalith and Erinoid, although it was sold under other trade names. During the 1930's, the European name persisted in this country, known simply as Galalith, but the more widely used American casein products were Ameroid and Aladdinite.

Casein itself is a product derived from skimmed milk. After forming into sheets and rods, it is hardened by the action of formaldehyde in which it is left to soak. This treatment requires from three days up to several months depending on the thickness of the material treated. The powdered form was mixed with dyes to produce various colors.

The Bonaz factory was located in D'Pyonnax on the Swiss border, in the mountains, because the factory originally had manufactured jewelry made from the horned animals which once abounded in those hills. But once the supply of horn was exhausted, the factory turned to plastic material which could imitate the natural element.

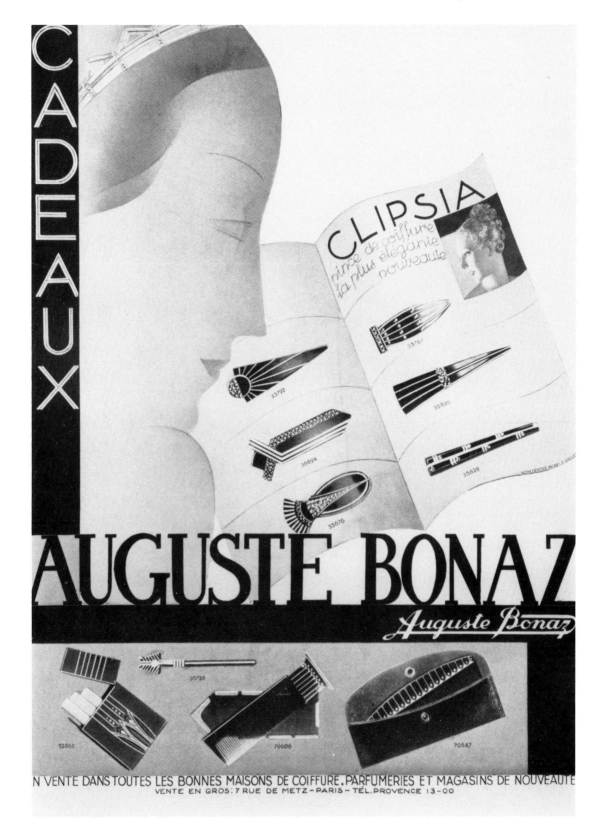

Plate B-19
Ginger Moro Archives

Plate #B-20

Location	Nomenclature	Circa	Description
December 1933 publication,			L'ILLUSTRATION (Paris) Advertisement, Auguste Bonaz. (See Plate 41.)

Plate B-20
Ginger Moro Archives

Kenneth Jay Lane

The name Kenneth Jay Lane has become synonymous with glamour. Famous for his dramatically designed jewelry for an international clientele, Kenneth Jay Lane also creates much of the breathtaking jewelry seen on the runways of the couture collections and on television shows such as *Dynasty, Dallas, Falcon Crest, and All My Children.*

Sharing the lifestyle of his most distinguished clients, he exemplifies the Kenneth Jay Lane philosophy, "Elegance, luxury, and good taste, never go out of style. I believe that every woman has the right to live up to her potential to be glamourous. I try to help her achieve that by creating affordable, beautiful jewelry that enhances her femininity."

Born in Detroit, Lane attended the University of Michigan, then came East to earn a degree in advertising design from the Rhode Island School of Design. He worked in *Vogue's* art department before joining Delman (shoes) and then *Christian Dior.* It was through his embellishment of shoes with rhinestone ornaments that motivated him to begin experimenting with jewelry.

"A whole new group of beautiful people began to exist," Lane said. "They started dressing up a lot and costume jewelry was rather dull...I believed it didn't have to be." The thought that fake jewelry could be as beautiful as the real thing grew on Lane in 1963.

He bought some plastic bangles at a dime store, covered them with rhinestones, crystal, leopard and zebra patterns and stripes, and a new era in costume jewelry was born.

Columnist Eugenia Shepard wrote at the time of Kenneth Jay Lane's rise in the costume jewelry world that "(it) has been nothing short of a comet!"

Since the early sixties, Lane has designed according to his own rules and has emerged as an urbane, elegant spokesman of style. Dinner partner and friend to some of the world's most glamorous women, Lane is both a participant and a mimic of the international social and fashion scene. Some of his favorite clients include: Jackie Onassis, Elizabeth Taylor, Audrey Hepburn, Nancy Reagan, and the British Royal Family.

"I work in less commercial ways than most manufacturers of costume jewelry," he says. "They work seasonally, but I do not believe there is a *season* for jewelry. I like to create jewelry that can be worn any season of the year. Glamour is to be desired all year long. I like my jewelry to be classic, something that is collected rather than bought for a season or as a throwaway."

Lane ignores the usual costume jewelry technique. Like a jeweler, he makes his designs in wax, or by carving or twisting metals. Known for his opulent jewelry and the richness of stone colors, he has many of the stones—particularly the larger ones—made exclusively for himself. The *plastic* stones, as KJL informed the author, are made with a secret formula worked out between Lane and a chemist who produces the *faux* gems exclusively for Kenneth Jay Lane jewelry.

Lane's trendsetting, witty, and colorful costume jewelry has captured high fashion. He was awarded the *Coty American Fashion Critics Award* for "Outstanding Contribution to Fashion." This award was followed by others including high accolades from: *Neiman Marcus, Harper's Bazaar, and Tobe Coburn.* Many other awards and citations came from colleagues in the jewelry industry.

For many years, Mr. Lane has been on the *International Best Dressed Men's List*, and since its inception, he has created unique jewelry for Diana Vreeland's *Costume Institute* exhibitions at the famed Metropolitan Museum of Art in New York.

Today, Kenneth Jay Lane's jewelry designs are sold throughout the world's department and specialty stores as well as in his own established shops such as the exclusive Rodeo Drive location in Beverly Hills, California.

Other exciting shops are located in the South Coast Plaza, (Costa Mesa, California); the Mirage, (Las Vegas, Nevada); Taj Mahal, (Atlantic City, New Jersey), and the Trump Tower, (New York City).

There are four Kenneth Jay Lane shops in London located in Beauchamp Place, South Molton Street, the Burlington Arcade, and on Queens Way.

The Paris location is on the Rue Castiglione, near the *Place Vendome*; another on the Rue Royale, near famed *Maxim's.*

Most recently, Kenneth Jay Lane shops opened a showplace in Vienna.

Los Angeles Magazine, January 1985, pictured Raquel Welch on its cover wearing KJL jewelry. Shown in the story about "America's 10 Most Beautiful Women," former First Lady Nancy Reagan is pictured wearing a fabulous parure by KJL consisting of earrings, necklace, and ring.

Kenneth Jay Lane's *faux* diamond and gilt belt copied expecially for the late Duchess of Windsor, was typical of "the Wallis style."

"She adored costume jewelry," said Mr. Lane during an interview at the famed Geneva auction of the Duchess of Windsor's spectacular collection. At the Duchess' request, KJL began copying the Windsor jewels in the sixties. It was then that he made a replica of the abovementioned *faux* diamond and gilt belt.

In England, KJL's shops go simply under the name, *Ken Lane*, and fashion-conscious writers admit that the first and foremost copycat "imitator of the real masterpieces, is American designer,

The A B C's of Plastic

By John D. Mollinak

**Reprinted by permission and courtesy of
Kyle Husfloen, editor,
The Antique Trader Weekly
Dubuque, Iowa
(First Published December 3, 1986)**

The years between 1925 and 1950 were years of tremendous innovation and expansion in the field of plastics. New "modern" synthetics were marketed in previously unavailable colors for new, widely varied uses. The users of plastics became more and more diverse as resins that would meet their requirements became available.

For the most part, the plastics of the 1920's, the 1930's and the 1940's are and were much different than the plastics of the 1980's. Because of this, there is much argument and ignorance about what types of plastics were used then. Understandably, there is a mist of uncertainty about the composition of old plastic items that come to light now.

In a scene repeated in countless shopping malls and armories, a customer and an antiques dealer chat about collectible plastic items on display in a hinged display case. Tradenames for these colorful old plastic baubles fill the air...like "Lucite," "Bakelite," "Catalin," and "Beetle," billowing up a cloud of confusion. Across town, a young couple drags home their prize; a "waterfall" china closet in blonde veneers with red plastic pulls on the doors and drawer. They refer to the pulls as "Celluloid," thinking...'it was the only kind of plastic that they had back then.'

To help melt away this misty fogbank of confusion about collectible plastics, this article is presented as a short summary of the characteristics and uses of four major categories of plastic and six specific plastics current from the "Twenties into the Fifties." The four categories and six plastics are: Acrylic plastic or "Lucite;" Bakelite or phenolic plastics, often referred to by the old tradenames "Bakelite" and Catalin;" Cellulose plastics, "Celluloid" and "Lumarith" respectively, and often-ignored Urea formaldehyde plastic "Beetle." This article also includes some guidelines to help in identifying these kinds of plastic. To find these guidelines, look at the charts at the end of the article.

Acrylic Plastic or "Lucite"

Acrylic plastic is often called "Lucite" by collectors and dealers. "Lucite" is a tradename that is registered to E.I. duPont deNemours and Company for methyl methacrylate plastic. This kind of plastic has been sold under the following tradenames among others:

"Acrylan"—American Viscose Corp.
"Acryloid"—Rohm and Haas Co.
"Cadco"—Cadillac Plastic Co.
"Chrystalix"—Rohm and Haas Co.
"Fiberfil"—Fiberfill Corp.
"Gala"—George Morrell Corp.
"Gering MMRW"—Gering Corp.
"Joda Acrylic"—Joseph Davis Plastics Co.
"Lucite"—E. I. duPont de Nemours and Co., Inc.
"Midlon M"—Midwest Plastics Products Co.
"Plexiglass"—Rohm and Haas Co.
"Rhoplexes"—Rohm and Haas Co.

This lightweight, transparent resin was first marketed in the 1930's. Dr. Otto Rohm was the developer of this resin, and Rohm and Haas was the first to market it.

Acrylic plastic is a synthetic; it is formed from some starting ingredients that become plastic when a third substance is introduced, called a catalyst. Herbert Simonds describes this process; "Methyl and ethyl esters are the best-known starting materials in the production of acrylics. These colorless materials polymerize easily in the presence of light, heat, and a catalyst such as benzoyl peroxide."

Acrylic resin had an unlimited range of color possibilities, but its greatest assets are its light weight, transparency, and good optical quality. When tinted, the combined strengths of this plastic make it take on a colorful and glimmering appearance. A table published by Rohm and Haas states that hues attainable have been "...theoretically unlimited..." and "...available in a wide range of transparent, translucent, and opaque colors."

Since it has such desirable characteristics, it is not surprising to learn that acrylic plastic has been used for the following applications: early contact lenses, various aviation applications as a substitute for glass, costume jewelry, buttons, reflectors for road signs and signals, display fixtures, clock cases, lighted parts of jukebox cabinets (AMI Model"A"), lighting fixtures, encasing for models and specimens, instrument covers for car dashboards, dial covers for radios, decorative items of all types car hood ornaments, car horn buttons, furniture.

Not all old transparent pieces of plastic are acrylic. Other plastics covered in this article that were used in transparent forms are cellulose nitrate, cellulose acetate, an obscure type of molded Bakelite, and urea. A plastic that this article does not deal with, polystyrene, also was used frequently in a transparent form. To compare and contrast the different types of obsolete transparent plastic, take a look at the guidelines at article's end.

The Phenolics or Bakelites: Molded Phenolics or "Bakelite"

Bakelite or phenolic plastic is derived from a mixture of formaldehyde and carbolic acid, also called wood tar acid or phenol. It was developed by Dr. Leo H. Baekeland between 1905 and 1910, and was named Bakelite in his honor. It was the first synthetic plastic, and the first plastic to find widespread industrial application.

Bakelite plastics fall into two types: molded, general purpose phenolic plastic and cast phenolic plastic. Although both are phenolic plastics and Bakelites by definition, the resins for molding and casting were prepared in different ways. Molded Bakelite will be considered first, then cast Bakelite. A list of some of the tradenames for molded phenolic products appears at the end of the article.

Resin for molded phenolic plastic was made in a reaction kettle that contained formaldehyde and phenol. The polymerization began when heat and an acid catalyst were introduced. Water formed during the reaction was drawn off, and the amber-colored mixture, called novolak, was poured out on to a hardening floor to cool. It was then ground into powder, mixed with lime, a lubricant, dye, and usually fillers. Combined with a chemical compound known as "hexa," this mixture was ready to be molded.

Molded Bakelite plastic has excellent insulating qualities that were enhanced by the impregnation of fillers, such as wood flour. Many industrial applications became feasible through the use of various fillers, hence the designation for phenolic plastics "general purpose."

It is often thought that molded Bakelites are always brown or black. While it is true that the amber color of the moded Bakelite resin prevented light colors from being produced, colors other than brown or black were available. J.H. DuBois lists the "most satisfactory..." colors for molded phenolics as: black, brown, medium brown, light brown, maroon, scarlet red, dark blue, dark green, walnut mottles, mahogany mottles.

Other colors may have been produced in molded phenolic products, but these were the easiest achieved and therefore the most common.

Transparent molded Bakelite was evidently available during the years being considered here. It was used for some high-heat applications, and for some decorative items as well. It was tinted into these colors, according to John Sasso: transparent clear, transparent red, transparent green, transparent light amber, opaque colors, assorted cloudy effects, assorted mottled effects.

A list of applications for molded Bakelite plastic follows. "General Purpose" Bakelite: automobile parts telephone receivers, handles of all types, housings of all types, clock cases, camera cases, buttons, coffee makers, containers, electrical applications of all types, radio cabinets, salt shakers, industrial uses with various fillers. "Transparent Molded" Bakelite: drawer and door pulls on furniture (look like cast phenolic plastic), industrial applications, farm applications (milking machine parts).

It does not appear that radio cabinets were made of this resin, but one possible use for this resin yet to be researched is that it was used for colorful trim on some radio cabinets of the 1930's and 1940's.

One of the great shortcomings of molded Bakelite and cast Bakelite is their low impact resistance. Also, both kinds of Bakelite darken, dull, and become brittle. For more information on Bakelite, and about molded Bakelite in particular, turn to the guidelines for identification at the end of the article.

The Phenolics or Bakelites: Cast Phenolics or "Catalin"

Cast Bakelite plastic is often referred to by the old tradename "Catalin." Its resin was prepared by a different process than the one used in making resin for molding. Other tradenames for this colorful and much sought-after synthetic were:"Aquapearl"—Catalin Corp., "Bakelite Cast Resinoid"—Bakelite Corp., "Catalin"—Catalin Corp., "Crystle"—Marbelette Corp., "Gemstone"—Knoedler Co., "Haveg 48"—Haveg Corp., "Joanite"—Joanite Corp., "Marbelette"—Marbelette Corp., "Opalon"—Monsanto Chemical Corp., "Plastitool"—Calresin Corp., "Plyophen"—Reichhold Chemicals, Inc., "Prystal"—Catalin Corp., "Textalite"—General Electric Corp.

---

[1]Bakelite and Catalin were tradenames belonging to competitive companies, and the tradenames were never substitutes or interchangeable. Each was a separate and distinct plastic product. (L. Baker)

Purified formaldehyde and phenol were used in the production of cast Bakelite plastic. These purified starting materials were combined with a caustic soda catalyst to make the resin. The resin was then agitated for eighteen hours at 150 degrees. Water formed during the reaction was only partially removed, as the amount of water left in the resin determined how translucent the plastic would be. After this eighteen hours of mixing, the caustic soda was neutralized and dyes were added. Following further agitation to insure uniform color, the resin was ready to cast.

The cast for the resin was made of metal, and generally had a space of 3/16 of an inch into which the resin or resins were poured. (In the case of jewelry or other small items, this gap was made smaller.) This gap of 3/16 of an inch was used in casts for radio cabinets and boxes.

Resins were often poured into the casts together to produce multicolored marbleization, often combinations of both color and different degrees of translucency being used. Most often, items were cast in one color, then combined with trim of contrasting colors.

All cast Bakelite pieces are thick, particularly by today's standards. They are translucent (except for the dark colors) and it is not unusual for pieces cast in this plastic to be highly figured with swirls. John Sasso remarked that this translucency and bright colors are generally the two most recognizable characteristics of cast phenolic plastic.

After the resin had hardened in the cast, the object that was formed was removed by force, sometimes by a jackhammer! Cast phenolic items came from the cast with a dull finish, and were tumblepolished with a mixture of waxes.

A partial list of the colors used for cast Bakelite objects would include: yellow, tan, green, turquoise, dark blue (not translucent), black (not translucent), red, orange, white, pink, dark green, maroon, many others.

The dark colors (black, dark blue, dark greens, brown) were not translucent, and were most often used as a backdrop for light, bright colors. At the other end of the spectrum, white and transparent shades of cast Bakelite were technically possible.

Some of the applications that were common for cast Bakelite before and after World War II were: clock cases, radio cabinets, costume jewelry, coat hangers, novelties, advertising items, handles for chrome serving pieces, lighted decorative pieces of juke-boxes (Wurlitzer 850), decorative pieces of light fixtures, other lighting applications, decorative boxes, statuary, and others.

By the 1950's, cast Bakelite plastic had fallen into deep disfavor because it had become prohibitively expensive to utilize. According to Howard Simonds, writing in 1956, cast phenolics were costing about $1.25 per pound per finished object, far above other materials that could be substituted for it.

For guidelines to identifying this collectible synthetic, please refer to the charts at the end of this article.

The Cellulostics: Cellulose Nitrate or "Celluloid"

Cellulostic plastics comprised a large portion of the pre-World War II plastics market. There are two kinds that will be considered in this section: first, cellulose nitrate or "Celluloid" and secondly, cellulose acetate or "Lumarith."

A partial list of tradenames for cellulose nitrate plastic in the United States includes those shown in an accompanying chart.

Cellulose nitrate plastic was first formulated in Europe and in England, but it was Isaiah and John Hyatt who made it commercially available in the U.S. through the formation of the Celluloid Manufacturing Company in 1870. This pioneer firm of the plastics industry was merged with the Celanese Corporation in 1941 to become the Celluloid Celanese Corporation. "Celluloid" was discontinued by the company in 1948 due to its flammable nature, but other firms continued to manufacture cellulose nitrate plastic well into the 1950's.

Cellulose nitrate plastic is the end-result of treating cotton fibers with nitric and sulphuric acids. This created a flammable mass that was washed and bleached when a certain acid concentration was reached. Soaked with alcohol, this mash was treated with camphor to plasticize it, dye was added, and a mixing on heated rollers to evaporate the alcohol followed. A large plastic cake was formed, then baked and sliced into uniform sheets or extruded into rods. Layering of several sheets of cellulose nitrate was not uncommon; the sheets were pressed into various forms, sometimes layering one color against another.

Cellulose nitrate plastic was often used to imitate ivory, so much that many tradenames included the word "Ivory." Nearly every possible hue and shade of color was used to dye cellulose nitrate; some of the colors appear in the list, ivory, green, gold, red, yellow, transparent colors of all types, multi-layered, multicolored cased effects, black, blue, various translucent effects, many others.

Often vertical or horizontal parallel line run through cellulose nitrate plastic, especially in those items that mean to simulate ivory.

Uses for cellulose nitrate plastic were legion. Some of these uses were: touring-car side curtains, detachable men's shirt collars, the ubiquitous dresser set, ping-pong balls, eyeglass frames, boxes, costume jewelry, knobs, keys for typewriters, toothbrush handles, toys, masks, rattles, Christmas tree ornaments, novelties, advertising "give-aways," thousands of dime-store items, myriad others...(At least one television cabinet was billed as pyroxylin!)

Cellulose nitrate plastic was very inexpensive to produce, but its Achilles heel was its flammability.

For this reason, it is wise to keep things made of it away from open flames or high heat. Even direct sunlight may damage cellulose nitrate collectibles. For some information about the identifying traits of cellulose nitrate plastic, look to the end of the article.

The Cellulostics:
Cellulose Acetate or "Lumarith"

Cellulose acetate plastic was developed at the turn of the century, but it was not until the 1920's and the 1930's that it was presented to consumers as a colorful alternative to quickly-burning cellulose nitrate plastic. Most cellulose acetate objects were produced by injection molding, although other modes of fabrication were sometimes employed.

Some of the tradenames for cellulose acetate plastic appear in the list shown elsewhere in this feature.

Cellulose acetate plastic was produced in a way similar to the manner that cellulose nitrate plastic was produced. Cotton fibers were treated with acetic acid, and the cotton mass was processed to the end-product of dyed cellulose acetate plastic sheets, which were usually ground on to sheets for molding.

Cellulose acetate was almost always dyed in wild, "loud" colors, and was used extensively for the big, bold fruit and floral jewelry of the late 30's and early 40's. A partial list of typical colors would include: fuchsia, plum, pink, mustard, orange, red, maroon, shocking pink, tan, green, turquoise, black, brown, many others.

Cellulose acetate was also used in transparent form, and is sometimes confused with acrylic plastic. It was also swirled on occasion in bright colors, resembling cast phenolics. Imitation mother-of-pearl, ersatz tortoise shell and tinted transparent colors were included in the wide repertoire of cellulose acetate colors.

Some items that were produced in cellulose acetate plastic were: colorful costume jewelry, transparent jewelry, transparent belts, decorative interior pieces for Chryslers and Studebakers, radio knobs and push-buttons, decorative pieces on radio cabinets (one model of the International Kadette had synthetic mother-of-pearl trim), novelties, toys, flashlights, and "dime store" items.

Cellulose acetate has one fatal flaw; it becomes disasterously and hilariously distorted when it is immersed in water for any length of time. To determine if a collectible is made of cellulose acetate plastic, take a look at the guidelines at the end of this article.

Urea Formaldehyde or "Beetle"

Urea formaldehyde, a molded synthetic known as "Beetle," was mass-marketed by American Cyanamid Corporation in 1929. It was introduced to close the "color gap" created by the limited color range of molded Bakelite. It could even be molded in some of the same machinery as phenolic plastic. "Beetle" was just one of a host of tradenames for this often ignored and misidentified synthetic. Some of the other tradenames for this resin are listed elsewhere.

Although it occurs in nature, urea was produced synthetically for the manufacture of this resin. The urea was manufactured in the form of white crystals which were combined with formaldehyde and an alkaline catalyst to produce the desired resin. A small portion of the water produced during the reaction was retained. This resin-water mixture was then purified, preparing it to be made into molding powder. To make this powder, lubricants, dyes, fillers, and a curing agent were added to the water-resin mixture, which was subsequently dried and ground.

The most desirable trait of urea-formaldehyde plastic was that it made a wide range of colors available for molded products. Some of the colors in this range were: blue, green, pastel blue, pastel green, pink, red, white, orange, and yellow.

These colors and myriad others can be found in various shades. It was theoretically possible to produce "Beetle" in transparent form or in cast-Bakelite-type swirls of several colors; even chips of various colors on white were often used.

Some of the objects that were molded from this resin appear in this list: radio cabinets, radio knobs, radio dials, many lighting applications that involved low heat, one-piece drawer pulls for metal cabinets, speedometer plates, thermometer casings, decorative lighted pieces for jukeboxes, food packages, cosmetic packages, and jewelry packages.

IDENTIFICATION GUIDELINES
FOR
MOLDED PHENOLICS/"BAKELITE"

Tradenames:

AQUALITE
ARCOLITE
AROCHEMS
BAKELITE
BAKELITE PHENOLIC
BECKOPOL
CATABOND
CATALIN PHENOLIC
CELORON
COLTROCK
COLTWOOD
CONSOWELD
CRYSTLE
DILECTO
DUREZ
DURITE

FIBERITE
FORMICA
GALA
GE PHENOLIC
GEMSTONE
HAVEG
HAVEG 43
HERESITE
HI-DEN
HYCAR-PHENOLIC
INDUR
INDURITE
LAMOROK
MAKALOT
MARBELETTE
MICARTA

MICHROCK
MICOID
MONOLITE
NEILLITE
NOEPRESS
91-LD
PHENOLITE
PLASKON PHENOLIC
PLASTITOOL
PLASTONE
PLENCO
PLYOPHEN
RAYCOLITE
RESINOX
R-4200
ROGERS BOARD

RICHELAIN
RYERCITE
SPRAYMASK
SUPER BECKASITE
SYNTHANE
SYNVAR-ITE-P
TAYLOR LAMINATED
    PHENOLIC
TEGO
TEMPLUS
TEXTOLITE
TREVARNO F92 SERIES
TUFFITE
UNIPLAST
VARCUM
VULCOID

Uses:

electrical parts
old telephone receivers
handles
housings

clock cases
camera cases
closures
coffee makers

car parts
containers
glue, paint, varnish
radio cabinets

salt shakers
industrial general
    purpose uses
    of all types

Colors

black
brown
medium brown

light brown
maroon
scarlet

dark blue
dark green
walnut mottle

mahogany mottle
painted or coated colors
    over black

unique characteristics NOT TRANSLUCENT
— Often has a strong, odd taste.
— Generally mottled or swirled colors; generally a mottle is black and another color.
— Many times these objects retain original shine.
— Low impact resistance.
— Thermosetting with high heat resistance.

typical damage/ware
Brittle.
Cracks, shards broken out.
Dark colors fade.
Shiny finish dull.
Heat damage in the form of crazing in the finish.

confused with...
Swirled polystyrene and opaque polystyrene that is not swirled.
Cellulose acetate.
Ureas.
Cast phenolics.

*(Author's note to reader: Ironically, Mr. Mallinak's article and above **Guideline Identification** for Bakelite, do **not** list jewelry under "uses." Study the colors available.)*

IDENTIFICATION GUIDELINES
FOR
CAST PHENOLICS/"CATALIN"

Tradenames:

AQUAPEARL	CRYSTLE	MARBELETTE	PRYSTAL
BAKELITE CAST	GEMSTONE	OPALON	TEXTALITE
RESINOID	HAVEG 48	PLASTITOOL	
CATALIN	JOANITE	PLYOPHEN	

Uses:

radio cabinets	novelties	trim on jukeboxes	statuary
jewelry	advertising "give aways"	decorative lighting	chessmen
coat hangers	handles	decorative boxes	animal figurines

Colors:

in various combinations and solids... translucent and non-translucent in dark colors; can be transparent...also black, browns, light browns, tan, yellow, red, white, dark green, green, turquoise, pastels, many more...

unique characteristics TRANSLUCENT; COLORFUL:

Heavy *translucent* swirling with pockets of transparency in some pieces.
Sometimes swirling absent.
Bright colors, primary colors, and pastels.
Radio cabinets and boxes have a thickness of $3/16$."
May have a slight taste. Smell when washed.
Heavy marbleization and combinations of two, three, or more colors.
Thermosetting; not as heat resistant as molded phenolics.

typical damage/wear

Heat damage. (Watch the tops of radio cabinets.)
Change in color; usually a darkening.
Factory-polishing worn off.
Cracks; shards broken out.

confused with...

Molded phenolics
Heavily figured polystryene (less thick than cast phenolics)
Swirled cellulose acetate
Urea

(Reader is directed to the chapter in this book, under the heading: FIFTY THUMBNAIL SKETCHES, particularly Sketches #16 &17.)

IDENTIFICATION GUIDELINES
FOR
TRANSPARENT PHENOLICS MOLDED

Tradenames:
"BAKELITE" perhaps others (DuBois lists the Bakelite Corp. as the developer of this resin.)

Uses:	**Colors:**
farm applications	transparent
(DuBois lists a	transparent red
milking machine,)	transparent green
industrial applications	transparent light amber
handles for drawer and	opaque colors
door pulls on some	assorted cloudy effects
furniture	assorted mottles
possibly radio cabinet	
trim	
possibly radio cabinets	
Seemingly used for	
small decorative	
pieces often.	

unique characteristics VERY SCARCE!
Strong smell when boiled. (Other phenolics have this characteristic, too.)
Thickness may be less than cast phenolics.
OPINION: May be evaluated on the same basis as cast Bakelite.

typical damage/wear
Discoloration.
Cracks.

confused with...
Cast phenolics (They can be virtually identical.)

IDENTIFICATION GUIDELINES
FOR
ACRYLIC PLASTIC/"LUCITE"

Tradenames:

ACRILAN	CHRYSTALEX	GERING MMRW	MIDLON M
ACRYLOID	FIBERFIL	JODA ACRYLIC	PLEXIGLASS
CADCO	GALA	LUCITE	RHOPLEXES

Uses:

early contact lenses	closures	light fixtures	car parts/hood ornaments
aviation applications	sign reflectors	instrument/dial covers	decorative pieces
glass substitute	display fixtures	encasing for models	furniture
costume jewelry	clock cases	nameplates	myriad others

Colors:
Transparent and a wide range of translucent, transparent, and opaque colors. Not always transparent, but valued for its transparency.

unique characteristics
— Reflects light around an angle of 42 degrees or less.
— Often used for curved dial and instrument covers.
— Acrylic plastic has no smell or taste.
— It is not suitable for high-heat applications.
— Acrylic plastic is smooth and lustrous, and can be
   used in varying thicknesses.
— It is not very flexible, is thermoplastic.

typical damage/wear
— Yellowing.
— Occasional crazing.
— Heat damage.

confused with...
Polystyrene, cellulose acetate, and
occasionally Bakelite or cellulose nitrate.

IDENTIFICATION GUIDELINES
FOR
CELLULOSTICS: CELLULOSE ACETATE

Tradenames:

AMPACET	JODA C/A	NIXONITE	TENITE I
BAKELITE C.A.	JODAPAC C/A	NIXON C.A.	TENITE ACETATE
CINELIN	KODAPAK I	PLASTACELE	VUEPAK
CLEARSITE	LUMARITH	PYRA-SHELL	
GEMLOID	MACITE	STRUX	
HEROCEL A	MIDLON A	TEC	

Uses:

"loud" costume jewelery	radio knobs/buttons	telephones	kitchen utensils
transparent costume jewelry	zippers	oil cans	toys
	chessmen	midget radio cabinets	flashlights
transparent belts	goggles	trim for radio cabinets	"dime store" items
Chrysler interior trim	sunglasses lenses	novelties	many others...

Colors:

fuchsia	mustard	green	mother-of-pearl
plum	orange	turquoise	imitations,
pink	red	black	sometimes in bizarre
shocking pink	maroon	many transparent colors	colors
salmon	tan	tortoise-shell imitations	

unique characteristics

Thermoplastic; some heat resistance.
Shiny, molded; often rather thick.
Bizarre, loud colors.
Flexible transparency.
Non-flammable; water is its *femme fatal*.
Forms of fruit, leaves, and big attention-getting designs common.

typical damage/wear

Dull.
Water damage or distortion.
Cracks; hunks broken out or off.
Chipping.

confused with...

Urea.
Some Phenolics.
Especially with polystyrene and acrylics.
Cellulose nitrate.

(Reader is directed to the chapter titled, FIFTY THUMBNAIL SKETCHES, Sketches #6 & #7.)

IDENTIFICATION GUIDELINES
FOR
CELLULOSTICS: CELLULOSE NITRATE

Tradenames:

AMERITH
CELLULOID
CINELIN
DURALIN
FABRIKOID

FIBERLOID
HERCULOID
ISINGLASS
KERATOL
MULTIPRUF

NITROL
NITRON
NIXONOID
NIXON CN
PYRALIN

PYROXYLIN
TEXTILEATHER
TEXTILOID

Uses:

side curtains
shirt collars
costume jewelery
dresser sets
ping-pong balls
television cabinets
     (very few)

radio cabinets
     (very few)
eyeglasses frames
boxes
business machine keys
knobs
toothbrush handles

toys
masks
rattles
desk sets
Christmas tree ornaments
novelties
advertising "give-aways"

souvenirs
thousands of "dime
     store" items...

Colors:

ivory
transparent clear
transparent shades of
     all colors

green
gold
red
black

blue
various translucent
     colors
cased colors

many others...
tortoise-shell
imitations

unique characteristics
The word "Ivory" often appears as part of tradenames.
Can be very thin; nearly always composed of sheets.
Look for evenly spaced lines in the plastic.
Burns up...quickly and completely.
Sometimes tastes or smells of camphor.
Is often slightly flexible. (Don't flex it too hard...)
Thermoplastic; very little heat resistance.

typical damage/wear
Heat damage.
Warpage.
Fading and yellowing.
Stains.
Layers chipping apart.
Cracks.

confused with...
Ureas.
Cellulose acetate.

(Reader is directed to the chapter titled, FIFTY THUMBNAIL SKETCHES, Sketch #9.)

IDENTIFICATION GUIDELINES
FOR
UREA: "BEETLE"

Tradenames:

ARODURES
BAKELITE UREA
BECKAMINE
BEETLE
CATALIN UREA
DAKA-WARE

FABREZ
GALA
INSUROK
LAMICOID
LAUXITE
PLASKON

PLASKON-UREA
PLIOFOAM
PLYAMINE
REPTONE
RHONITE
RICHELAIN

SYLPLAST
SYVA-ITE U
SYNVAROL
UFORMITE

Uses:

lighting fixtures/shades
lamp parts
radio knobs, dials, cabinets
midget radio cabinets
one-piece drawer/door
     pulls for metal and

kitchen cabinets
speedometer plates
thermometer casings
lighting parts on
     jukeboxes
food/cosmetic packaging

costume jewelery
kitchen containers/
     cannisters
glass substitute, especially
     in lighting applications
clock cases

buttons
switch plates
lighting applications
     with low heat
     exposure

Colors:

transparent shades of
     all hues
pastel shades of all
     colors

white
blue
green
red

pink
orange
yellow
occasional cast-phenolic

type multi-color
mottles, swirls

unique characteristics
Shiny, molded plastic.
VERY COLORFUL, not "loud" like cellulose acetate.
Design limitations with this medium required very "clean " looks with very little surface decoration;
     occasionally louvers, but no intricate decoration unless it is applied.
Urea objects maintain color better than "Celluloid."
Urea has no taste. Urea has no smell.

typical damage/wear
Fading or changes in color.
Water, humidity damage.
Heat damage; cause cracks to open. (Watch the top of radio cabinets.)
Cracks, shards broken out.
Surface discoloration.

confused with...
Acrylics.
Cellulose nitrate.
Phenolics.

Tradenames for Cellulose Nitrate Plastic

"Amerith"	Celluloid Mfg. Co./Celanese Celluloid Corp.
"Celluloid"	Celluloid Mfg. Co./Celanese Celluloid Corp.
"Cinelin"	Cinelin Co.
"Duralin"	Respro Inc.
"Fabrikoid"	E. I. duPont de Nemours and Co. Inc.
"Fiberloid"	Fairfax Co.
"Herculoid"	Hercules Powder Co., Inc.
"Isinglass"	
"Keratol"	Textileather Corp.
"Multipruf"	Elm Coated Fabrics Co. Inc.
"Nitrol"	Monsanto Chemical Corp.
"Nitron"	Monsanto Chemical Corp.
"Nixonoid"	Nixon Nitration Works
"Nixon CN"	Nixon Nitration Works
"Pyralin"	E. I. duPont de Nemours and Co. Inc.
"Pyroxylin"	various companies
"Textileather"	Textileather Corp.
"Testiloid"	Textileather Corp.

Tradenames for Cellulose Acetate Plastic

"Ampacet"	American Molding Powder and Chemical Co.
"Bakelite C.A."	Bakelite Corp.
"Cinelin"	Cinelin Corp.
"Clearsite"	Celluplastic Corp.
"Cellulate"	National Plastics Corp.
"Gemloid"	Gemloid Corp.
"Herocel A"	Hercules Powder Co., Inc.
"Joda C/A"	Joseph Davis Plastics Co,
"Jodapac C/A"	Joseph Davis Plastics Co.
"Kodapak I"	Eastman Kodak Co.
"Lumarith"	Celanese Celluloid Corp./Cellanese Corp. of America
"Macite"	Manufacturers' Chemical Co.

"Midlon A"	Midwest Plastics Products Co.
"Nixonite"	Nixon Nitration Works
"Nixon C/A"	Nixon Nitration Works
"Plastacele"	E.I. duPont de Nemours and Co., Inc.
"Pyra-Shell"	Shoeform Co.
"Strux"	Aircraft Specialities Co.
"TEC"	Tennessee Eastman Corp.
"Tenite I"	Tennessee Eastman Corp.
"Tenite Acetate"	Tennessee Eastman Corp.
"Vuepak"	Monsanto Chemical Corp.

Tradenames for "Beetle," (Urea Formaldehyde)

"Arodures"	U.S. Industrial Chemicals
"Bakelite Urea"	Bakelite Corp.
"Beckamine"	Reichhold Chemicals, Inc.
"Beetle"	American Cyanamid Corp.
"Catalin Urea"	Catalin Corp.
"Daka-Ware"	Harry Davies Molding Co.
"Fabrez"	Reichhold Chemicals, Inc.
"Gala"	George Morrell Corp.
"Insurok"	Richardson Co.
"Lamicoid"	Mica Insulator Co.
"Lauxite"	Monsanto Chemical Co.
"Plaskon"	Plaskon Division, Libbey-Owens-Ford Glass Co.
"Plaskon Urea"	Barrett Division, Allied Chemical and Dye Co.
"Pliofoam"	Goodyear Tire and Rubber Co.
"Plyamine"	Reichhold Chemicals, Inc.
"Reptone"	Sun Chemical Corp
"Rhonite"	Rohm and Haas Co.
"Richelain"	Richardson Co.
"Sylplast"	Sylvan Plastics, Inc.
"Synvar-Ite U"	Synvar Corp
"Synvarol"	Synvar Corp.
"Uformite"	Rohm and Haas Co.

Section III
Appendix B

Collectible Plastics

Newsletter of
The Society for Decorative Plastics

Catherine Yronwode and Dean Mullaney, Editors
Vol. 1, No. 1, October-November 1984
(By Permission)

The Major Types of Collectible Plastic:

For the purposes of this introduction, we are defining "collectible" plastics as those produced between 1868 (when synthetic plastics were invented) and the period immediately after the Second World War (when the use of cast phenolics declined to near nothing in the United States, and the finishing off of flash-marks was abandoned). Excluding such natural plastics as shellac and such non-collectible and recent plastics as polyethylene, we can take a look at plastics as they stood at their heydey, during the late 1930's.

Pyroxylin
("Celluloid," "French Ivory," "Pyralin," "Vegetable Ivory," et cetera):

This is the earliest form of synthetic plastic. It was invented in 1868 by John Wesley Hyatt, who was searching for a way to simulate ivory, for use in making billiard balls. Pryoxylin (which, by the way, is not hard enough to make billiard balls from) is chemically known as cellulose nitrate. It is highly flammable (being a close chemical "relative" of gun cotton) and it tends to turn yellow with age. It was often produced in a striated ("ivoroid") form, as well as an irridescent "mother-of-pearl" laminated form much used in toiletry articles. "Celluloid" was a brand name for products made by The Celluloid Corporation of New York, New York. Other brands included Nixonoid (Nixon Nitration Works, Nixon, New Jersey), Xylonite (British Xylonite Co., Ltd., London, England) and Nacara (Fiberloid Corp., Indian Orchard, Massachusetts). In addition to its decorative uses, Celluloid also formed the basis for the early "nitrate" film stock and gave its name to the "cels" on which cartoon animators paint each frame of an animated feature. Pyroxylin plastics are fairly light in weight and become soft when heated. Many articles of pyroxylin were made by heating and forming thin sheets. The material is rather soft, and small dents or even burns can be sanded out with fine steel wool. Celluloid articles were not made after WW II.

Cellulose Acetate
("Tenite," "Similoid," et cetera):

An outgrowth of cellulose nitrate, this was an attempt to produce a similar product without the dangerous flammability of the pyroxylins. It had limited use in the costume jewelry trade and also was made into cutlery handles, but it is most often encountered in the form of knobs and handles in cars of the 1930's and 40's. It has one fatal flaw: it tends to develop a characteristic crackling on the surface with age and exposure to light. In time this can lead to the entire article falling apart into tiny little chunks. Colors were varied, imitation horn and marble being two of the more popular types. Cellulose acetate was expensive to manufacture and was used mostly when its ability to have metal rods and fittings molded into it without heating or drilling repaid the extra cost of manufacture. Cellulose acetate was always molded, never cast. It is hard and slightly brittle. It does not have the "greasy" feel of the phenolics.

Casein Plastics
("Ameroid," "Kyloid," "Dorcasine," "Casolith," et cetera):

This plastic is made from milk proteins. It was invented in 1904. Because it takes a long time to cure, and because it warps when manufactured in large sizes, it was commercially available in sheets ¼ inch thick at the most or rods no larger than ⅝ inch in diameter. This limited its use to the realm of buttons and buckles, where its beautifully glossy surface, its wide color range, and its ease of lamination and carving made it very popular. Casein plastic cannot be molded; it must be cut or carved from stock rods or sheets. Laminated layers, cut away in "cameo" form are a dead giveaway of casein products as no other type of plastic from the 1930's-40's was routinely shaped in that way.

Bringing Back The Shine

Celluloid and Catalin objects retain their original polish far longer than do today's softer plastics, but even so, exposure to 50 years of dishwater, air pollution and dust can take its toll. To bring back the original shine, use either regular jeweler's compounds such as tripoli and rouge—or, for even easier results, try Turtle Wax Buffing Compound (red), wash off excess, follow with Turtle Wax Rubbing Compound (white), and finish with a clean dry cloth. You'll find these products in the automotive section of your local discount store, where they sell for around $1.80 per large can. (1984 pricing)

Phenol Formaldehyde ("Bakelite," "Catalin," "Marblette," "Agatine," "Gemstone," "Durite," "Durez," "Prystal," et cetera):

This was the major class of "Art Plastic" in the 1930's. Its inventor was L.H. Baekeland (hence "Bakelite") and he discovered it in 1908. There are two basic groupings of phenolic plastics—the cast and the molded. The molded types came first and they include both the early formulas for resins incorporating wood flour (powdered wood) and those which were free of filler and thus clear or colored with dyes. The most typical use of the name "Bakelite" is to describe the darker-toned, wood-flour filled plastics (such as those which were used for early telephones and are still used in situations where the material's non-conductivity of heat and electricity is vital). However, "Bakelite," being a tradename for products manufactured by the Bakelite Corp of New York and Bakelite, Ltd. of London, can also properly be applied to cast resins too - if they were made by that company. The most popular name in cast phenolic was not Bakelite, however, It was "Catalin," a tradename of the American Catalin Corporation of New York. It was the Catalin Corp. which came up with the slogan "The Gem of Modern Industry" to describe its wide variety of cast phenolic shapes. These ranged in color from yellow, orange and red through green, blue and purple. Catalin is most widely encountered in the form of costume jewelry, cutlery handles, and small decorative boxes, lamps, desk sets and the like. It is quite heavy, has a very slight "greasy" feel, and will not soften at heats under that of boiling water. It is about as hard as brass and can be worked with files, grinding tools and abrasive cutters. It buffs to a high and durable polish. Molded phenolics originated around the First World War and continue to this day (although the non-filler or clear-colored types are not much in vogue). Cast phenolics hit the scene in 1930 and were gone by around 1945-50; their manufacture was too labor-intensive for them to be economical past that point because each piece had to be individually cast in a non-reusable lead mold and then carved, buffed and tumble-polished.

Other Plastics of the 1930's:

The period between the two World Wars saw rapid changes in the chemical industries. Acrylic resins, so common today, had just been invented, as had vinyl, soon to dominate the recording industry. Polystyrene made its bow then, and furfural-phenols were in use in industrial applications. A great future was predicted for ethyl cellulose but by 1937 it was still in the experimental phase.

Urea Formaldehyde ("Beetleware," "Plaskon," "Duroware," "Hemcoware," "Uralite," et cetera):

The early phenol formaldehydes were dark in color, due to impurities, and thus the resultant items made from them were usually given a dark tone through dyeing, to mask this. Urea formaldehyde, on the other hand, is naturally light, and thus it was used to create injection-molded products in the pastel range of colors. One set of molds could be used to make stove handles, for instance in either black (phenol) or white (urea). Urea formaldehyde also formed the light half of the "Formica" color range, with the darker tones being handled by phenol formaldehyde. Urea's great disadvantage, however, is that it is a lightweight, cheap-feeling product. It is the archetypal "plastic," brittle, of indescript color, shiny rather than glossy, and not very strong. Anything smaller than a bread box which was molded out of urea could have been molded out of phenolics for a slight increase in cost and with an even greater increase in aesthetic pleasure to the collector of today. A number of classic art deco designs were wasted on cheap urea castings for jewelry and cosmetic containers, radios, clocks and the like. If found in phenolics they are worth a fortune; in urea they are frustrating "might-have-beens."

The Five Groups (Recap)

For most purposes the field of decorative plastic from the first half of the century can be narrowed down to the five major types listed above. Once again, they are: PYROXYLIN ("Celluloid"), PHENOLICS ("Bakelite" and "Catalin"), CELLULOSE ACETATE ("Tenite"), CASEIN PLASTICS ("Ameroid"), UREA FORMALDEHYDE ("Plaskon")

Of these five, Cellulose acetate is rarely encountered in the area of decorative or "art" objects and Casein is limited by its chemical properties to use in the making of buttons, belt buckles and dress clips. Urea is readily identifiable as the "cheap" feeling, brittle stuff. Pyroxylin is the "Celluloid" of which a million vanity sets were made from the late Victorian period on through the advent of *Art Deco* styling. Molded phenolics such as "Bakelite" began as dark, dense utilitarian objects, but by the Thirties, when the problem of clear, bright colours had been solved, they were used extensively for radio and clock housings designed in streamlined forms. The cast phenolics such as "Catalin" were used for small decorative items, notably jewelry, cutlery handles, desk sets and novelties.

Having memorized these five general classifications of collectible plastic, the collector (and the antique dealer) need never again hold aloft that napkin ring in the form of a scottie dog and say, "It's old. I think it's Celluloid."

("From Hours to Minutes," Eve Main. Modern Plastics, May 1937. Courtesy, Catherine Yronwode and Dean Mullaney Archives).

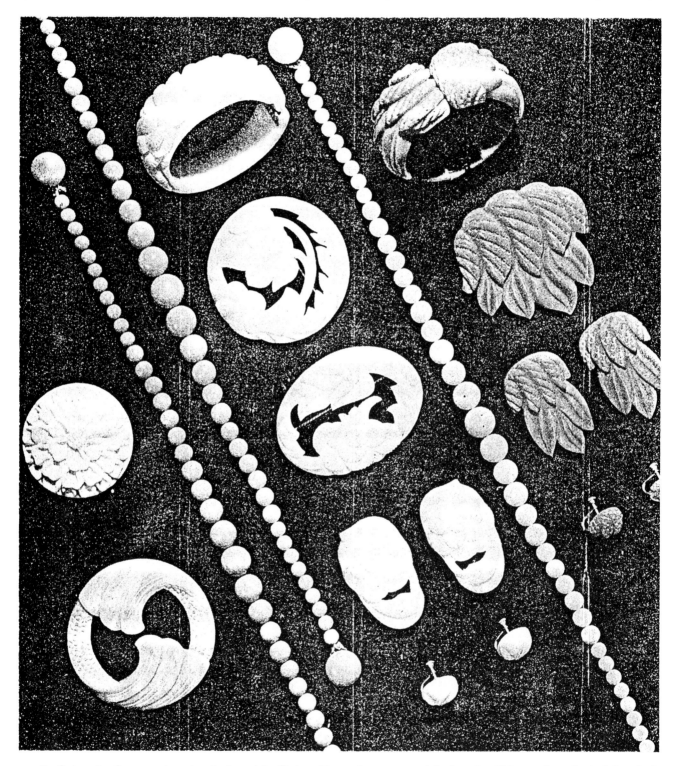

Craft jewelry from cast resin, designed to fit in with contemporary style trends. Strings of graduated beads in pastels and bright colors highly polished, are popular for beach and town wear with light spring and summer ensembles. Deeply carved hinged bracelets, huge clips and brooches, and dainty earrings add zest to costumes for all occasions. The pieces are turned out in vast quantities by skilled craftsmen aided by machines especially constructed for the fabrication of cast resin jewelry. Low material and low fabrication cost make it possible for women to afford several sets or pieces to complement daytime and evening apparel. *(Jewelry by Ace Plastic Novelty Corp., of cast resin fabrication, cut from Marblette, NOT "Bakelite.")*

"The desire for personal adornment is the foundation upon which has been built one of the oldest and most important industries—the making of jewelry. All through the ages, man has fashioned trinkets for his women folks and himself from materials supplied for the most part by nature. Pre-historic man found it necessary to devise some method of fastening his clothing of skins, and because bone was nearest at hand and familiar to him, he skillfully adapted it to his needs. His bone fastenings were first of all practical, then carved with original designs inspired by his surroundings which though crude, possessed a natural beauty.[1]

"Brooches and rings were the first jewels made from metal followed by necklaces, bracelets, chains and carved stones. Different countries have contributed their interpretations of personal ornamentation: Egyptian goldsmiths prepared massive gold bracelets for the Queen of Zer in 5400 B.C.; Assyria favored bronze jewelry elaborately decorated; the Minoan gems of Crete, 1600 to 1400 B.C. included necklaces and beads cut from amber, amethyst, agate and crystal; the best Greek jewelry dates from the 5th Century B.C. and includes pieces of delicate filigree and others enameled in color; Persian women bedecked themselves with necklaces of pearls, lapis, turquoise, emerald and jasper; Anglo-Saxon craftsmen worked in gold filigree and enamel; Middle Age jewelry was engraved, inlaid and set with all the precious stones. During the Renaissance, the jeweler's art became increasingly important in Italy, France, Germany and England.

"There have probably been fewer radical changes in the jeweler's art than in any other industry because the purposes for which jewelry is used are the same that have existed throughout the ages although styles, of course, have kept abreast of other fashion trends. Old-time craftsmen worked upon their metals and stones with primitive tools. Each piece required a great amount of painstaking labor and consumption of much time and concentration. Later, laborious hand methods were augmented and supplanted by machinery, which made possible more rapid production and brought attractive pieces within the reach of a greater range of people. This tendency toward using machinery has perhaps represented the greatest change in all the history of jewelry manufacture and the principal difference between ancient and modern art lies in the craftsmanship and tools the workers were able to bring to bear upon raw materials. The materials used have not changed a great deal except for the introduction of new ones to supplement older substances.

"Cast resins, one of the newer man-made materials which appeared less than ten years ago,[2] have speedily become indispensable for the fabrication of all types and kinds of sports and costume jewelry. Through their use, much of the ancient craftsman's feeling and spirit is maintained although work previously done by hand is now accomplished with the aid of ingenious machines developed especially for carving and fabricating these plastic materials. Actually, it is a species of hand work facilitated by means of rapidly revolving grinding wheels. However, the principles involved are different. For example, the cameo was originally wrought at great expense of time and labor by the craftsman who held the stone firmly in one hand or in a vise, and with the other hand moved his cutting tool over the surface to carve it.[3] Today's machinery for fabricating cast resins works directly opposite. A stationary grinding wheel moves at a fast rate of speed while the operator holds the piece to be carved in both hands and guides it against the wheel, cleverly working out intricate patterns. Then, with a minimum of polishing, the piece is ready for findings which are attached by a foot treadle operated machine."

The extensive article by Eve Main was accompanied by illustrative material featuring examples of cast resin fabricated products of the Ace Plastic Novelty Corporation. The cast resin items were cut from Marblette, and the full production of Ace Plastic Novelty Corporation was marketed solely though manufacturing jewelers who assembled and distributed the plastic parts.

Mr. A.D. Seidman was president of this company which was one of the earliest to turn to producing costume jewelry from plastics. Seidman was an innovator, beginning with a staff of two to three workers, and building up to a work force of 135-150 talented craftsmen and operators. From a company with a mere 2400 square feet, it grew to providing plastic jewelry and other fabricated women's accessories, requiring manufacturing areas of 20,000 square feet with a special department for designers and artists.

"Plastic jewelry," wrote Eve Main, "is not in any sense a substitute for pieces made from other materials. It has created a comfortable niche all of its own because of its adaptability, its decorative value and its brilliance. It is equally effective used alone or to complement other materials; in fact, plastics combine harmoniously with metal or wood and are even seen in combination with leather, lending a touch of color and charm to more conventional materials."

At the time the May 1937 article was written, Mr. Seidman predicated that "strings of graduated beads, highly polished" would be coming for the spring and summer fashions. The lightweight plastics made beads of this material favored for beach and town activities.

Eve Main tells how beads were available in "myriads of color—white, red, royal blue, turquoise, coral, pink, maize, French violet, lilac, and green." The Ace Plastic Novelty Corp. was actually turning out two thousand gross per day in addition to deeply carved bracelets, clips, earrings, pins and rings. "Handpainting in bright colors on the under side of transparent resin" was becoming a favorite pattern. Because cast resins resisted heat, (thermoset), they were gaining favor over cellulose plastics which were not as durable.

Ace Plastic Novelty Corp. was a large manufacturer of plastic jewelry which today might incorrectly be called "Bakelite," whereas the plastic used was Marblette, which is in the same class as Bakelite and other phenolic plastics.

[1] Preceding the use of bone as a pinning device was the thorn. (Unpublished manuscript, "From Ancient Bodkin to Period Hatpin" by Lillian Baker.)

[2] Eve Main's article, "From Hours to Minutes" was published in May 1937. Therefore the cast resins referred to as appearing "less than ten years ago," refers to the advancement of the plastic industry from 1927.

[3] Eve Main refers to cameos made of *stone*, (gemstones). The earliest cameos were actually made of *shell*, and are probably still the most popular natural element for cameos hand-carved for royalty and for the masses. Hardstone, not gemstones, (sometimes referred to as "pebble stones"), were used in carving earliest cameos and the ancient tool was "a kind of mandrel that was spun in primitive fashion by a bow." (See *Cameos: Gems of Intrigue and Imagination*, Lillian Baker, published August 16, 1978, "The Antique Trader.")

Section III
Appendix C

Cameo Biographies About The Collector/Dealers Featured In This Book

Dorothy Buhrman

Dorothy Buhrman has been an avid collector and wearer of distinctive *art deco* and *moderne* jewelry, which includes designs manufactured in plastics. She is owner/partner with Wanda G. Baker, the author's daughter, of two shops in which much vintage jewelry is displayed and sold. Together, these young collector/dealers have established a growing resource for fashionable plastic jewelry. In fact, the first "showcase" concept was designed and built at their Sherman Oaks, California store, and many others in the antique/collectibles shops and malls have followed suit. Dorothy has appeared in films, on television, and has been a professional "voice-over" actress for many years. An attractive young lady, she is a perfect model for the type of jewelry she favors, and many are the jewelry pieces "sold off her back," so to speak. But she retains her favorites, of which just a few are a pictured herein. (Contact: Showcase Antiques, 21531 Sherman Way, Canoga Park, CA 91303, and 13603 Ventura Blvd., Sherman Oaks, CA 91423.)

Ginger Moro

When I interviewed Ginger Moro whose partial collection is featured on many of the photographs in this book, it was most interesting to learn of her exciting background which I'm pleased to share via a letter she wrote about her buying/selling experiences as a collector and dealer. She told about herself "on the prowl in Paris" as follows:

"I was an actress under contract to Paramount when I jumped ship in Paris at the end of a U.S.O. tour of American bases in Europe. Since I had only $5 and two years of college French, the remaining members of the U.S.O. troop which returned to the United States, believed for sure that I'd be home in two weeks. Sixteen years later, I reappeared, 'decorated' in Bakelite jewelry.

"While I was in Europe, I worked in French films and sang in Mediterranean cabarets by night. By day, I combed the flea markets looking for jewelry and art. When all the available space in my 6th floor walk-up apartment was usurped by my objects d'art, I opened an antique boutique in Paris.

"That was twenty years ago. I tried, unsuccessfully, to interest the conservative French in *Art Deco* jewelry, but it was too soon for the French and they said it would never sell. (Which proves that 50,000 Frenchmen can be wrong!) So I packed up my chrome and Bakelite and bundled it off to America where it was enthusiastically received!

"Every year I take vintage American costume jewelry to Europe and return with Continental treasures. It's a happy exchange.

"I'm in awe of the characteristic styles of plastic jewelry design of the 1930's and 1940's. The German machine age was primarily heavy chrome links with Bakelite used as decorative accents. Germany also manufactured wonderful chrome mesh and enamel jewelry.

"The French have a sophisticated and elegant style, suited to the chic and petite Parisienne. Belgian design is a combination of both, and of course the inventor of Bakelite, Dr. Baekeland, was born in Belgium.

"The English mixed brass elements with their plastics making them unique.

"Considering the devastation caused by two World Wars, vintage European plastic jewelry is relatively rare and is therefore priced accordingly.

"Now American Bakelite is chunky, clunky, and delightfully humorous. In the United States, it's the jazzy color and originality of design that counts and makes pieces collectible. Whereas in France, one discreet pin is worn on an exquisitely tailored lapel, here in Uncle Sam's country, we pile on the bracelets and cover jeans jackets with figural pins— the more pizazz the better. *Vive la difference!*

"*Call it Celluloid, Galalith, or Bakelite.* In any language, plastic jewelry has seduced two generations of collectors and is working on a third."

Readers can contact Ginger Moro by writing to her at P.O. Box 64376, Los Angeles, CA 90064.

Christie Romero

Anyone who has attended Christie Romero's jewelry workshops will verify her popularity as a teacher whose classes include a "hands on" practice as well as demonstrations, techniques, and simple repairs of antique and vintage jewelry. A majority of her students have repeated more than one of her multi-session classes slated annually at several community colleges and adult schools in Southern California.

Christie Romero is a collector and dealer, researcher and lecturer, who specializes in early to mid-20th century vintage jewelry. She is an expert on Mexican silver jewelry, and speaks with authority about fashionable and collectible plastic jewelry.

Her expertise on Mexican silver jewelry makes her a favored speaker for programs which have been sponsored by the International Society of Appraisers, and the National Association of Jewelry Appraisers. During the summer of 1991, she was invited as an expert on the subject, to lecture at the 12th annual course in antique jewelry and gemstones, at the University of Maine.

Christie's initial introduction and interest in plastic jewelry began with a simple purchase of a pair of plastic dress clips at an antique show. The design and the fact that they were characteristic of the 1930's era of unique jewelry fascinated her. Her natural curiosity about this type of jewelry led to further acquisitions and research. Major acquisitions remain in her private collection, with some of these pieces exhibited herein.

She is the proprietor of *Christies's Treasures*, and sells privately (by appointment), and to the trade.

Interestingly enough, Christie was a "rock and roll" entertainer, and when performing in select night clubs, found the wearing of colorful plastic jewelry lightweight, attractive, and complementary to her varied programs. She is now retired from the entertainment field and devotes full time to her teaching and lecturing career, while at the same time conducting her business, Christie's Treasures. (Contact: P.O. Box 1904, Hawaiian Gardens, CA 90716.)

Catherine Yronwode and Dean Mullaney

Catherine Yronwode and Dean Mullaney are the founders of The Society for Decorative Plastics, and as editors of the newsletter, *Collectible Plastics*, introduced themselves to their membership in Vol.1, No.1, October-November 1984 issue. Although involved in paper collectibles, (everything from fruit crate labels to illustrated children's books), their greatest passion is the beautiful cast phenolics of the 1930's. The objects include many items other than plastic jewelry and women's accessories, but they were most generous to the author in allowing reprints of pertinent information from their copyrighted newsletter. They also made available their extensive archives from which many sources of information with historical reference to plastic jewelry were obtained and thereby shared with readers of this book. Permission to use and reprint such useful and informative material was given without reservation, credit and sources are given throughout this work and a reprint of their definitive break-down of types of collectible plastics appears in Appendix B. Included are excerpts with proper source credit noted. Readers may contact Catherine "Cat" Yronwode by writing to P.O. Box 1099, Forestville, CA 95436.

Section IV
Unit I

Cross Reference Index
Designer Names

Section IV
Unit II

Cross Reference Index
Jewelry & Accessories

Section V

Glossary of Jewelry Terms and Types Including a Nomenclature for Plastics in Simple Terms

Accessories

Jeweled accessories held a prominent place in late 19th and 20th century high fashion, especially as introduced by Coco Chanel in the 1920's and into the 1930's. Accessories were utilitarian but combined utility with beauty of design. The lorgnette, buckles, short hatpins and hat ornaments, dress clips, sash pins, beaded bags and purses were very popular, and the "necessaries" included: coin purses, vanity cases, card cases, and tiny writing tablets complete with silver case and lead pencil. These accessories added an expression of charm to the individual costume. The *Art Deco Period*, c.1925, brought the powder and rouge compact, with bright lipsticks, and even the elongated cigarette holder which gave a contrived saucy stance to the faddish fashion models of the era.

Aigrette

A hair ornament consisting of a plume or spray of glitter, often accentuated by either a jewel or buckle. Worn in the hair, or attached to a head-band, *aigrettes* were still being worn through the 1920's and early 1930's.

Alloy

Combination of metals fused together. A base metal mixed with a precious ore to make it workable, to harden it, or to change its color.

Antimony

The mineral, *stibnite*, used to impart hardness in alloys. Antimony is now another word for a tin-white colored metal used extensively in costume jewelry castings. It expands as it solidifies, and becomes brittle. Antimony is a "pot metal" base for rhodium plating or other types of gilding.

Arabesque

Flowing scrollwork, often in low relief, epitomized by curlicues of line.

Art Deco (1910-1930)

A stilted, stylized design which was named after the 1925 *L'Exposition Internationale des Arts Decoratifs et Industriels Modernes*, held in Paris, France. Much of the *Art Deco* design was a transition from the earlier *Art Nouveau*, and as with the *nouveau* epoch, was inspired by the art of the

American Indian, ancient Egyptian, and Greek and Roman architecture. The early 1920's interest in *Cubism* and *Dadism* as a new art form, greatly influenced the *Art Deco* period. The King Tut traveling exhibit, in the 1970's, renewed the craze for Egyptian design jewelry. Additionally, the mysteries of the Pyramids and a continuing revival of astrological studies, lent itself to *Art Deco* designs which in turn were incorporated in the *Art Moderne* period following 1930.

Art Moderne (1935-1945)

It is generally accepted that the period of the 1920's to the 1930's is the *Art Deco* period. The decade of 1940-1950 is considered the "modern" period, an era in which just about any conceivable type of design—whether it be flamboyant or contrived with delicate fancy—survived. However, the *Art Moderne* period (1935-1945) avoided such frivolous swirls and instead "streamlined" into crisp geometric lines, all designs of decorative and utliitarian art form. "Modern" seems to be a term giving license to all creativity in any form, be it eccentric or strictly along conventional jeweler's line. The *Art Moderne* period expresses the conflict between machine and nature, which is so evident in *Art Deco*. But *Art Moderne* contains somewhat less contrived artistry, although some pieces do appear as near absurdities. Most *Art Moderne* jewelry combines phenolics and modern metals such as chrome and rhodium. However, there have been great jewelry pieces executed in 3-dimensional *Art Moderne* form, designed by the famed artists, George Braque and Salvador Dali.

Artificial (see Imitation and Synthetic)

Art Nouveau

Refer to Lillian Baker's book, *Art Nouveau & Art Deco Jewelry*, published by Collector Books, Paducah, Kentucky, 1981. This is the first book entirely devoted to these two periods which produced some of the most collectible jewelry sought after in the 1980's. A note from the author states, "A simplistic but hearty definition of *Art Nouveau* and *Art Deco* design, is the triumph over functional line by artistic merit." Its full meaning is in the text.

Bags (see Purses)

Baguette

A narrow rectangular-cut stone most often chosen for diamonds. A *baquette-cut* was influenced by the interest in Cubism of the 1920's. When associated with emeralds, it is called an "emerald-cut."

Bakelite (also see Plastics)

A trademark for a synthetic resin chemically formulated and named after Belgian chemist L. H. Baekeland (1909). This newer plastic was for molding items formerly created in the highly flammable Celluloid or in hard rubber molds. It is capable of being molded and carved, and some *art nouveau* and *deco* jewelry pieces were crafted in Bakelite.

Bandeaux (see Tiara)

Baroque

Bold, ornate, heavy-looking ornamentation.

Barrette

Another name for barrette is "hair clasp," particularly those into which a beautiful silk or grosgrain ribbon bow could be inserted. Barrettes are available in elegant gold or silver plate, highly chased and engraved, and some were also offered in sterling and gold karat. Metallic barrettes were marketed through the 1920's and from the twenties to the present time. Many handsome barrettes are made of various plastics, including those set with rhinestones, gems and gemstones. Sterling barrettes were more popular after the 1930's.

Bead

An ornament of varied shapes and sizes, with a hole end to end into which a needle can be inserted for stringing or mounting. Most glass beads came from Czechoslovakian, Italian and American glass-blowing factories. However, René Lalique is known to have made and sold beads through his catalogue and shop. Beads are made from gemstones, metals, shells, seeds, ivory, bone, stone, horn, papier-maché and plastics. Glass beads are made on a blowing rod and then pierced for stringing on thread, wire and many natural and man-made fibres.

Belts

Metallic discs and chains were worn to accentuate a small waist. The chasing and engraving on the metal was executed to pick up the pattern of the lace on the garment being worn, or to complement the fashionable design of the frock. Buckles often were designed with *art deco* motifs, combining *plastics* with metals.

Bezel

A groove or flange which holds a stone secure in its setting.

Billiken (or Billikin)

An original good luck charm conceived and patented in 1908 by Florence Pretz, from Kansas City, Missouri. The Craftsman's Guild, and The Billiken Company (Chicago), were the principle manufacturers of this novelty.

The original American design was first copied by the Eskimos in walrus tusk ivory, and whale's teeth. From 1925 through 1965 copies were manufactured in Germany, Czechoslovakia, and Japan. These were fabricated in glass, porcelain, metals and plastic.

According to researcher/collector, Dorothy Jean Ray, the artist/designer Florence Pretz was influenced by Asian figures such as Buddha or Taoist gods. Another influence was Palmer Cox's pixie-like "Brownies." It is interesting to note that according to Ms. Ray, "Kewpies" came after Billikens.

Dorothy Jean Ray's article, "The Billiken," is available from *Alaska Northwest Publishing Co.*, 130 Second Ave. South, Edmonds, WA 98020. This fine work appeared in *The Alaska History and Arts of the North Quarterly Journal*, winter 1974, *Vol. 4, No. 1*. It contains fascinating history, photographs and excellent references. A must for Billiken buffs.

Box Setting

A stone enclosed in a box-shaped setting with edges of metal pressed down to hold it in place. Sometimes referred to as a "Gypsy" mounting.

Bracelets

Bracelets have been popular since time immemorial. *Art Deco* artisans produced "jointed" wide-cuffed bracelets and unjointed bangle-type bracelets, the latter often given in friendship. Adjustable bracelets were worn by both ladies and infants and had an adjustable "expando" mechanism. Because Queen Victoria's Prince Consort presented her with a wedding ring in the form of a pair of entwined serpents, bracelets with this motif were very much in vogue during her long reign. With discovery of King Tut's tomb, the serpent again became a symbol on many pieces of jewelry, and most eloquently in the bracelets of the *Nouveau, Deco,* and *Moderne* eras. The bangle bracelet was originally called a "bangle ring," although it was made to fit around the wrist. It resembled an enlarged ring and was called "bangle ring" because the piece was very narrow and resembled a wedding band. The adjustable cuff or band bracelet was another innovation of the 1890's, as was the coil or mesh wire bracelet. Coil bracelets were adjustable in that being a coil the bracelet could be stretched to fit. The "wedding band" type of bracelet could also be expanded with either end separating and then popping together after it was placed on the wrist. As late as 1910, the stiff band or cuff bracelet was still preferred and measured from 1" to 2" wide. High relief and much *niello* work (black tracery enamel) were featured on cuff bracelets, especially those imported from the Orient. Catalin or Marblette plastic bracelets of the *deco* and *moderne* periods gained enormous popularity during those periods (1930-1940) followed by the enormous appeal of flexible wrist ornaments of rhodium studded with rhinestones and imitation gemstones of foiled crystal to dazzle the fashion world. Bracelets became so fashionable that they were worn in varied quantities and designs, sometimes at wrist or as arm-bands like some colorful tatoo. The wristwatch band of the 1960's and 1970's became bracelets with hidden timepieces, thus a piece of jewelry which was not only decorative but functional.

Brass

A yellowish-gold color metal which is primarily an alloy of copper, tin, zinc or other base metal. Brass is the base for much gilded or gold-washed jewelry of the *deco* period.

Brooch (see Pins)

Buckles

Buckles were wrought for belts, cummerbunds, sashes, shoes, capes and hats. Some belt buckles were actually brooch-pins with simulated hasps. The buckle was pinned in front of a sash, belt, cummerbund or hat. Buckles were finished in Roman gold, rose gold, antique gold, silver, French gray, oxidized metals, or gun metal and were made of the plastics and chrome of the *deco and moderne* periods. They were most fashionable after the turn-of-the century. When the belt buckle was designed to meet at an angle, rather than in a horizontal manner, it was called the "new dip" belt buckle. Shirtwaists were "in" at this same period and women demanded buckles that matched pins and studs, as well as hatpins, buttons, and collar stays. Colonial-type shoe buckles came in oxidized silver and were used to accent a brown or black calfskin pump with a very high tonque. The clasp of the tonque fit into the colonial buckle, and the shoe was called "Colonial Pump" because this type buckle was a reproduction of the earlier fashion. Many colonial-type shoe buckles were of beautiful cut steel. The color of the metal was known as "French Gray," and the steel was often hand etched within its square shape. Soon these types gave way to many new shapes, particularly the oblong. In the 1915-1925 era, there arrived a new color, "brown jewelry," which was a kind of seal-brown tone of metal and plastic which went very well with the popular brown fabric coming into vogue at the beginning of the twentieth century. In the second decade of the twentieth century, the sash buckle with the simulated hasp was introduced on wider cummerbund-type belts which were worn closer to the hips rather than to the waist, a fashion note of the *deco* period. Small waists were "in" until after World War I, when the flapper girl costume brought the so-called "waistline" to well below the curve of the hip—a fashion revived today. Since the 1970's, belts of fabric and leather have been shown with detachable buckles which are made in various shapes, metallic content, fine cloisonné enameling, and many kinds of plastics.

Buttons (dress)

Some dress buttons came in sets of three and were joined by a very delicate lovely link chain which prevented loss. The stud end was worn inside the blouse which, prior to 1900 was called a "waist."

From 1900 to 1920, the waist was then called a "shirt," even for women. During the *deco* period, it became a "blouse," and has remained thus to the present day. Buttons were beautifully engraved, enameled, with raised borders, and some were set with garnets, pearls or turquoise. Identical buttons in miniature were made for children's wear, although often simpler in design. Buttons not only came in the round, but were bar shape, oblong shape and oval shape. During the *deco* and *moderne* periods, buttons had beautifully curved designs, wonderfully engraved with lovely rippled or ribbed cable patterns. These were made of both natural and man-made materials—and especially glass and plastics. Most metallic buttons were die-stamped, but others were handcrafted. The *deco* and *moderne* plastic buttons were often enhanced by foiled rhinestones of many colors, sizes and shapes. New machine manufacture and plastic compositions which lent themselves to injection molding, produced extraordinary designs, shapes and colors. With modern methods of fastenings and invisible closures made possible by modern space technology thermal plastics, buttons are now more decorative rather than functional, and in many cases have become obsolete. In 1985, new interest arose in the use of buttons as adornments, and has increased in 1990.

Cabochon

A stone without facets, and shaped like a dome.

Cage (see Mountings)

Cameo

Conch shell, onyx gem, coral and various gemstones which were carved in either relief or intaglio. Cameos are also molded in synthetics such as plastic or glass. Cameos usually depict a scene or portrait, but may be symbolic. Ivory and wood can also be carved into a cameo, but natural elements cannot be molded.

Cartouché

A shield or scroll with curved edges used particularly on gold or silver for a monogram. A *cartouché* should not be confused with an escutcheon. An escutcheon is a plate of metal added or applied to the top of a signet or monogram type hatpin head, or to any other piece of jewelry such as a ring or brooch.

Casting

To form a plastic or liquid substance into a particular shape so as to form the shape, (most often in metal). The heated metal is poured and then allowed to harden and take shape in the mold.

Casting usually is associated with metallic work, whereas molding is more descriptive of an injection type of process such as for plastic or for molding glass. One can also mold a pliable material into a particular shape, such as clay, plaster-of-Paris, thermoplastic resins, cellulose acetate, rubber, etc., so these molds can be used for castings or reproduction work.

A mold is a cavity into which anything is shaped, thus regulating the size, form, pattern, or design of an object. (See Templet and Prototype.)

Celluloid (also see Bakelite & Plastics)

A trademark of Hyatt Bros., Newark, NJ (1868). It is a composition mainly of soluble guncotton and camphor, resembling ivory in texture and color. Celluloid was also dyed to imitate coral, tortoise-shell, amber, malachite, etc. Originally called *xylonite*, Celluloid is the word most often used to describe any imitation ivory, bone or tortoise. But there were many other imitators of such natural elements: "ivorine," "French ivory," "tortine," and the like. Celluloid should not be confused with the harder and more resilient plastics known as Bakelite, Catalin, Beetle or Marblette. Celluloid, being highly flammable, lost favor to phenolic resins of the 1930's. Celluloid was first used as synthetic ivory in the manufacture of billiard balls.

Celtic Design

Primarily junctured lines and discs affiliated with the ancient Celtic Cross. The designs are derived from Gaulic, British, Irish, Scotch, and Welsh symbols and have been incorporated in much modern design revived in the 1930's.

Champleve (also see Enameling)

An enameling technique in which areas of metal are cut, etched or routed and filled with enamel. Unlike *cloisonné*, the cells are cut rather than formed by wires, (*cloisons*). *Champleve* is most commonly applied to copper or bronze. The metals are gilded on exposed and visible surfaces.

Channel Setting

A series of stones set close together in a straight line with the sides of the mounting gripping the outer edges of the stones.

Chasing

The ornamentation of metal with grooves or lines with the use of hand-chisels and hammers. Obverse (front) chasing is called *intaglio*; chasing from the reverse side, (back) is called *repousse*.

Chatelaine

A decorative clasp or a hook from which many chains are hung to accommodate various household accessories such as thimbles, scissors, keys, nail files or to display jeweler's conceits such as watches, seals, and other decorative implements. From *chatelaines* hung various "necessaries," such as a miniature fan, glove buttoner, or a dog whistle. There were also grooming devices: an ear spoon for cleaning the ears, a sharp pick for cleaning under the nails, as well as a toothpick.

Very short *Chatelaine* chains were called *chatelettes*. They measured from 2" to 6" in length. An ornamental pin or brooch was attached, although the jewelry could be worn separately. The *chatelette* chain had a swivel at the end of the chain from which to hang a watch. The brooch was in the popular bowknot or pansy, wrought in *baroque* fashion or an unusual twisted design. Early *chatelaines* were worn at the waist, but in more recent times, the clasp-type was pinned to the dress or waist, then caught up at the end of the chain and pinned again by another ornament. Silver card cases, coin holders and vanity cases comprised the *chatelaines* of the 1925-1940 years, when the *chatelaine* ring was introduced. From the tiny, short chain, came a clasp which secured a handkerchief, and vanity cases equipped to hold scent pills, a little mirror, straight pins, coins, a lipstick, and powder puff. The introduction of rhinestone studded *plastic* evening purses during the *deco* period ended the long-reigning *chatelaine*. Over-sized bags and purses became recipients of "modern" women's "necessaries," including cosmetic cases, wallets, address books, and other toiletries too numerous to mention.

Chrome (also called Chromium)

The word comes from the Greek "chroma," which means color. Chrome is a metal that forms very hard steel-gray masses that gleam a silver color. Less than 3% mixture of chromium to steel produces an extremely hard alloy. It is used for plating base metals that easily corrode. It receives its name from the green, orange, yellow, red, etc., colors which emanate from the oxide and acid which contacts specific minerals and yields chrome-green, chrome-yellow and other color pigments. Chrome-plated jewelry is not common since it was an experimental metal proving to be more expensive that silver-color platings of nickle and pewter. One may occasionally come upon a chrome and plastic brooch or bracelet from the *Art Deco* or *Art Moderne* periods. These pieces are highly collectible not only because of scarcity, but because the combination and designs of the periods lent uniqueness to each and every piece.

Clasps

The "push-pin" type clasp is the oldest form of clasp on a bracelet or necklace. Brooch clasps had simple hooks under which a pin-shank was held in place. Eventually, safety-type devices were added. The "ball-catch" safety type of clasp consists of a ¾" circle with a small lever-type tab which completes the round, securely locking the brooch-pin. This "ball-catch" was innovated in 1911 and helps date pins and brooches.

A "spring-ring" clasp is in the shape of a tiny circle with a push-pin on a spring which opens and springs shut for closure of a necklace or bracelet. This is the most common type of clasp device and is found on most modern jewelry made after the turn-of-the-century.

Ornamental clasps were worn until the 1930's, when there came the simple screw-barrel type usually found on beads. This was followed by a chain with an open "fish-hook" type of appliance which could hook into the linkage of the chain, thus making it adjustable to the size of the wearer.

Prior to die-stamped jewelry and again in the 1930's, clasps were usually incorporated in the overall design of necklaces, pendants, chains, chokers and bracelets. All finer designed, more expensive pieces, had such clasps, including high fashion jewelry from 1925-1975. Some designers fashioned fabulous clasps to be worn either at the back or as an ornament to be shown at the side of the neck or directly in front to further enhance the wearer. KJL jewelry are good examples of this ornamental clasp.

New types of safety clasps, with and without safety chains, have entered the jewelry trade, but these are usually found on expensive gold and gemstone jewelry.

Claw-set (sometimes called "Tiffany-set")

Tiny claws or prongs which are curved to secure a stone in its setting.

Clips (dress clips, fur clips and sweater clips/guards)

These are devices to clasp, clamp, or hold something tightly or securely together.

A dress clip could be purely decorative or used to hold a collar in place or for a neck closure. In the 1930's, dress clips worn singly or in pairs, were favored as decorative pieces of jewelry. Many were manufactured in plastic, some were of pot metals, studded with colored paste stones or rhinestones. These were set into varied patterns influenced by the *Deco* and *Moderne* movements. Dress clips were made in hundreds of shapes and sizes. All had clips rather than the sharp dual-pronged device of the fur clip or the jagged-toothed "crocodile" type opening of the sweater clip/guard.

Fur clips were most ornate and had a spring-loaded device with sharp dual-pronged pins for insertion into a thickness of fur or fabric. Both dress and fur clips could be worn in turbans and in fur hats.

Sweater clips (or sweater guards), consisted of two decorative and functional clips linked together by a short chain. These clips (guards), could be highly decorative when worn with evening sweaters that were beaded, sequined or embroidered. The clips were clasped to an open sweater which was draped over the shoulders, thereby keeping the sweater from slipping or being lost. Clips were simple or ornate.

Cloisonné (also see Enameling)

A type of enameling in which thin wire made of silver, gold, bronze or copper is gilded, then bent to form cells (*cloisons*). Each cell or *cloison* is then filled with enamel. Each color is in a separate compartment, each compartment separated by this thin wire.

Combs

Combs did not become purely ornamental until about 1880. Before that time, they were not only decorative but functional. In the mid-twenties, the "Gibson Girl" hairdo was popular and the comb again became functional.

Early combs were generally made of real tortoise-shell, bone, sterling, gold and ivory. After 1900, imitation materials were more popularly used, especially in America. These *plastics* were much less expensive to produce. However, in the late sixties, concern for endangered species such as the tortoise, elephant, and tusk-bearing sea animals precluded the use of those materials in all types of adornments, including combs and jewelry. Therefore, it was not simply a matter of monetary concern, but the concern for animal species which influenced the manufacture of modern-day combs, using the many new compositions and plastics readily available.

Back combs usually had three or more teeth and often the crest of the comb was hinged for easy insertion and more comfortable wearing. Fancy combs were set with brilliants, Bohemian garnets and other ornamental gemstones. Imitation tortoise-shell and ivory combs came under many trademarks such as: NuHorn, Tuf-E-Nuf, and Stag, the latter manufactured by Noyes Comb Co., Binghamton, New York. Imitation tortoise-shell combs were manufactured by Schrader & Ehlers (New York), makers of the "Olive Dore Combs." Early producers of the real tortoise-shell combs were Sadler Bros., So. Attleboro, MA, and Wagner Comb Co., of New York. However, most of the more artful combs were imported from Europe.

As with most fashions, the vogue for changing hair-styles dictated the return of decorative hair articles, including some combs flashing with rhinestones or dripping with ribbons and silk flowers. Others have plastic geegaws attached to accent specific types of hair arrangements. Since the latter half of the twentieth century and especially with the production of stage and television spectaculars, hairdressers have utilized combs to stylize tresses in upswept, curly or lank updo, poodle cut, pony tail and all the dozens of other transformations of "hair raising" excitement a *coiffeur* could conjure.

Conceits

A term used to represent curiously contrived and fanciful jewelry, a jeweler's artifice or jeweled accessories which are quaint, artificial, or have an affected conception that flatters one's vanity. To be "plumed with conceit" signifies an awareness or an eccentricity of dress.

The *Delineator* (March 1900) reported a "new high-fashion" at the beginning of the century, stating that "dainty neck conceits" were becoming an important item in women's wardrobes. "...there is no bit of finery so truly feminine," the article stated, "or possessing so many charming possibilities as the tie or collar of ribbon, velvet, chiffon or lace..." Each of these "neck conceits" was fastered with an unusual and attractive brooch, which is as stylish today as at the beginning of this century.

Another neck conciet was the close-fitting "stock," a wide velvet ribbon folded around a stiffened foundation. Fastened on the side of the velvet ribbon was a jeweled ornament. The actual fastening of the ribbon was to the back, but the jewel pinned at the front gave the impression that the jewel was the clasp. This "stock" is now referred to as a "choker" or "dog collar."

The neckware of the turn of the century could change a blouse or shirtwaist into varied costumes to be worn with close-fitting skirts of the period. The waistline of the skirt was accentuated with a small jeweled clasp that often matched the brooch worn at neck or at the shoulder. In the 1950-1960 period, these small "conceits" were called "scatter" pins.

Millinery for all seasons was given brilliancy by some of the more elaborate creations and conceits of jewels such as dull gold enameling in colored alloys, crystal cabochons, wide buckles of gold, cut steel and rhinestones. Added to all this were the popular hat ornaments and small and oftentimes odd-looking beaded or plastic hatpins. Cloche hats and turbans were made vogue-ish by the addition of a brilliant ornament or clip made of plastic.

Depose

A French word similar to U.S. "copyright" or "patent." The word is sometimes stamped on an article implying the article is meant for export or is imported from France.

Die Stamping

To cut a design into metal for mass production and reproduction. This superseded handwrought and custom-made molds and hand-made jewelry. Today, prohibitive labor costs of mold-making and casting have caused this process to become a lost art in mass-produced jewelry in the competitive market. Almost all costume jewelry is now die-stamped.

Dragon's Breath

Simulated Mexican fire opals, made of glass, popular from 1910 through the 1930's.

Dress Clips (see Clips)

Earrings

Earrings are rather easily dated. The earliest were lightweight, hollow-gold and were made with wire hooks which went through pierced ear lobes. Wire *posts* were made after 1900. From 1900-1930 came screw-backs and after 1930, the ear clip was introduced. Fancy "pierceless" eardrops gained popularity after 1930. Prior to 1930, most women wore pierced earrings, primarily studs and/or short drops. However, during the *Art Deco* period, the more daring wore elongated designs simply dripping with marcasites and imitation stones. Lightweight plastics for all kinds of earrings became popular in 1930 to the present time. In the 1970's, earpiercing became the rage, resulting in a renewed interest in dangling, opulent, fashionable earrings.

Electroplating (or Electro-Plating)

This plating is achieved by immersing jewelry into an electro-magnetic acid bath which deposits a thin layer of gold, silver or other metal on to a lesser metal, such as nickle or pewter. The lesser metals used by jewelers are referred to as "pot-metal," "base metal," "white metal," or "jeweler's metal."

Enamel (also see Basse-Taille, Champleve, Cloisonne, Limoges, Niello, Plique-A-Jour and Guilloche)

Enameling is a firing of melted glass. The powdered glass mixture is composed of feldspar, quartz, soda, borax, calcium phosphates and kaolin. Metallic oxides produce the various desired colors. There is little transparent, see-through, colorless enameling; rather a better and more definitive term is "translucent." However, the word "transparent" has been an accepted term for *plique-a-jour* enameling which permits light to pass through as in stained glass.

There are several important types of enameling:

Basse-Taille - Metal plate cut to various depths into which translucent enamel is poured, thus achieving a 3-dimensional effect. The depth of relief produces shadings from light to dark. The deeper the metal is cut, the darker the color; where shallow routing occurs, the shading is almost transparent. This routing is worked *intaglio*, the opposite of *repousse.*

Champleve - An enameling technique in which areas of metal are hand cut, etched or routed and filled with enamel. Unlike *cloisonne*, the cells are cut rather than formed by wires. *Champleve* is most commonly applied to copper or bronze. The metals are gilded on exposed and visible surfaces.

Guilloche technique differs in that the designs are machine-turned and etched, and then enameled. This is a much faster process and many boxed sets of hatpins, matching stud buttons, buckles; brooches and medallions are representative of this technique; *Guilloche* patterns consist of interlacing curved lines.

Cloisonne - Enameling in which thin wire of silver, gold, bronze or copper is bent to form cells, (*cloisons*), and then filled with enamel. Each color is in a separate compartment, each compartment separated by thin wire that has often been gilded.

Limoges enamel - A colorful application of enamel which depicts a portrait or scene similar to that rendered on canvas.

Niello enameling - The lines or incisions of a design are contrasted with the color of the metal, i.e., gold, silver, etc., by applying in several layers a mixture of sulphur, lead, silver and copper. This addition appears black when filled into the engraved metallic work. *Niello* is a blackish enameling process, providing contrasts in highlights and darkness of the design.

Plique-a-Jour - A translucent *cloisonne* in which there is no metal backing for the enamel work. During firing, a metal supportive base is used until firing ceases. Then, when the piece has cooled and the enamel has hardened, the finished product no longer requires the base, so this support is removed. It is a most cautious procedure, requiring highly skilled craftsmanship and technique.

Engraving

Cutting lines into metal which are either decorative or symbolic. Method used in monogramming a crest, *cartouche*, or escutcheon.

Escutcheon

Small metal plate used atop an ornament or ring, for monogram or signet.

Facet

Small flat surface cut into a gemstone, glass, shell or plastic. Its purpose is to refract light or enhance the design.

Faux (pronounced "foe")

Literally, the word means "false light." Used in the context of jewelry, it specifically means that the gems or gemstones reflect a "false light," in that the brilliance is achieved by highly faceted glass with a foiled backing, or by grooving, carving, or cutting plastics. Fashion jewelry of the finest quality can be described as being set with *faux* turquoise, rubies, emeralds, or sapphires. Usually the glass or plastic stones are of the finest craftsmanship and could pass for the genuine article.

Festoon

A garland of chain or chains decorated with ornamental drops or pendants which lay on a curve against a woman's upper bosom or draped across a man's chest. A *chatelaine* chain could well be worn in festoon fashion, meaning it would be draped from shoulder to shoulder, forming a curve at the center fall.

Filigree

To apply thread-like wire and decorate into a lace, lattice or cobweb work.

Fin de Siecle (French, meaning "end-of-the-century")

This is a popular expression in art, fashion, society and in describing high fashion jewelry, denoting "decadence" or "restlessness." It can also mean "daring" or *avant garde*, or to use a more flattering definition: *"ahead of its time."*

shown as the emblem of charity, hope, joy and abundance. They also have the reputation of curing epilepsy and being an all-around pain killer. St. John writes of the emerald in his Apocalypse.

The diamond has always been regarded as the most precious stone. It was believed that if a guilty person wore a diamond, it turned red; but in the presence of innocence it would retain its original purity and brilliance. The diamond was reputed to be a preserver against epidemics and poisons; that it calmed anger and fomented conjugal love. The ancients called it "the stone of reconciliation." It symbolizes constancy, strength, and innocence.

In ancient times, the opal was considered a splendid stone, but due to the belief that it attracted misfortune, it had the effect of lowering the desirability of the stone except by those who were born in October. This, of course, was a mere superstition seemingly founded on a Russian legend that had come into France. It was reported that the Empress Eugenie had a horror of the opal and at the sight of one in the *Tuilleries*, she was actually terrorized.

The language of gems, their significance and the superstitions connected with gems and gemstones have been documented in great depth in many books on stones and lapidary work. In fact, whole volumes have been written about the curiosity of gems, gems as talismans, the lore of gems, and so forth. It is another fascinating aspect of jewelry which deserves avid pursuit.

It is always fashionable among lovers and friends to note the significance attached to various gems and gemstones, and to give these as birthday, engagement and wedding remembrances.

Birthstones and Their Significance

Month	Stone (Modern v. Ancient)/Significance
January	Garnet (unchanged)/Insures constancy, true friendship, fidelity.
February	Amethyst (formerly included pearl)/Freedom from passion and from care.
March	Aquamarine (formerly Bloodstone)/Courage, wisdom, firmness in affection.
April	Diamond (unchanged)/Emblem of innocence and purity.
May	Emerald (unchanged)/Discovers false friends and insures true love.
June	Pearl (formerly Agate or Cat's Eye)/Insures long life, health and prosperity.
July	Ruby (formerly included Coral)/Discovers poison, corrects evils resulting from mistaken friendship.
August	Peridot (formerly Sardonyx or Moonstone)/Without it, no conjugal felicity, so must live unloved and alone.

Findings

Metal parts used by jewelers for finishing an ornament or attaching an ornament to a pin or link.

Foil

Silver, gold, or other thin leaf of metal used to back imitation gemstones or faceted glass to improve their color and provide greater brilliance.

Frame (see Mountings)

"French Ivory" (also see Celluloid, Bakelite, and Plastic)

An imitation of ivory tusk in grained Celluloid or plastic. "French Ivory" is a registered trademark. Other ivory imitations, not quite as good, were Ivorette, Ivorine, Ivory Pyralin, and DuBarry Pyralin. In the 1870's, there was a shortage of ivory for billiard balls and a $10,000 prize was offered to anyone who could produce a substitute. John Wesley Hyatt mixed nitric acid and cellulose (guncotton), to make *Celluloid*. It was the first plastic to look like ivory. "French Ivory" products were produced by J.B. Ash Co. (Rockford, Illinois). Since *Celluloid* was highly flammable, it was eventually replaced with *Bakelite* and other fire-retardent plastics. *Celluloid* is a copyrighted name and patented product, but has become an accepted generic term for most thermoplastic "meltable" plastics or resins.

Fur Clip (see Clips)

Gems and Gemstones

Genuine gems and gemstones are created by natural mysterious forces. Plastics have been synthesized to produce inexpensive replicas of the natural elements.

Traditionally, the gems designated as "precious" are diamond, ruby, sapphire, and emerald. All other stones are considered ornamental or ornamental gems. The term "semi-precious" is considered obsolete. The modern view is that all gems are "precious" according to individual taste or preference. However, the values of the traditionally classified precious gems are usually far greater than other natural stones. Therefore, "gemstones" is the word used when referring to gems other than the diamond, the ruby, the sapphire and the emerald.

The faceted portion of a gem or gemstone - the top of the stone - is called the "table." The bottom of the stone is called the "pavillion." The point or the center is known as the "culet."

For many centuries past, jewels were considered medicinal. It was believed that some stones possessed unquestioned healing power. Hebrew tradition states that the Tablets of Moses were of sapphire, and the Hebrew word "sappir" means "the most beautiful." It also symbolizes loyalty, justice, beauty and nobility. Hence the "royal blue" or "purple of nobility." Emeralds from India, Persia and Columbia (South America) are most valuable. Emeralds are

September   Sapphire (formerly included Chrysolite)
/Frees from evil passions and
sadness of the mind.

October   Opal (unchanged)/Denotes hope and
sharpens the sight and faith of the possessor.

November   Topaz (unchanged)/Fidelity and friendship.
Prevents bad dreams.

December   Turquoise (unchanged, but additions of
Lapis Lazuli and/or Blue Zircon)/Sucess
and prosperity in love.

The language of gems and gemstones has changed in modern times. From the earliest of times, jewelry was worn primarily by men, and the gems and gemstones formerly related to birth-month were more popular with men than with women who began to wear "jewelry for the masses" after the turn of the century.

Anniversaries and Jewels

Twelfth ....Agate
Thirteenth ....Moonstone
Seventeenth..................................Amethyst
Eighteenth ....Garnet
Thirtieth..Pearl
Thirty-fifth ....Coral
Fortieth ....Ruby
Forty-fifth ....Sapphire
Fifty-fifth ....Emerald
Sixtieth..Diamond

Jewelry Designs were Inspired by Flowers

January.....................Carnation or Snowdrop
February ....Violet or Primrose
March..................................Jonquil or Violet
April ....Daisy or Sweet Pea
May ....Hawthorn or Lily of the Valley
June...........................Rose or Honeysuckle
July............................Larkspur or Water Lily
August............................Gladiolus or Poppy
September ....Morning Glory or Aster
October......................Calendula or Cosmos
November ....Chrysanthemum
December ....Narcissus, Holly or Poinsettia

Plastic "stones" and floral designs are found in collectible 20th Century Fashionable Plastic Jewelry

German Silver

Metal which has no actual silver content but is an alloy of copper, zinc and nickel with the highest content being nickel which gives it a silvery-white color. It is a common base for plating. Also called "nickle silver," "french gray," or "gun metal."

Gilt (or Gilded)

A method used after the invention of electro-gilding. Gilding (gilt) is a process of plating a die-stamped piece of base metal to give it a real or pseudo gold or silver color. Most often, and more abundant, are gold color ornaments which have been gilded, rather than silver-color gilt. Most fashion or costume jewelry is rhodium plate rather than silver gilt. Gilding is considered inferior to rolled plate or electroplating.

Gold

Precious metal ore containing alloys which vary depending on desired color and hardness.

Gold colors range from green to dull yellow, to bright pink and even red. White color (the color of platinum or silver) is achieved by alloying nickel and a small percentage of platinum to gold. Thus, white gold is an alloy of gold with silver, palladium, platinum or nickle.

Platinum is more a 20th century metal and is represented in jewelry after the turn of the century, particularly used during the *Art Deco* period.

Gold is twice as heavy as silver, which is perhaps the reason why a more solid silver was used while gold was plated, filled or rolled with inferior alloys. Platinum is even heavier than gold which explains why it was not used for early *baroque* pieces.

The term carat or karat is for the fineness of gold. Example: 18K or 750-18/24 or 750/1000th, representing 85% pure gold content.

Gold Electroplate (see Electroplating)

Gold-Filled

Joining a layer or layers of gold alloy to a base metal alloy, then rolling or drawing out as required for thickness or for thin sheeting of material.

Granular Work

Gold or silver metal applied in decorative designs which resemble tiny grains or pin-heads, roundly shaped.

Gypsy Setting (also known as Bezel)

A type of setting where the top of the stone is exposed just above the metal casing.

Guilloche (see Enamel)

Hair Ornaments (also see Combs and Barrette)

Hair ornaments have existed even in early tribal cultures. Early hair ornaments were functional as well as decorative, providing a pick used for cleaning and separating tangles in the hair. Hair ornaments preceded the invention of primitive combs. Once combs came into being, hair ornamentation became symbolic and decorative.

From 1850 through the 1925 era, hair ornaments were made in high baroque style in both gold and sterling silver. Most of the metal was cut, pierced or engraved with some fine *repousse* work. The entire ornament, including the teeth, were of inlaid ivory, bone and tortoise. From 1910-1930,

228

hair ornaments were made of either Celluloid or other plastics embedded with brilliants.

Ordinarily, hair ornaments have simply a stem or a pair of teeth, whereas combs have as many as four to nine teeth, depending on the size and style of the comb. Atop the stem or pair of teeth, is the ornamental decoration used to enhance the hairstyle and fashionable dress. Although delegated to the attic after the 1950's, hair ornaments are once more in style, lending a touch of glamour and femininity to the wardrobe. Many are made of plastic.

Hair Pins (or Hairpins)

The *Tortoise Brand* trademark was that of Rice & Hochster Makers (New York), a firm manufacturing three shapes of hair pins: straight, loop and crimped. They sold for $.25 per dozen boxes in the 1920's-1930's and were available in three colors: shell, amber, and black. Hair pins come in various lengths from 1"-3", and in several gauges of wire.

Hair pins were made of rolled gold decorated with birds, butterflies and stars and these were worn in great profusion throughout the headdress. In 1921, Swartchild & Co. (Chicago) advertised in their catalogue "The Neverslip Hairpin" for holding an eyeglass-chain securely to the hair. The chain extended from the curve of the hair pin to the small loop at the side of the spectacles or eye glasses. Celluloid hair pins were made for a very short period, (1910-1930).

Hallmark

An official mark first adopted in England. The mark is incised, punched or stamped on gold or silver to show quality and to signify purity of metal according to "sterling" or "karat" standard. Other countries' hallmarks indicate origin, patent, manufacture, etc. Most of the countries in Europe "punched" their gold and silver wares with "hallmarks." As early as 1363, England had already passed laws stating that every master goldsmith shall have a "quote by himself," and the same mark "shall be known by them which shall be assigned by the King to survey their work allay." That meant all goldsmiths' work had to be assayed before it could be marked by the king's authority. Such individual marks would certify the ore content of both gold and silver.

By 1857, the word "Sterling" became universally used except in the United States. Until 1894, no State protection was given in the United States to purchases of either gold or silver, and the buyer could only trust the reputation of the maker and dealer.

State laws regulating the stamping of the words "Sterling," "Coin," "Coin Silver" on wares of silver or metals purporting to be silver, were first passed in 1894. Massachusetts was the leader in this regard, but many other States followed suit within the next decade. These laws were similar within each State and they specified that any wares

which were marked "Sterling," or "Sterling Silver," must contain 925 parts of fine silver in every 1,000 parts. "Coin" and "Coin Silver," were to contain 900 parts of fine silver in every 1,000 parts. Persons were subject to misdemeanor charges if they attempted to sell merchandise marked "Sterling," or "Coin Silver" that did not contain the lawful quantities of pure silver.

Regarding the hallmarking of gold: it had become law that no article was to be offered for sale that did not plainly stamp the exact number of twenty-fourth parts of pure gold or portion of gold the article actually contained. Any person found guilty of violation of the provisions of this act could be fined up to $1,000, or imprisoned in a "common jail" (not to exceed one year or both), "at the discretion of the court."

Hallmarking became so strict that even portions of a particular piece of jewelry had to be marked. For instance, the front of a pin could be marked "Sterling"; but if only the front was sterling, the back would be stamped thus: "Sterling front."

Trademarks should not be confused with *Hallmarks*. A trademark is the name of a manufacturing company or of the artisan. A hallmark is a guarantee of the quality of the ore contained in the merchandise.

Mass production brought new codes, and many European countries then allowed their retailers of jewelry to have their own mark. Therefore, many manufacturers, craftsmen, designers and/or artists, remain unknown. Retailers oftentimes left the jewelry unmarked, except for hallmarking, and placed their own identity (name of retail outlet or advertising slogan) on fancy boxes made especially for the trade. Liberty & Co. (England) is a prime example. Their artists and jewelers were compelled to remain anonymous, and all the "modern works" and "Orientalia" were marked or labeled with the Liberty Co. trademark. Tiffany & Co., (New York) is another example where fine jewelers remained anonymous, except for a few proteges who developed a following of their own and built on their own reputations. In many instances, jewelers who designed and manufactured mass-produced jewelry for department store trade became actual "jobbers" and the backbone of a multi-million dollar industry. This was particularly true of the 1930's plastics trade.

In a 1980 survey taken from the "Yellow Pages" nationwide, there were no less than 5,000 jewelry wholesalers, and more than 56,000 jewelry retailers. Yet in the high fashion jewelry manufacturer/designer category, there are fewer than 100 recognized names in the entire industry. This book is one small step toward recognizing the plastics jewelry industry, and provides some archival record of its achievements and accomplishments. The pictorial record herein serves as a chronical for historical reference to the plastics jewelry trade of the 20th century, (1906-1992).

Twentieth Century Fashionable Plastic Jewelry

Marks Mistaken for Name of Manufacturer/Designer/Jeweler

R.P. ....rolled gold or silver plate
E.P. ....gold or silver electoplate
G.F. ....gold filled (usually preceded by numeral, i.e. 14K G.F. or 10K G.F.)
N.S. ....nickle silver
G.S. ....German silver
B.M. ....Britannia metal
W. M. ....White metal
G.E.P. ....Gold electro-plate

Hat Pin (also see Hatpin)

A man's decorative pin worn on a hat or cap and particularly in recent times as an insignia on hats worn by both men and women in the armed forces. Hat pins have also become collector's items, especially those of political campaigns or Olympic commemoratives. The hat pin is unlike a woman's hatpin (one word), a pinning device absolutely necessary to securely anchor ones hat to the hair or head. A hat pin has been worn in men's hats from the earliest of times to designate his so-called "station in life," his religious order, his peerage, family crest and so forth. **Hats** and **Hat Pins** are given much archival information in the titles mentioned under **Hatpin** (below).

Hatpin

The author has written the first world-wide definitive work on the subject of hatpins, titles: *The Collector's Encyclopedia of Hatpins and Hatpin Holders*, published by Collector Books (1976), (second limited edition, 1990, Elbee Publications). A supplemental work was published by Collector Books (1983), title: *Hatpins and Hatpin Holders: An Illustrated Value Guide*. Both are available to readers seeking a fascinating story about this functional, decorative, historical and political piece of jewelry - the hatpin.

The *woman's* device is spelled as hatpin (one word), so as to differentiate from a man's hat pin, which was worn for decorative purposes and as a means of identity. *The Encyclopedia Brittanica* has recently accepted this definition.

It has long been settled among researchers and historians reporting on jewelry and jeweled accessories, including international writers of high repute, that when referring to a woman's pinning device, the item is correctly spelled hatpin (one word).

All modern encyclopedic reference works show both *hat pin* and *hatpin*, and clearly point out the difference between the two separate "collectibles."

Since language is the great communicator for educational purposes, among other reasons, an agreed upon term makes understanding and communication simpler. As the author of the first and only worldwide definitive encyclopedic work on the subject of hatpins and hatpin holders, it was my responsibility to devise the proper nomenclature and terms relative to the subject.

When referring to a woman's pinning device, it's not only archaic to use the out-moded term hat pin, but confuses readers of advertisements—particularly if the ad does not have a photo or graphic illustration. There's no doubt whatsoever as to the meaning or description hatpin, – one word – to describe the strictly feminine use of the functional, decorative, and historical piece of jewelry known as a hatpin, used to anchor a hat upon the hair and head of women.

Historically speaking, men did not wear hat "pins." Rather they wore hat badges or *ensigne*, which was a type of ornament worn on the hat or cap of men of prominence. Thus, when one man approached another, he could tell by this badge of "station" who was subservient and thereby tip the hat first, or await the salute of the other, This mode and manner still exists in many countries and particularly in the military.

Originally, a badge was worn by knights to mark or distinquish them and to provide heraldic cognizance. Men could be recognized by what was worn on the head as to his "station" in life, i.e., butcher, baker, sheperd, painter, Cardinal, Pope, Bishop, and King, etc. Recently, the Green Berets adopted a military head covering accented by a special badge. These badges were functional for identification, and of course were quite decorative. More recently, both men and women collect hat pins from the Olympics, souvenirs of travel (especially the wide variety of colorful pins with feather and brush accents offered in Austria and Switzerland for Alpine sport hats). Newly found clubs for collectors of souvenir hat pins make it even more necessary to separate the actual *period hatpin* from the pins that were never used as "anchors" or pinning devices.

Hardly a week goes by that a phone call does not reach my number seeking certain "olympic" souvenir pins, political badges—a completely different genre than the period hatpin. Another reason for separating hat pins from hatpins. There *is* a distinct difference.

After the invention of the pin-making machine (1832), the pin became a common commodity and the *Spectator* (London), called the pin a "trifle"; yet prior to the invention which so many take for granted—pin making—people were taxed to pay for the Queen's pins, and the penalty for stealing hand-made pins was hanging! Pins were so valuable they were bequeathed in wills and could only be purchased on New Year's Day. So came the term "pin money." Yet after pins became plentiful, it was indeed common to hear such phrases as " I don't care a pin for her." Shakespeare's Prince Hamlet said he didn't set his life at a "pin's fee." But then a Prince could afford what a pauper could not.

When women took to wearing hats instead of bonnets, the term hat *pin* had a derogatory meaning; that is, women could wear "pins" but not badges. There were a few exceptions when a Queen, for instance, could wear her "badge of office," and to this day, Queen Elizabeth wears hers on her hat or ribbon. In following up my research, it seemed more and more evident that the term hat pin (as used from 1850-1910) was begrudgingly assigned to women's pinning devices needed to keep the bonnet or chapeau atop the hair and head. With the cutting of bonnet strings, women found women with no "station" in society were delegated to wearing a "pin" such as a hatpin and hairpins. They wore "hat ornaments"...not badges. Eventually hat pin was hyphenated (hat-pin) and finally evolved into the accepted spelling hatpin, (one word) which first appeared in Webster's New International Dictionary of the English Language (1918).

The Encyclopedia Britannica never mentioned the hatpin as a woman's pinning device, until 1975, when it adopted the word and definition which I, "as the hatpin authority," provided. Harold Newman's An Illustrated Dictionary of Jewelry (Thames and Hudson, Ltd., 1981) recognized the need for a specific term for describing the item used to secure a lady's hat, "used especially from Victorian times until c. 1940," and makes the distinction between a hatpin—a badge—a hat pin.

Lillian Baker is founder of the International Club for Collectors of Hatpins and Hatpin Holders (ICC of H & HH): 15237 Chanera Ave, Gardena, CA 90249; (213) 329-2619.

Illusion Setting

A setting in which the stone is made to appear larger by cutting metal in shape of the gem-table, thus giving the stone the illusion of being a heavier carat.

Imitation (also see Synthetics)

To make out of other materials a substance resembling the natural elements, i.e., paste or rhinestones for gems; hard rubber, dyed and then molded into coral-color flowers; plastic tortoise shell; "French Ivory," an imitation of ivory, bone, etc. Imitation is not the same as synthetic.

Intaglio

To cut a design deeply on the obverse or front side of a gem or other type material. Intaglio is the opposite of repousse work done in metals.

Japanned

The process known as Japanning is the darkening of wire by immersing the wire into black Japan, a by-product of coal-oil. Japanned metals were introduced particularly for mounting jewelry mountings, including the pinning devices.

Jewelers (1925-1935)

For biographical information about some of the noteworthy Art Deco and Art Moderne jewelers, artisans, designers, manufacturers and retailers of this genre of jewelry, refer to the author's book, Art Nouveau and Art Deco Jewelry, published by Collector Books (1981). Makers of some plastic jewelry are mentioned in this definitive study of 20th century plastics jewelry which are fashionable and collectible.

Lorgnette

A lorgnette is a pair of eyeglasses or an opera glass which is attached to a handle. A lorgnon is actually a single glass such as a monocle, but ordinarily speaking, lorgnon could be a substitute word for lorgnette.

Most lorgnons fold, and there were tiny ones especially made for chatelaines. Some were so small, they were called "glove lorgnons."

Frames for lorgnettes could be simple or ornate. Some were jewel encrusted or encased in tortoise-shell or mother-of-pearl. Some had crests engraved in solid gold. Shell and horn, however, were the best sellers and were made by European craftsmen.

There were wrist chains used especially for the glove lorgnon. Chains and lorgnons frequently go together and the same decorative treatment was usually applied to both. In 1880, lorgnettes made of zylonite (plastic) were offered for sale.

The Art Nouveau period produced exquisite lorgnettes which folded in half on a small hinge and could slide into the handle. The demise of the lorgnette came with the Great Depression of the 1930's when theatres and other places of luxury were less frequented. The sobering event dictated a less "affected" stance by high society in the face of mass poverty. The Art Deco period (1925-1930) produced an interesting display of plastic lorgnettes, with geometric designs studded with rhinestones and artificial glass gems. These plastic lorgnettes were lighter in weight than the metallic counter parts, and these were stylishly worn on silk cords.

Marquise Cut

Popular cut for diamonds in which the stone is brilliantly faceted. The diamond's oval shape is gradually narrowed until opposite ends are pointed.

Mounting

A specific adaptation of a stone or artifact within a cage, frame, or setting comprised of various metals, wood or plastic.

Necklaces (see Lavaliere, Pendants, Charms and Beads)

Nodder (also called Bobbler, Springer, Trembler or Tremblant)

A short spring which causes an ornamental head to bobble or bounce freely. Several short springs or wires could be utilized on a bouquet of metallic or plastic flowers set with brilliants. The ornament would sparkle as it moved and caught the light. Figural animals, birds, and flowers had spring devices which would cause the head, feet or blooms to bobble in motion.

Openwork (see Piercework)

Paste

Another term for fine quality glass imitation of a gem or gemstone.

Parure

Matching jewelry containing three or more pieces such as a necklace, choker, brooch, earrings, bracelet and ring. *Demi-parure* consists of only two or three matching pieces, but the modern term for matched jewelry consisting of two to three pieces is a *set*.

Pavé Set

Stones placed so closely together that almost no metal shows between them. This was a favored type of setting for rhinesotnes c.1950-1960.

Pendants

In 1910, the vogue for low collars invited all sorts of pretty neck ornaments such as pendants, medallions, *lavalieres* and brooches. The most favored was the pendant, which was more often enhanced by a black *moiré* ribbon than by a chain.

The delicate metal work was invariably the cool gray of platinum, the new 20th century precious ore coming into prolonged use. Many of the beautiful pendants included fine wires twisted into filigree work, and much of the metal had a very thin edge or depth. Enamel work was very popular, and the pendants of the 1925-1940 period reflect this vogue. Pendants remain in the fashion jewelry domain, with some pendants being detachable from a necklace or heavy linked chain.

Phoenix

A bird represented by the heron or eagle motif in Egyptian mythology. According to legend, it was consumed by fire but rose from the ashes. Thus, the Phoenix symbolizes resurrection and an emblem of immortality. It also appears in Chinese symbolic motifs. *Art Deco* designs stylized the heron and eagle and these variations appear on much of the *Deco* and *Moderne* plastic jewelry pieces.

Pierce Work

Die-cast frame which is cut and engraved with a great deal of open work in the metal or plastic.

Pin

Origin of the word is thought to be from the Latin "spina," a thorn found on the Spina Christi tree. Natural thorns are still used as pinning devices in some parts of the world. A pin is a device for attaching or securing many things. It can be strictly functional, decorative, or both.

Pins (or Brooches)

Because yesteryear clothing lacked today's modern laundry techniques, collars, frills, ribbons, etc., were detachable. Many of the collars and cuffs, etc., were pinned in place by exquisite "lace pins," most often of delicate filigree or open work.

A small pin, which has long since been forgotten, was the novelty "safety pin," that came in vogue around 1901. These were offered in 10K gold and were sometimes called "negligee collar pins," and they resembled a very narrow barrette or bar pin. They were also called "handy pins," sold in pairs in a myriad of designs executed in a choice of gold front, gold filled, sterling silver, or black enamel.

The bar pin is usually a one or two inch horizontal pin of gold or silver, with many innovations and variations of the jeweler's art. It was worn at the collar or neckline of a woman's garment, and sometimes used to join a detachable collar to the frock. A *plastic* bar pin was the *first Celluloid* piece of Jewelry, c.1909. It was hand made by George Berkander.

Sterling silver brooch pins were most often engraved or had open lacework or filigree work. The *baroque* scroll patterns were the most desirable in Victorian times, but this gave way to *Art Nouveau* designs, and finally the renditions of the *Deco* and *Moderne* jewelers.

Cape or jersey pins were two pins attached by a chain. Much in demand during the turn of the century, they drifted out of vogue during the 1920's only to be all the rage in the 1930's. Variations on this theme are seen in the "sweater pins" worn in the 1950's-1960's when twin sweater sets were in fashion. The matching long-sleeved sweater was fashionably worn over the shoulders, and a sweater-guard pinned each side, drawn by the short chain to keep the sweater from slipping.

There were many types of pinning devices, such as veil pins, cuff pins, stickpins, and "beauty pins," the latter worn in place of studs on women's "shirtwaists" (the name for blouses in America). In France, women's blouses were called "*chemisettes.*" Both "shirtwaists" and "*chemisettes*" imitated the Renaissance-sleeve: fullness at the cuff, which was accented by cuff buttons.

The main difference between pins and brooches is that pins are first and foremost utilitarian and then decorative, whereas brooches are primarily decorative. Today, we refer to all kinds of decorative brooches as either pins or brooches. If the object is exceptionally large in dimension or laden with gemstones, or of grandoise design, the piece is called a brooch.

Plastics (also see Bakelite and Celluloid)

Term applied to a group of synthetic chemical products with the distinct quality enabling them to be molded, carved, laminated or pressed into many shapes, sizes and design. Tortoise, horn, mother-of-pearl, wood, marble, jet, and amber were all made in *plastics*, as are gems and gemstones.

Plastic jewelry is not an imitation of earlier jewelry, but is an art form highly collectible today. A layman's simple nomenclature for plastics, in glossary form, follows:

Casein - A milk product which can be chemically changed into a glue-type substance, or "plastic." It is easily and quickly dyed, and was available in translucent, transparent, and opaque forms. Mottled effects were produced by compounding two or more colors or by a system of spray-dying which can then be used to simulate horn and other mottled effects. Casein was often substituted for natural horn and mother-or-pearl used in the button industry. Casein is not flammable.

Casting - Liquid substance of chemically formed plastic which is poured into a mold so as to form a particular shape. The ultimate product that comes out of the mold is sometimes used as is, but more often is worked in various ways by hand-cutting, sawing, turning, drilling, grinding, polishing, sanding, routing, or other procedures necessary to produce the final article.

Flexibility - A term used to describe a type of plastic that is capable of bending without breaking, such as some Celluloid products.

Injection molding - Heat-softened plastic material is forced under pressure into a mold which enables the plastic to take on the *shape* of the article.

Laminated Articles - Plastic into which sheets of paper, wood, fabric, etc., are impregnated with a resinous composition. Under heat and pressure, the plastic and other materials used become a single unit.

Resinoids - Plastics more commonly termed as thermoplastics, which are "meltable" when heat is applied.

Thermoplastic - Plastic or resinoids which have the property of softening under heat. All molding materials are firstly thermoplastic and will remain permanently soft when heat is applied. Thermoplastic materials must be cooled before the articles can be removed from the mold. Thermoplastic articles of jewelry and other dress accessories will retain their shapes under normal temperatures, but will become mishapen if exposed to high heat or direct sunlight. Thermoplastic products are more easily cracked, damaged, or broken than are articles of thermoset plastics.

Thermoset - Chemically transforming a thermoplastic into a hardened product which becomes a permanently formed article which remains unaffected by pressure or heat.

Prototype

The original first model to be copied in either the method of casting or molding. A prototype is actually modeled after an original conception of a design or pattern done on the drawing board. Jewelry designers provide renditions on paper, from which a prototype is made for casting or molding a piece from which a die can be produced for mass production. (See Casting and Die Stamping.)

Repoussé

Decorating metal by pushing out from behind or the reverse side in order to create a raised design in relief. The opposite of intaglio.

Rim

The outside edge of a set stone.

Rings

The "father of jewelry" was Prometheus. According to Pliny, Hercules cut Prometheus loose from the chains which fastened him to Mount Caucasus. Prometheus supposedly made a ring out of one of the links, bezel-set a portion of the rock against which he had been chained, and created what's considered the first ring and the first "gem."

There's a great deal of sweet romance and legend bound up in the wedding ring. When the first glow of Christianity lighted the world, Pliny the Elder told of a custom his people had borrowed from the ancients of the Nile, that of giving a ring of iron to pledge a betrothal. Such customs from the dim past and the ceremonies which have evolved today, have definitely changed from those early times.

In 1893, Prince Albert presented Queen Victoria with a wedding ring in the form of a serpent. Because of the presentation, and the 1922 opening of King Tut's Tomb, the serpent design is found in many forms of jewelry, through the Art Deco period and into the late 1930's.

In 1900, rings with colored stones were not in vogue for engagement rings. The fashionable engagement ring was a solitaire diamond or smaller stone set in a simple mounting.

"Anti-rheumatic" rings came in just before the turn of the century. They were of gold shell on the outside, with gray metal on the inside.

In 1901, the *Delineator* reported that beautiful rings "proper for a man" would be a solitaire diamond, cat's eye, or other precious stone mounted in a gypsy or handsome carved gold setting.

Women did not consider rings their province until the early 18th Century, and then they were mostly "glove rings," worn on the forefinger. Prior to that, most men of nobility wore rings as seals. The period when rings were most commonly worn by both sexes begins from 1875 to the present day.

In the *Deco* period, several rings were displayed and considered vogue-ish. But during the depression and post WWII, only rings signifying betrothal or marriage were worn by women. By the early 1960's, and to the present time, rings of all sizes and designs are worn singly or in multiples.

"Token rings" were the most desirable gift for the betrothed from 1880 to around 1910. Such a ring, with clasped hands, was called "Mizpah." Translated, "Mizpah" means: *The Lord watch between me and thee when we are absent one from another.*" These rings were greatly exchanged during World War I, and revived again during World War II.

"Costume" rings of imitation stones, lesser metals and plastics were prized during the 1930's; again in the 1950's, and again in the 1970's to the present time.

Double-ring ceremonies were initiated during

WWII. In the 1940's, it was common practice to present the "girl of my dreams" with a class ring in lieu of a proper engagement ring. Many a war-bride lacked the traditional diamond engagement ring, but in subsequent years of prosperity, a diamond ring was given on a 10th or 20th anniversary—although tradition has it that the diamond is the jewel for the 60th anniversary. Perhaps the separations of war brought a quickening of needs to make up for lost time, or a realization and urgency to "live today." In any event, self-indulgence and the joy of giving to a loved one made the jewelry industry prosper, grow, and soar in popularity. Rings for any occasion prevailed above all else in purchases of jewelry. Grandmother Rings, Birthstone Rings, Valentine Day rings, Anniversary rings, Friendship Rings, Souvenir Rings, Betrothal Rings, Class rings, initial rings and just about any other event could be commemorated in rings fashioned with gems, gemstones or imitations and synthetics.

Rococo Style

An enriched and embellished ornamentation with much profusion of shellwork, scrolls, flowers, figures and an excess of broken, irregular curves framing a major theme of the piece. To work in *Rococo* style is to add a *Baroque* (or heavy type of ornamentaition) to *Rococo*.

Rococo ornamentation was revived in the 1930's, departing from the continuous flowing and gentle lines of *Art Nouveau*. *Rococo* design has always influenced, more or less, fashionable jewelry from one epoch into another. Modern jewelry is no exception.

Rolled Gold

A thin leaf of gold used in plating lesser metals. Method varies from rolling to electroplating a coat of gold over an inferior metal.

Roundels

Tiny round beads often used as separators.

Scarf Pins

Scarf pins were made for both ladies and gentlemen as seen in the 1890-1930 catalogues. By the 1920's they were already being called "cravat" and "tie pins" for men, and "scarf pins" for women.

No distinction was made between male or female styles. Many of the pins had a spiral device which kept them from slipping out; others had fancy innovations such as small shafts at the heads which would secure them against slippage or loss.

Scarf pins offered no end to diversity of design and were set with gems, gemstones, imitation stones, and synthetics.

Advertisements for scarf pins most often read: "set with brilliants" which usually referred to a glass "diamond" or doublet of a popular gem such as garnet, opal, ruby, moonstone, or turquoise.

Setting (see specific type)

A means of incorporating gems, gemstones (genuine, synthetic or imitation), into metal or other elements, with designs known as Bezel, Box, Channel, Claw, Gypsy, Crown, Illusion, Metal Cup (for rhinestones), *Pavé*, and Tiffany.

Shank

A circle forming a ring, or that portion of a ring which is finally joined to the center or focal point. Also, a pin-shank, the utilitarian part of a brooch, stickpin or hatpin, which is then attached to the ornamental object or head, (as in the hatpin).

Signet

A design in a ring or a fob, often utilized as a seal because of its *intaglio* carving or engraving. The design usually portrays an initial, crest, or is symbolic. *Intaglio* work may be either in stone, gem or metal.

Silver Gilt (also see Vermeil)

Process of applying a thin coat of gold or yellow lacquer over silver, to produce a rich golden color.

Square Cut Stone

Another design cut for gems and rhinestones.

Sterling

A British term referring to the highest standard of silver, fixed at 925 parts of pure silver to 75 parts copper. The word originated with immigrant Germans who came across the English Channel to England. They settled in a geographic area from which they took the name "Easterlings." Jewelers by trade, these Germans who had resettled in England, were called upon to refine silver for coinage. In 1343, the first two letters were dropped from the word, "Easterling," resulting in the nomenclature—"sterling." It denotes the highest purity of silver. All British sterling is hallmarked. (See Hallmarks.)

Sterling silver, besides being coinage and utilized for conventional, familiar pieces of jewelry, was also produced as: veil clasps, ornamentation for elastic garters, ornately executed sash slides and buckles (so favored in 1925-1935 Periods). Additional uses were trimmings for silk and grosgrain belts, hat marks, folding pocket combs, key rings, umbrella straps, bag or trunk checks, belt buckles, slides, ladies' hatband buckles, armlets (garters), hatpins, and frames for purses and bags. All of these so-called "conceits" were wrought in *Nouveau* and earlier design motifs. Sterling silver was, without doubt, the preferred metal for *Art Nouveau* design in Great Britain, Germany, Bohemia, Scandinavia, and the United States.

Swivel (or Tongue Clip)

A prong-snap connector which is mounted in a movable part, then joined by a hook-ring which is connected to the ends of watch chains into which the watch is snapped and hung. Also utilized on chatelaines.

Synthetic

The term differs from imitation. Synthetic stones are created by man's intelligent application of the chemicals which nature has produced through natural means. When referring to synthetic gems or gemstones, we refer to the recent developments of man-made diamonds from pure carbon, and the Chatham emerald which is a synthetic speeding-up process of obtaining emeralds. In the art of synthesizing, man attempts to *duplicate* nature, whereas in chemical imitations, man seeks to merely *imitate* it.

Doublets and triplets are stones consisting of two or more layers of material which are adhered to the top layer of a genuine gem. If one were to remove a doublet, triplet or quadruplet from its setting and look at it from its side, under a magnifying glass, the materials can be seen where they were glued together. Ordinarily, a fine paste or a glass substance is glued to the genuine stone to make a gem appear larger. This process is not considered either synthetic or imitation. In one word: it is outright *fraud*. Nonetheless, it was an accepted practice for many years, and may even continue to the present day.

A fine example of man's ingenuity for creating a synthetic product is the cultured pearl. This is produced by man creating an "unnatural" imitation within the oyster. Technically, a cultured pearl could be called synthetic, but since it is not "manufactured" by man, but is rather produced by the workings of nature, it is called *cultured*. With man harnessing the atom, and with more understanding of the workings and configurations of atoms, it is not too unrealistic or too far reaching to suppose that some day in the not too distant future, many if not all gems will be synthetically produced in competition with the natural gem.

"Synthetic" is a term for a man-made material produced as a substitute and is usually a substitute for a more expensive natural element such as elephant tusk ivory.

Synthetic is not synonymous with artificial. "Synthetics" are man-made, such as the production of metallic alloys, i.e., bronze, (alloy of copper and tin); steel (alloy of iron, carbon and other elements); or glass ("paste"). All of these man-made products are not "artificial." They represent man's ingenuity. *Artificial leather*, made from plastic, is a *synthetic man-made material* which imitates the natural. Variations of plastics were also synthesized to create exquisite artificial precious gems and gemstones. (Bronze was the first man-made *synthetic*.)

Template (or Templet)

To make a permanent record or copy of a pattern or design, usually on a thin plate or board which can then be traced or reproduced in a given media.

Tiara

The word is derived from a royal Persian headdress but is now accepted as any decorative jeweled or flowered headband or semi-circle worn by women for formal wear. The difference between a tiara and a diadem is that the latter is worn as a symbol of power or a crown of dignity. A *bandeaux* is a semi-circle, usually of bendable plastic, used as a decorative hair accessory to keep hair swept back from forehead. Most popular in 1940-1960.

Tortoise-Shell

A yellowish-brown grained substance which is the hardplate shell from the back of the tortoise. Now an endangered species, the material can no longer be used in the making of decorative objects, including jewelry. Imitation tortoise-shell was manufactured from plastic, and is still imitated in the newer compositions of soft and hard plastics. Sadler Bros. (South Attleboro, Mass.) made imitation Tortoisene, used primarily for combs, hair ornaments and fine jewelry. Natural tortoise-shell was also used for these purposes and tortoise *pique* work is highly sought after by collectors.

Trademarks (see Hallmarks)

Trembler (or Tremblant) (see Nodder)

Triangular Cut

A cut for gemstones, in a triangular shape.

Vermeil

Silver, bronze or copper that has been gilded. Also a red (vermillion color) varnish applied to a gilded surface to give high luster. Ordinarily, one thinks of *vermeil* as a gold wash over sterling silver. (See Gilt or Gilded.)

Vermicelli

The word in Italian means, "little worms." This aptly describes the thin gold wire which is twisted in a decorative design resembling squirming worms. *Vermicelli* should not be confused with granular work. (See Granular.)

Watches and Wrist Watches

There are many books on the subject and the reader is urged to research them. The reader should also venture into the many old catalogues which provide enlarged drawings and engravings of the innerworks of watch movements as well as the outer decorative cases, including hunting cases, "pie-crust" cases and simple bezeled cases. A summary appears in the Glossary section of the author's book, *100 Years of Collectible Jewelry: 1850-1950*, now in its 5th printing, (Collector Books, 1978). Revised and updated values appear in the later editions. Up until WWI, the pocket watch and the decorative lapel watch were fashionable. But with the wearing of military uniforms and with women doing factory work requiring untypical clothing from that worn in the past, both sexes adopted the wrist watch first initiated in the British army.

From 1920-1930 there were very stylish *Art Deco* flat, evening watches for men, worn with evening dress and without a chain. Some of the flat watches for men held a combination cigar cutter. *Art Deco* watches, in sterling or platinum, set with marcasites in silver, and diamonds in platinum, were prized by women during this same period. Plastics were utilized in the manufacture of watch cases and strap-bands, c.1935-1990.

Section VI
Bibliography - References - Recommended Reading

Anderson, Frank J., *Riches of the Earth*, Windward, a Division of W.H. Smith Publishers, Inc., New York. (1981)

Baker, Lillian, *Art Nouveau and Art Deco Jewelry: An Identification and Value Guide*, Collector Books, Paducah, Kentucky (1981, updated 1990)

Baker, Lillian, *The Collector's Encyclopedia of Hatpins and Hatpin Holders*, Collector Books, Paducah, Kentucky (1976)

Baker, Lillian, *The Collector's Encyclopedia of Hatpins and Hatpin Holders*, second printing, limited edition, Elbee Publications, 15237 Chanera Ave., Gardena, California 90249. (1988)

Baker, Lillian, *Fifty Years of Collectible Fashion Jewelry: 1925-1975*, Collector Books, Paducah, Kentucky (1986, updated 1990)

Baker, Lillian, *Hatpins and Hatpin Holders: An Illustrated Value Guide*, Collector Books, Paducah, Kentucky 1983, (updated 1992)

Baker, Lillian, *One Hundred Years of Collectible Jewelry (1850-1950)*, Collector Books, Paducah, Kentucky (1978, updated 1991)

Ball, Joanne Dubbs, *Jewelry of the Stars: Creations from Joseff of Hollywood*, Schiffer Publishing Co., 1469 Morstein Rd., West Chester, Pennsylvania 19380. (1991)

Bauer, Dr. Jaroslav, *Minerals, Rocks, and Precious Stones*, Octopus Books, Ltd., London. (1974)

Cherry, Raymond, *General Plastics*, McKnight and McKnight, Bloomington, Indiana (1941)

Davidov, Corinne and Ginny Redington Dawes, *The Bakelite Jewelry Book*, Abbeville Press, Inc., 488 Madison Ave., New York, New York 19922 (1988)

Di Noto, Andrea, *Art Plastic - Designed for Living*, Abbeville Press, Inc., New York, New York (1984)

Dormer, Peter and Ralph Turner, *The New Jewelry: Trends and Traditions*, Thames and Hudson, Ltd., London (1985)

Harris, Godfrey, *The Fascination of Ivory: Its Place in Our World*, The Americas Group, 9200 Sunset Blvd., Suite 404 Los Angeles, California 90069 (1991)

Hillier, Bevis, *Art Deco of the 20's and 30's*, Studio Vista/Dutton, New York (1968)

Hughes, Graham, *Modern Jewelry*, Crown Publishers, Inc., 419 Park Ave., South, New York, New York 10016 (1963)

Lalique, Marcet Marie-Claude, *Lalique Par Lalique*, copyright Societe Lalique, Paris (1977)

Lesieutre, Alain, *The Spirit and Splendor of Art Deco*, Paddington Press, Ltd., 30 E. 42nd St., New York, New York

Lockrey, A.J. *Plastics in the School and Home Workshop*, Governor Publishing Corp., New York, New York (1937)

Lynnlee, J.L., *All that Glitters*, Schiffer Publishing Ltd., 1469 Morstein Rd., West Chester, Pennsylvania 19380 (1986)

McNulty, Lyndi Stewart, *Plastic Collectibles: Price Guide*, Wallace Homestead Book Co., P.O. Box 5406, Greensboro, North Carolina 27403 (1987)

Menten, Theodore, *The Art Deco Style*, Dover Publications, Inc., New York, New York (1972)

Miller, Harrice Simmons, *Costume Jewelry: Official Identification and Price Guide*, The House of Collectibles, 201 E. 50th St., New York, New York 10022 (1990)

Mulvagh, Jane, *Costume Jewelry in Vogue*, Thames and Hudson, Inc., 500 - Fifth Ave., New York, New York 10110

Schiffer, Nancy, *The Best of Costume Jewelry*, Schiffer Publishing, Ltd., 1469 Morstein Rd., West Chester, Pennsylvania 19380 (1990)

Schiffer, Nancy and Kelley Lyngerda, *Plastic Jewelry*, Schiffer Publishing, Ltd., 1469 Morstein Rd., West Chester, Pennsylvania 19380 (1987)

Shields, Jody, *All That Glitters: The Glory of Costume Jewelry*, Rizzoli International Publications, Inc., 597 Fifth Ave., New York, New York 19917 (1987)

Articles - Magazines - Periodicals - Catalogues

Angeles, published monthly by California Magazines Partnership, Los Angeles, California, "Plastic Fantastic: Bakelite Teasures from the Thirties," July 1989.

Art Deco Catalog, October, 14 - November 30, 1970, Finch College Museum of Art, New York.

The Antique Trader Weekly, Dubuque, Iowa, Dec. 10, 1974. "Collecting Art Deco," Stanley Baker.

The Antique Trader Weekly, Dubuque, Iowa, (Article, Vol. X), "Collecting Costume Jewelry of the Twenties and Thirties," Marion Cohen.

The Antique Trader Weekly, Dubuque, Iowa, (Article, Vol. IV), "Early Plastic Jewelry," (November 26, 1974), Eleanor Gordon & Jean Nurenberg.

The Antique Trader Weekly, Dubuque, Iowa, Sept. 21, 1988. "Celluloid: Grandma's Plastic, Poor Man's Ivory," Francine Kirsch.

Antiques & Collecting, Sept. 1989. "Costume Jewelry: The Basics in Bangles and Beads," Elizabeth Baroody.

Collectible Plastics Newsletter, The Society for Decorative Plastics, published by Eclipse Enterprises, P.O. Box 1099, Forestville, CA 95436 USA, Vol. I, Numbers 1 thru 15.

Connoisseur Magazine, July 1985, The Hearst Corp, New York, "Bakelite Envy," by Andrea DiNoto.

Connoisseur Magazine, March, 1989, "Gems That Heal - for Peace of Mind."

Hobbies Magazine, September, 1985, "Jewelry of the Art Deco Period," by Mildred Jailer.

International Club for Collectors of Hatpins & Hatpin Holders, (Founded August 1977), Monthly Newsletter - *Points*; Semi-Annual *Pictorial Journal*. Information: Send SASE to ICCofH&HH,15237 Chanera Ave., Gardena, California 90249. Founder and Editor: Lillian Baker.

Los Angeles Times, Friday, Feb. 16, 1990, "Return of the Celluloid, Rhinestone and Old Paste," by Suzanne Stone.

Los Angeles Times Magazine, Oct. 8, 1989, "Objects D'Artisans," by Jane Applegate.

Los Angeles Times Magazine, Feb. 4, 1990, "Faking It, " by Barbara DeNatale.

Long Beach Press Telegram, Jan. 7, 1990, "Bakelite is Back," by Dave Wielenga.

Modern Plastics Magazine, Oct. 1936, "Cast Resins - and How They are Used," by D.K. Bancroft.

Modern Plastics Magazine, (Series 1936-1937) "Beach Jewelry," "Floral Carved Rings"; "Carved Stylized Floral Pins, Dress Clips and Belt Buckle"; "Horse Head Pins and Scarf Clasp"; "Horses and a Dagger"; "A Dog and a Giraffe"; "Fruits and Vegetables"; "Dangler Pin."

Modern Plastics Magazine, Dec. 1936, "Plastic Modes," by Eve Main.

Modern Plastics Magazine, May 1937, "From Hours to Minutes," by Eve Main.

Modern Plastics Magazine, June 1937, "Seashore Suavities," by Eve Main.

Modern Plastics Magazine, Sept. 1936, "Equestrian," by Eve Main.

Modern Plastics Magazine, Oct. 1937, Directory Listings (Industrial Designers and Fabricators).

The National Button Bulletin, Vol. 47, No. 1, Feb. 1988, "Plastic Buttons," Pg. 5 thru 17. (Address: Mrs. Arlene M. Westrom, 1212 - 10th Ave., S.E., Puyallup, Washington 98372).

Ornament Magazine (previously, *The Bead Journal*), Los Angeles, California 19924, "Amber and Its Substitutes," Vol. 2, No. 3, Pg. 15-20 (1976). Vol. 3, No.1, pg. 20 (1976) "Plastic Imitations"

Schroeder's Insider & Price Update, Monthly Newsletter published for the antique and collectible marketplace, Aug. 1983-Sept. 1985, Jean Cole, Editor. Schroeder Publishing Co., Inc., 5801 Kentucky Dam Road, Paducah, Kentucky 42001.

Additional Sources and References

Compact Collectors Club Newsletter, "Powder Puff," P.O. Box Letter S, Lynbrook, New York 11563.

Daily News, Palm Beach, Florida, February 10, 1991. "Faux Jewelry Designer Has Genuine Spirit," Maureen O'Sullivan, Fashion Editor.

Egg's, "Collector's Issue," New York, March 1991. "Ken and Nan's Excellent Adventure," Timothy Hawkins.

International Herald Tribune, July 18, 1989. "A Pearl Designer's String of Successes," Suzy Menkes.

The Mail, London, April 5, 1987. "Femail on Sunday: on a Jewel of an Idea," Kathy Phillips.

Northwest, Magazine, November 1986. "Kenneth Jay Lane: Faking It With Style," Patricia Lynden.

Press Telegram, Long Beach, California, July 1989. "Plastic Fantastic."

Press Telegram, (Lifestyle Section), January 7, 1990. "Bakelite is Back," Dave Wielenga.

Vanity Fair, November 1988. "The Fast Lane at Home," Gita Mehta.

Vintage Fashion & Costume Jewelry Newsletter & Club, P.O. Box 265, Glen Oaks, New York 11004.

Vogue, December 1990. "Talking Fashion," Julia Reed.

Section VII
Price Guide

Plate 1
Top to Bottom ....Pin (4) ....ea. 125.00-135.00
Center ....Beads 250.00-275.00
Center, Top ....Earrings (clip)...........125.00-135.00
Center, L-R ....Earrings (2 pr). ....ea. 125.00-135.00

Plate 2
Top, Row 1 ....Buckle 80.00-85.00
Row 2, L-R ....Necklace.................375.00-425.00
Row 2, L-R ....Necklace.................285.00-300.00
Row 2, L-R ....Necklace.................300.00-350.00
Center ....Brooch 150.00-225.00

Plate 3
Center ....Necklace.................495.00-525.00
Row 1, L-R ....Pin.......................210.00-235.00
Row 1, L-R ....Pin........................95.00-110.00
Row 2, L-R ....Brooch 65.00-75.00
Row 2, L-R ....Pin........................85.00-110.00

Plate 4
Left to Right...............Necklaces (6) ....ea. 25.00-35.00

Plate 5
Top, L-R....................Brooch 35.00-45.00
Top, L-R....................Ring Box 35.00-45.00
Top, L-R....................Ring 45.00-65.00
Top, L-R....................Earrings 35.00-45.00
Center ....Earrings 10.00-15.00
Bottom, Left ....Purse 135.00-175.00
Center, Right ....Jewelry Box 25.00-35.00
Bottom, Right ....Bracelets (3)...........ea. 35.00-65.00

Plate 6
Left, Top to Bottom .....Earrings (2pr) ....ea 95.00-125.00
Left, Top to Bottom .....Brooch 65.00-75.00
Center, Top to Bottom .Bracelet 95.00-125.00
Center, Top to Bottom .Bracelets (3) ....ea. 75.00-85.00
Center, Top to Bottom .Bracelets (3).......ea. 150.00-165.00
Center, Top to Bottom .Bracelets (3)...........ea. 75.00-85.00
Right, Top to Bottom....Bracelet 150.00-195.00
Right, Top to Bottom....Bracelet 125.00-135.00
Right, Top to Bottom....Bracelets (8)........ea. 125.00-135.00

Plate 7
Row 1, L-R ....Earrings 35.00-45.00
Row 1, L-R ....Clip 35.00-45.00
Row 1, L-R ....Clips (pr) 35.00-65.00
Row 1, L-R ....Buckle (not shown) 45.00-55.00
Row 2, L-R ....Clips (pr) 45.00-65.00
Row 2, L-R ....Clips (pr) 75.00-95.00
Row 3.....................Hat Ornament 25.00-30.00
Row 4, L-R ....Clips (pr) 30.00-45.00
Row 4, L-R ....Set 65.00-85.00
Row 4, L-R ....Clips (pr) 35.00-45.00
Row 5, L-R ....Clip 25.00-35.00
Row 5, L-R ....Clip 25.00-35.00
Row 5, L-R ....Buckle 45.00-65.00
Row 5, L-R ....Clips (pr) 35.00-45.00

Plate 8
Top ....Necklace.................195.00-225.00
Center ....Pin.........................75.00-85.00
Center, L-R ....Bracelet 95.00-125.00
Center, L-R ....Bracelets (2)...........ea. 50.00-65.00
Bottom.....................Pins (2) ....ea. 125.00-135.00
Bottom, Center...........Bracelet 45.00-55.00

Plate 9
Top ....Back Comb.................65.00-75.00
Bottom, Left ....Hair Ornaments (pr.) 35.00-45.00
Bottom, Right ....Comb 95.00-135.00

Plate 10
Row 1, Top to Bottom..Buckle (2 piece)...........65.00-95.00
Row 2.....................Set 75.00-95.00

Row 3.....................Bracelet 145.00-195.00
Row 4.....................Buckle (2pc.) 45.00-55.00
Row 5, L-R ....Brooch 35.00-45.00
Row 5, L-R ....Brooch 95.00-145.00
Row 5, L-R ....Clips (pr) 55.00-75.00
Row 6, L & R ....Pin (2) ....ea. 55.00-75.00

Plate 11
Top to Bottom ....Belt 125.00-135.00
Top to Bottom ....Buckle 75.00-85.00
Top to Bottom ....Buckle 125.00-135.00
Row 4, L & R ....Buckle ....ea. 95.00-110.00

Plate 12
Left to Right...............Hatpin Holder 85.00-125.00
Left to Right...............Hatpin Holder 65.00-95.00
Bottom.....................Tiara 75.00-95.00
Top, Left ....Hatpins (3) ....ea. 25.00-45.00
Top, Right..................Hatpins (2) ....ea. 45.00-65.00
Center Bottom.............Hatpins (3) ....ea. 35.00-75.00

Plate 13
Center ....Pendant/Necklace 250.00-325.00
Top, L-R....................Brooch 45.00-65.00
Top, L-R....................Brooch 65.00-85.00
Top, L-R....................Brooch 95.00-125.00
Center ....Brooch 95.00-125.00
Center ....Button 4.00-5.00
Bottom, Left ....Pendant 75.00-85.00
Bottom, Left ....Pendant 45.00-85.00
Bottom, Right ....Set 125.00-165.00

Plate 14
Top to Bottom ....Necklace...................95.00-125.00
Top to Bottom ....Necklace.................750.00-795.00
Top to Bottom ....Necklace.................125.00-135.00
Top to Bottom ....Necklace.................750.00-795.00

Plate 15
Row 1, L-R ....Clips (pr.) 25.00-35.00
Row 1, L-R ....Pin.........................15.00-20.00
Row 1, L-R ....Brooch 20.00-25.00
Row 1, L-R ....Earrings 15.00-25.00
Row 2, L-R ....Set 45.00-55.00
Row 2, L-R ....Brooch 55.00-65.00
Row 2, L-R ....Earrings 10.00-15.00
Row 3.....................Bracelet 45.00-55.00
Row 4.....................Bracelet 25.00-35.00
Row 5.....................Bracelet 45.00-55.00
Bottom.....................Earrings 25.00-35.00

Plate 16
Top, L-R....................Pin.......................125.00-175.00
Top, L-R....................Brooch 55.00-65.00
Top, L-R....................Pin........................85.00-95.00
Center, L-R ....Brooch 95.00-125.00
Center, L-R ....Brooch 85.00-110.00
Center ....Set 35.00-55.00
Bottom, L-R ....Combs (3).................ea. 5.00-10.00
Bottom, L-R ....Buttons (3.) ....set 5.00-10.00

Plate 17
Row 1, Top to Bottom ..Buckle (2 pc.) 35.00-45.00
Row 2.....................Set 55.00-75.00
Row 3, L-R ....Buttons (3) ....set 45.00-65.00
Row 3, L-R ....Buckles (2 pc.).............45.00-65.00
Row 3, L-R ....Buttons (6) ....set 35.00-45.00
Row 4, L-R ....Belt 95.00-125.00
Row 4, L-R ....Set 65.00-75.00

Plate 18
As Pictured ....Buttons ....ea. 10.00-25.00

Plate 19
Top to Bottom ....Purse 295.00-325.00
Top to Bottom ....Purse 95.00-125.00

Plate 19 (Cont.)
Top to Bottom ....Purse 110.00-135.00
Top to Bottom ....Purse 95.00-135.00
Plate 20
Top, L-R......................Bracelet.....................85.00-125.00
Top, L-R......................Bracelet.....................35.00-45.00
Top, L-R......................Bracelet.....................25.00-35.00
Center, L-R ....Bracelet.....................55.00-95.00
Center, L-R ....Bracelet.....................75.00-95.00
Center, L-R ....Bracelet.....................25.00-35.00
Bottom, L-R ....Bracelet.....................75.00-95.00
Bottom, L-R ....Bracelet.....................65.00-75.00
Bottom, L-R ....Bracelet.....................25.00-35.00
Plate 21
Top to Bottom,
Row 1, L-R.................Earrings 35.00-45.00
Row 1, L-R.................Buckle.......................35.00-45.00
Row 2, ...Bracelet.....................35.00-45.00
Row 3, L-R.................Necklace....................35.00-45.00
Row 3, L-R.................Pin............................45.00-55.00
Row 3, L-R.................Pin............................45.00-55.00
Row 4, L-R.................Earrings 35.00-55.00
Row 4, L-R.................Earrings 25.00-35.00
Row 4, L-R.................Earrings 35.00-55.00
Plate 22
Top, L-R......................Bracelet.....................95.00-125.00
Top, L-R......................Bracelet.....................35.00-45.00
Top, L-R......................Bracelet.....................75.00-95.00
Center, L-R ....Bracelet.....................65.00-85.00
Center, L-R ....Bracelet.....................95.00-125.00
Center, L-R ....Bracelet.....................55.00-75.00
Bottom, L-R ....Bracelet.....................195.00-225.00
Bottom, L-R ....Bracelet.....................95.00-125.00
Bottom, L-R ....Bracelet.....................35.00-55.00
Bottom, L-R ....Bracelet.....................165.00-195.00
Plate 23
Top to Bottom
Row 1, L-R.................Brooch 150.00-175.00
Row 1, L-R.................Pin............................15.00-20.00
Row 1, L-R.................Brooch 75.00-95.00
Row 2.........................Necklace....................45.00-65.00
Row 3.........................Bracelet.....................95.00-125.00
Row 4, L-R.................Earrings 35.00-45.00
Row 4, L-R.................Pin.......................................No Price
Row 4, L-R.................Pin............................10.00-20.00
Row 4, L-R.................Earrings 25.00-35.00
Row 5, L-R.................Earrings 30.00-45.00
Row 5, L-R.................Earrings 35.00-50.00
Row 5, L-R.................Earrings 25.00-35.00
Row 5, L-R.................Earrings 35.00-45.00
Plate 24
Left, Top to Bottom .....Bracelet.....................225.00-275.00
Left, Top to Bottom .....Bracelet.....................95.00-115.00
Left, Top to Bottom .....Bracelet.....................115.00-145.00
Left, Top to Bottom .....Bracelet.....................115.00-145.00
Left, Top to Bottom .....Bracelet.....................115.00-145.00
Left, Top to Bottom .....Bracelet.....................115.00-145.00
Left, Top to Bottom .....Bracelet.....................115.00-145.00
Right, Top to Bottom....Bracelet.....................25.00-35.00
Right, Top to Bottom....Bracelet (left) 25.00-40.00
Right, Top to Bottom....Bracelet (center) 35.00-45.00
Right, Top to Bottom....Bracelet (right) 45.00-55.00
Right, Top to Bottom....Bracelet.....................75.00-95.00
Right, Top to Bottom....Bracelet (left) 55.00-75.00
Right, Top to Bottom....Bracelet (right) 35.00-55.00
Plate 25
Top
Row 1, L-R.................Earrings 35.00-50.00
Row 1, L-R.................Pin............................150.00-175.00
Row 1, L-R.................Bracelet.....................75.00-95.00
Row 2, L-R.................Pin............................75.00-100.00

Row 2, L-R.................Key chain...................35.00-55.00
Row 2, L-R.................Bracelet.....................150.00-195.00
Row 3, L-R.................Bracelet.....................30.00-50.00
Row 3, L-R.................Bracelet.....................65.00-85.00
Row 4, L-R.................Pin............................65.00-85.00
Row 4, L-R.................Ring..........................65.00-85.00
Row 4, L-R.................Ring..........................175.00-235.00
Plate 26
Top Row,L-R ....Ring..........................35.00-55.00
Top Row,L-R ....Ring..........................45.00-55.00
Top Row,L-R ....Ring..........................65.00-85.00
Bottom Row,L-R ....Ring..........................15.00-25.00
Bottom Row,L-R ....Ring..........................45.00-65.00
Bottom Row,L-R ....Ring..........................55.00-75.00
Left, Top to Bottom .....Bracelet.....................150.00-200.00
Left, Top to Bottom .....Bracelet.....................125.00-150.00
Left, Top to Bottom .....Bracelet.....................250.00-325.00
Left, Top to Bottom .....Bracelet.....................250.00-300.00
Right, Top to Bottom....Bracelet.....................85.00-125.00
Right, Top to Bottom....Bracelet.....................75.00-90.00
Right, Top to Bottom....Pin............................45.00-65.00
Right, Top to Bottom....Brooch......................295.00-350.00
Right, Top to Bottom....Bracelet.....................85.00-125.00
Right, Top to Bottom....Bracelet.....................85.00-125.00
Plate 27
Row 1, L-R.................Pin............................195.00-225.00
Row 1, L-R.................Bracelet.....................125.00-140.00
Row 1, L-R.................Bracelet.....................125.00-135.00
Row 2.........................Set 150.00-175.00
Row 3, L-R.................Bracelet.....................115.00-130.00
Row 3, L-R.................Bracelet.....................115.00-130.00
Bottom......................Eye Glasses 45.00-65.00
Plate 28
Top Row L-R ....Bracelets (4)........ea. 275.00-325.00
Center, L-R ....Large Cuffs (6) ....ea. 145.00-165.00
Bottom, L-R ....Bracelets (8)
                          Polka Dot ....ea. 275.00-375.00
                          Multicolored ....ea. 135.00-150.00
                          Reverse Carved ea.145.00-155.00
Plate 29
Top, L-R......................Brooch 110.00-135.00
Top, L-R......................Brooch 195.00-225.00
Top, L-R......................Earrings 125.00-145.00
Center........................Set 525.00-575.00
Center........................Brooch 115.00-135.00
Plate 30
Top to Bottom ....Set 450.00-525.00
Plate 31
Top ....Bracelets (2)........ea. 135.00-165.00
Top ....Pins or Clips (4)...ea. 135.00-200.00
Top ....Pin............................225.00-265.00
Center........................Pendant 75.00-95.00
Bottom, L-R ....Pins (2) ....ea. 45.00-65.00
Bottom, L-R ....Pin (center) 45.00-65.00
Bottom, L-R ....Pin (bottom)................65.00-85.00
Bottom, L-R ....Set 145.00-165.00
Plate 32
Top to Bottom ....Necklace...................375.00-425.00
Top to Bottom ....Necklace...................325.00-365.00
Top to Bottom ....Necklace...................295.00-325.00
Top to Bottom ....Necklace...................345.00-365.00
Top to Bottom ....Necklace...................375.00-425.00
Plate 33
Row 1, L-R.................Pin............................195.00-245.00
Row 1, L-R.................Pin............................165.00-195.00
Row 1, L-R.................Pin............................145.00-165.00
Row 2, Center.............Pin............................265.00-285.00
Row 3, L-R.................Scarf/Brooch Combo 35.00-55.00
Row 3, L-R.................Brooch 65.00-85.00
Row 3, L-R.................Pin............................65.00-85.00
Row 4, L-R.................Pin............................95.00-125.00

Plate 33 (Cont.)
Row 4, L-R ....Brooch 185.00-225.00
Plate 34
Row 1, L-R ....Buckle 25.00-45.00
Row 1, L-R ....Buckle 25.00-45.00
Row 1, L-R ....Pin...........................35.00-55.00
Row 1, L-R ....Hairpin 3.00-5.00
Row 2, L-R ....Necklace.....................65.00-85.00
Row 3.........................Necklace.....................25.00-35.00
Row 4.........................Necklace.....................25.00-35.00
Plate 35
Top, L-R.....................Hatpins (9) ....ea. 25.00-55.00
Bottom.......................Brooch 5.00-10.00
Plate 36
Top and Bottom..........Earrings (5)...........pr. 95.00-150.00
Center.......................Pendant Set 135.00-155.00
Plate 37
Top to Bottom ....Cigarette Case (4)..ea. 195.00-225.00
Top to Bottom ....Pin...........................85.00-110.00
Top to Bottom ....Pin...........................85.00-110.00
Plate 38
Left to Right................Set 495.00-525.00
Plate 39
Top ....Watches (2)........ea. 110.00-135.00
Top, Left ....Bracelets (2)...........ea. 35.00-55.00
Center.......................Watches (3).......Clear 90.00-110.00
Black 65.00-85.00
Bottom......................Pin...........................110.00-135.00
Plate 40
Top, Left ....Brooch 20.00-35.00
Top, Right..................Necklace.....................25.00-45.00
Center.......................Set 95.00-135.00
Bottom......................Set 35.00-55.00
Bottom, Center...........Brooch 45.00-55.00
Plate 41
Top, L-R.....................Hair Ornament 185.00-225.00
Top, L-R.....................Hair Comb 65.00-85.00
Top, L-R.....................Barrettes (2)..........ea. 85.00-110.00
Top, L-R.....................Pin with Pendant 145.00-165.00
Center.......................Hair Ornament 145.00-165.00
Bottom, L-R ....Hair Ornament 145.00-165.00
Bottom, L-R ....Barrettes (pr.)......ea. 110.00-125.00
Bottom, L-R ....Hair Ornament 145.00-155.00
Plate 42
Row 1, L-R.................Pin...........................145.00-195.00
Row 1, L-R.................Buckle 45.00-65.00
Row 1, L-R.................Pin...........................65.00-95.00
Row 2........................Buckles (shoe).........pr. 20.00-30.00
Row 3, L-R.................Pin...........................175.00-200.00
Row 3, L-R.................Scarf Slide 125.00-150.00
Row 3, L-R.................Pin...........................85.00-95.00
Row 4, L-R.................Pin...........................75.00-95.00
Row 4, L-R.................Brooch 85.00-115.00
Row 4, L-R.................Pin...........................35.00-55.00
Row 5, L-R.................Pin...........................85.00-125.00
Row 5, L-R.................Earrings 10.00-15.00
Row 5, L-R.................Pin...........................145.00-195.00
Plate 43
Full Page ....Hatpins (10) ....ea. 15.00-35.00
Plate 44
Full Page ....Hatpins (9) ....ea. 10.00-25.00
Plate 45
Top ....Bracelet (2)..Carved, ea. 45.00-55.00
Plain, ea. 25.00-35.00
Center.......................Bracelet with Watch ..150.00-175.00
Center.......................Bracelet 65.00-85.00
Bottom, L-R ....Bracelet 75.00-85.00
Bottom, L-R ....Bracelet 35.00-45.00
Bottom, L-R ....Bracelet 45.00-65.00
Left ....Bracelet 55.00-75.00
Top, Center ....Fur Clip 25.00-35.00

Top, Left ....Hatpin 25.00-35.00
Top, Left ....Hatpin 20.00-30.00
Top, Left ....Hatpin 20.00-30.00
Center........................Earrings 15.00-20.00
Center, Right ....Earrings 25.00-30.00
Center, Left ....Brooch 65.00-75.00
Plate 46
Full Page ....Set 950.00-1,100.00
Plate 47
Top to Bottom ....Set 250.00-325.00
Top to Bottom ....Hat Ornaments........ea. 15.00-35.00
Plate 48
Full Page ....Buttons ....ea. 2.00-20.00
Plate 49
Left to Right................Pendant Necklace 150.00-225.00
Left to Right................Pendant Necklace 185.00-225.00
Center.......................Necklace...................125.00-150.00
Top, Right..................Hat Ornament 15.00-25.00
Center.......................Clip.............................65.00-75.00
Bottom, L-R ....Hatpin 15.00-20.00
Bottom, L-R ....Hatpin 85.00-110.00
Bottom, L-R ....Hatpin 45.00-65.00
Plate 50
Top, L-R.....................Pin...........................110.00-135.00
Top, L-R.....................Rings (6) ......Lucite, ea. 15.00-20.00
Insects, ea. 25.00-35.00
Bottom, L-R ....Earrings 135.00-165.00
Bottom, L-R ....Pin...........................25.00-35.00
Plate 51
Top, L-R.....................Necklace...................275.00-350.00
Top, L-R.....................Cufflinks....................25.00-35.00
Bottom......................Bracelet 135.00-150.00
Plate 52
Top to Bottom ....Set 35.00-50.00
Top, Center ....Earrings 10.00-25.00
Plate 53
Top, L-R.....................Pin.............................75.00-125.00
Top, L-R.....................Pin.............................75.00-125.00
Top, L-R.....................Pin.............................85.00-135.00
Center, Left ....Bracelet 25.00-45.00
Center, Right ....Brooch 120.00-145.00
Bottom......................Necklace...................295.00-350.00
Plate 54
Top, Left ....Earrings 55.00-75.00
Top, Right..................Pin.............................65.00-85.00
Center, Left ....Pendant with Chain 45.00-65.00
Bottom, Left ....Necklace...................175.00-225.00
Center, Right ....Cuff...........................55.00-75.00
Bottom, Right ....Brooch 125.00-150.00
Plate 55
Top ....Bracelet 275.00-300.00
Center.......................Necklace.....................85.00-110.00
Bottom......................Beads 295.00-350.00
Plate 56
Top to Bottom ....Necklace...................325.00-385.00
Center.......................Necklace...................275.00-325.00
Plate 57
Top, Left ....Earrings 65.00-75.00
Top, Right..................Pendant with Chain 55.00-75.00
Bottom, Center...........Earrings 55.00-75.00
Center.......................Necklace...................275.00-325.00
Plate 58
Top ....Bracelet 125.00-150.00
Bottom......................Necklace...................245.00-295.00
Plate 59
Left ....Bracelet 25.00-45.00
Right ....Earrings 25.00-35.00
Plate 60
No Price Available
Plate 61
No Price Available

Plate 62
No Price Available

Plate 63
Row 1, L-R.................Clip 40.00-50.00
Row 1, L-R.................Bar Pin.........................60.00-75.00
Row 1, L-R.................Clip 40.00-50.00
Row 2, L-R.................Bar Pin.........................40.00-50.00
Row 2, L-R.................Pin...............................35.00-45.00
Row 2, L-R.................Bar Pin.........................60.00-75.00
Row 3, L-R.................Clip 40.00-50.00
Row 3, L-R.................Clip 40.00-50.00
Row 3, L-R.................Clip 45.00-55.00
Row 4, L-R.................Clip 25.00-35.00
Row 4, L-R.................Clip 40.00-50.00
Row 4, L-R.................Clip 30.00-40.00
Row 5, L-R.................Clip 55.00-65.00
Row 5, L-R.................Clip 60.00-75.00
Row 5, L-R.................Clip 60.00-75.00

Plate 64
Row 1, L-R.................Clip 30.00-35.00
Row 1, L-R.................Clip 35.00-40.00
Row 1, L-R.................Clip 40.00-50.00
Row 2, Left................Clip 25.00-35.00
Row 2, Right..............Clip 30.00-35.00
Row 3........................Set 50.00-80.00
Row 4, L-R.................Bar Pin......,.................45.00-55.00
Row 4, L-R.................Belt Buckle 50.00-60.00
Row 4, L-R.................Bar Pin.........................60.00-65.00

Plate 65
Row 1, Left................Pin.............................175.00-225.00
Row 1, Right..............Scarf Clasp 100.00-125.00
Row 2, L-R.................Pin...............................75.00-85.00
Row 2, L-R.................Bracelet.....................300.00-350.00
Row 2, L-R.................Pin...............................50.00-65.00
Row 3, Left................Pin.............................200.00-250.00
Row 3, Right..............Pin.............................175.00-190.00
Row 4, L-R.................Pin.............................110.00-125.00
Row 4, L-R.................Belt Buckle 100.00-125.00
Row 4, L-R.................Pin...............................95.00-110.00

Plate 66
Row 1, L-R.................Pin.............................150.00-165.00
Row 1, L-R.................Pin............................. 175.00-185.00
Row 1, L-R.................Pin.............................175.00-185.00
Row 2, L-R.................Pin.............................175.00-185.00
Row 2, L-R.................Pin.............................175.00-185.00
Row 2, L-R.................Pin.............................175.00-185.00
Row 3, Left................Pin.............................150.00-165.00
Row 3, Left................Pin.............................175.00-185.00
Row 3, Left................Pin.............................175.00-185.00
Row 4, Center.............Pin.............................175.00-185.00

Plate B-1
Row 1........................Pin...............................95.00-125.00
Row 2, L-R.................Bar Pin.........................35.00-55.00
Row 2, L-R.................Bracelet.....................145.00-165.00
Row 2, L-R.................Bracelet.....................145.00-165.00
Row 3, L-R.................Pin.............................110.00-135.00
Row 3, L-R.................Bracelet.....................145.00-165.00
Row 3, L-R.................Ring.............................10.00-15.00
Row 4, Left................Pin...............................75.00-95.00
Row 4, Right..............Earrings 115.00-135.00

Plate B-2
Left to Right.................Necklaces (5) ....ea. 45.00-65.00

Plate B-3
Row 1........................Earrings 10.00-15.00
Row 2........................Bracelet.......................20.00-30.00
Row 3........................Bracelet.......................25.00-35.00
Row 4, L-R.................Earrings 25.00-35.00
Row 4, L-R.................Pin and Locket.............20.00-35.00
Row 4, L-R.................Earrings 15.00-20.00

Row 5........................Bracelet.......................25.00-35.00
Row 6, Left................Earrings 20.00-25.00
Row 6, Left................Earrings 10.00-20.00

Plate B-4
Full Plate ....Lucite Buttons............ea. 2.00-6.00

Plate B-5
Row 1........................Brooch 75.00-95.00
Row 2........................Bracelet.....................85.00-125.00
Row 3, L-R.................Earrings 45.00-55.00
Row 3, L-R.................Pin...............................35.00-45.00
Row 3, L-R.................Pin...............................75.00-95.00
Row 3, L-R.................Earrings 35.00-45.00
Row 4, L-R.................Slides (2) ....ea. 35.00-45.00
Row 4, L-R.................Bracelet.......................65.00-85.00
Row 4, L-R.................Pin...............................45.00-55.00
Row 5, L-R.................Brooch 95.00-125.00
Row 5, L-R.................Pin...............................65.00-85.00
Row 5, L-R.................Pin...............................45.00-65.00
Row 6........................Bracelet.....................95.00-135.00

Plate B-6
Top...........................Necklace...................300.00-350.00
Top, Center ....Pin...............................65.00-85.00
Center, Left ....Bracelet.....................165.00-185.00
Center, Right ....Bracelet.....................165.00-185.00
Bottom......................Necklace...................300.00-350.00
Bottom, Center...........Brooch 245.00-265.00

Plate B-7
Row 1, Left................Buckle 55.00-75.00
Row 1, Right..............Clips (pr.) 45.00-65.00
Row 2, L-R.................Bracelet.......................95.00-145.00
Row 2, L-R.................Buckle 35.00-45.00
Row 2, L-R.................Clip 45.00-55.00
Row 3,.......................Necklace......................65.00-85.00
Row 3, Center.............Hat or Cravat Pin...........35.00-45.00
Row 4, L-R.................Buckle 55.00-75.00
Row 4, L-R.................Bracelet.......................25.00-35.00
Row 4, L-R.................Bracelet.......................65.00-85.00

Plate B-8
Row 1........................*Lorgnette*....................85.00-110.00
Row 2, Left................Bracelet.......................95.00-110.00
Row 2, Right..............Earrings 65.00-85.00
Row 3........................Hatpins (6) ....ea. 10.00-25.00
Row 4........................Purse 150.00-225.00

Plate B-9
Row 1........................Watch Fobs (3)........ea. 65.00-75.00
Row 2........................Bracelet.....................145.00-165.00
Row 3........................Necklace...................235.00-275.00
Row 3, Center.............Brooch 235.00-275.00
Row 4........................Brooch 245.00-255.00

Plate B-10
No Price Available

Plate B-11
No Price Available

Plate B-12
No Price Available

Plate B-13
No Price Available

Plate B-14
No Price Available

Plate B-15
No Price Available

Plate B-16
Top, Left ....Brooch 65.00-85.00
Bottom, Left ....Ring.........................110.00-125.00
Center, Right ....Bracelet...................125.00-150.00

Plate B-17
No Price Available

Plate B-18
No Price Available